Women in Social Work
Who Have Changed the World

Women in Social Work Who Have Changed the World

Edited by Alice Lieberman
University of Kansas

LYCEUM
BOOKS, INC.

Chicago, Illinois

© 2010 by Lyceum Books, Inc.
Published by
LYCEUM BOOKS, INC.
5758 S. Blackstone Avenue
Chicago, Illinois 60637
773-643-1903 fax
773-643-1902 phone
lyceum@lyceumbooks.com
www.lyceumbooks.com

6   5   4   3   2   1   09   10   11   12   13

ISBN 978-1-933478-29-6

Printed in the United States of America.

Library of Congress Cataloging-in-Publication Data

Lieberman, Alice A.
Women in social work who are changing the world / Alice Lieberman.
    p.   cm.
Includes bibliographical references and index.
ISBN 978-1-933478-29-6 (pbk. : alk. paper)
1. Women in charitable work.   2. Social service.   I. Title.
HV541.L54   2010
361.3092'2—dc22

                                                    2009031204

How important it is for us to recognize and celebrate our heroes and she-roes!

—*Maya Angelou*

Contents

Part III: Bringing Social Work to the Rest of the World

Acknowledgments

I want to thank all of the women who agreed to be featured in this book. Each was interviewed by the chapter author or authors, and each read (and in some cases, reread) their chapters for accuracy. And I am especially grateful to the chapter authors, some of whom went to heroic lengths to interview their subjects. All are leaders in social work education and research, and work on this book certainly constituted a detour from their other scholarly pursuits. Finally, I want to acknowledge the hard work of three anonymous reviewers, whose contributions have added immeasurably to this book.

The stories in this book are ultimately about hope, for a more just world and for the potential of the social work profession to make important contributions to that world. That hope manifests in the students we have all had over the years. In my own experience, some of the gutsiest, smartest, most creative, and adventurous social workers I have known are those who once occupied a chair in my classroom. Readers of this book have probably not yet heard of Amy Khare, Samantha Finke, Jen Dawdy, Melinda Lewis, and so many more. But they, and those others whose names you will likely never hear, make that hope burn brighter.

My dean, Mary Ellen Kondrat, has been extremely supportive of this work, and no one could ask for better colleagues or a better environment for teaching, scholarship, and just plain camaraderie than the University of Kansas. David Follmer, the publisher of Lyceum Books, provided the opportunity for us to bring these stories to a wider audience. Wynne Korr, Dean and Professor of the School of Social Work at the University of Illinois at Urbana-Champaign, gave the manuscript what we thought was the final once-over, but her comments were so helpful and so right on that a number of pieces changed substantially as a result of her critique.

Acknowledgments often include a salute to one's family. This one is no different: it doesn't get any better than being a partner or parent to the McDonald boys, Tom, Ethan, and Jared. I would also like to acknowledge my mother, Sally Lieberman. At the time that this book was being written, and approaching her ninth decade, she moved to Lawrence, Kansas, to be with my family. She undoubtedly would have chosen otherwise had adverse health matters not intervened. But she has not looked back, has established a new life for herself, and takes great pleasure in her identity within the retirement community as my mother.

A final indulgence: at some recondite level that I will never fully understand, this book was propelled forward by two people who are no longer here. Liane Vida Davis was the associate dean of the School of Social Welfare here at the University of Kansas until her death in 1995, at the age of fifty-three. She was an exceptional thinker, writer, friend, and proud, unreconstructed feminist activist. Until her death at the age of fifty, Deborah Gerner was a colleague in the Department of Political Science, also at the University of Kansas. She was a Middle East scholar and a committed advocate for international peace. The hope of both of these women was that the next generation of activist practitioners and scholars might accomplish what they could not in their brief lifetimes: worldwide gender equality and a hope for peace in the world's troubled regions. I can imagine both of them reading this book, deeply satisfied that the work continues and hopeful that those in the succeeding generation who read this book will be inspired to carry it forward.

Alice Lieberman
September 1, 2009

Preface

The social work profession has always attracted to its ranks those who see social inequity and oppression in the lives of individuals, families, and communities, and want to make profound changes on behalf of those systems. Indeed, this is our raison d'être. Although others may lay claim to an overarching goal of social and economic justice, social work is the only profession for which social justice is a core value, which drives its unique purpose among the helping professions.

The fifteen remarkable women profiled in this book—all social work colleagues—have lived this core value. Each has used the teachings of the profession to enable profound social change in communities around the world. Their work has taken them to places as far flung as North Korea and as close to home as Chicago, and they have engaged in work that is at times as mundane as digging latrines and at others as complex as helping mediate nuclear nonproliferation agreements between adversarial governments. The character of each woman's work is different, and certainly the environments in which they practice are different, but all can claim a large measure of responsibility for lasting improvements in the lives of marginalized persons in the United States and around the world. I hope that reading about them will inspire you to consider your own career path and to broaden your ideas about the applicability of the values, knowledge, and skills one learns in social work schools.

What Can I Learn from This Book?

A careful reading of this book reveals some general themes and lessons. First, all of these women have operated from a strong belief in our collective need to remedy social injustice and oppression. Thus, whether they came into social work by design or by serendipity (and there is a little of each in this book), it was clear from the start that the core values of the profession were a solid fit with their worldviews. But, given this homogeneity in philosophy, it is remarkable to think about how different their life circumstances are. One difference is in religious or spiritual beliefs and the consequences of following those beliefs. For example, three of these women are members of the clergy as well as social workers. A number of others make strong statements of commitment to religion. Yet others note how they observed, as children, religious discrimination in their own communities (discrimination often directed at their families). But whether it is Catholicism, Judaism, Zoroastrianism, Islam, or Christianity, nearly all of our subjects speak of how religion informed both their outlook on our human obligations and their aspirations.

Another great difference among these women is in the social class into which they were born. The range of their experience runs from life in a one-room mud structure with parents and siblings to royalty and privilege. Regardless, all witnessed the cruelty, oppression, and ignorance to which many of their fellow citizens have been subjected and then vowed to do something about it.

A third notable element is that nearly every single one of these women pointed to a parent as her greatest influence, and in most cases, to their father. This should not be surprising: the literature in both social work and psychology describes positive outcomes for women who had quality relationships with their fathers growing up, in the United States and around the world (see Cooper, 2009; Radin, 1986). But the fact is particularly important to point out here, as it demonstrates a convergence between lived experience and the abstractions of scholarly literature.

Fourth, despite the great differences in their accomplishments, every one of these women has attested to the critical importance of their social work education to their work. Even though that education looks very different in each country of study, the central pedagogy remains the same. Thus, education was the point at which the meeting of head and heart occurred.

With only a few exceptions, none of these women had a long-range career plan; in fact, one explicitly advises against having one. Instead, they took advantage of opportunities that presented themselves— opportunities to innovate in established environments or to create something entirely new (at great risk, in some cases). But such adventures can have a cost, and some of those have been noted here as well. For example, to the extent that they discuss their contemporary family lives, these women collectively reveal that, if one is going to have a life partner, then he or she has to be a partner who shares one's ambition, or else that relationship is likely to dissolve.

Finally, each of these women could be described as, for lack of a better word, "charismatic" leaders: they have been able to engender a shared vision among many other talented, generous people who have then adopted that vision as their own. But as with any good leader, they all note that, though the vision may have been theirs, those other individuals who joined them on the journey share in the credit for their achievements. Success, as they would say, has many mothers.

The Selection Process

The women who are featured in this book were chosen by their colleagues. In some cases, a prospective author made the case for the inclusion of a particular person. In other cases, a decision was made to interview someone and then a willing author was found. In quite a few instances, there was a desire to include someone in the book, but either that person declined our invitation for an interview or it was not possible to find someone who could span the language barrier. At every step, from the initial questions of whom to include to the final manuscript preparation, an extensive vetting process was undertaken. The resulting product is one of which the contributors to this volume are all proud, and we continue to be in awe of the women who have permitted us to tell their stories.

As you read this book, you will see that, as was alluded to earlier, the tie that binds all of these women is perseverance, intelligence, and courage. On this foundation, they acquired knowledge and skill—the same core knowledge and skill that you have acquired in your education. We hope that you, too, will combine your own stellar personal qualities with your formal social work education (as well as lifelong learning!) to change the world for your fellow citizens.

References

Cooper, S. (2009, August). Associations between father-daughter relationship quality and the academic engagement of African American adolescent girls: Self-esteem as a mediator? *Journal of Black Psychology, 35,* 404–425.

Radin, N. (1986). The influence of fathers on their sons and daughters. *Social Work in Education,* 8, 77–92.

PART I

Change Our World from Within
Social Workers in the Corridors of Power

Reflecting on his just-completed presidency in 1910, Theodore Roosevelt, in the speech "Citizenship in a Republic," given at the Sorbonne in Paris, said this about those who engage in the highest levels of civic life:

> It is not the critic who counts; not the man who points out how the strong man stumbles, or where the doer of deeds could have done them better. The credit belongs to the man who is actually in the arena, whose face is marred by dust and sweat and blood; who strives valiantly; who errs, who comes short again and again, because there is no effort without error and shortcoming; but who does actually strive to do the deeds; who knows great enthusiasms, the great devotions; who spends himself in a worthy cause; who at the best knows in the end the triumph of high achievement, and who at the worst, if he fails, at least fails while daring greatly, so that his place shall never be with those cold and timid souls who neither know victory nor defeat.

A century later, the sentiment still rings true, albeit with an expansion of pronouns to include the feminine. And the five women we profile in this section have certainly gotten into the arena, spent themselves in worthy causes, and experienced triumph and defeat.

These women rose to the pinnacle of important extant power structures and, from that perch, were able to effect great social change.

Ambassador Wendy Sherman (chapter 1), Senator Barbara Mikulski (chapter 2), and Ada Deer (chapter 5) have asserted leadership in very different ways but all within the U.S. government. Minister Alicia Kirchner (chapter 3) has used her critical position in the Argentine power structure to bring change consistent with social work values to that country. Dr. Nazneen Mayadas (chapter 4), a longtime educator in the United States, led the social work effort for the UN High Commissioner for Refugees as its social services section chief.

For their willingness to get into the arena, to leave the safety of what they knew to be their spheres of competence, to fail nobly in some cases, and to keep reaching for success, the reward for these five social workers has been to change the world.

CHAPTER ONE

Ambassador Wendy R. Sherman

A Social Worker at the Forefront of Foreign Policy

Alice Lieberman

We all go through life hearing the names of people who populate the various realms of our world, but we are often surprised when those people turn out to be closer to us than we imagined. Such is the case with Ambassador Wendy R. Sherman, whom former secretary of state Madeleine Albright (2004) called "a shrewd and resilient veteran of numerous Washington wars who [can] learn any subject faster than anyone I [know]" (p. 233). This is one of the reasons Secretary Albright chose Sherman for the position of State Department counselor, in 1997. In her memoir, *Madame Secretary*, Albright further details the logic behind her choice: "The position . . . is of special importance because it has no formal place in the bureaucratic hierarchy and has little staff. To be useful, the [counselor] must give the Secretary better advice than she receives elsewhere, then have the drive to make sure that advice is implemented should it become policy. . . . I had been friends with Wendy for a long time and knew I could count on her loyalty and her gift for separating meat from bull" (p. 233).

And so it was, on her formal appointment by President Clinton and subsequent confirmation by the U.S. Senate, that Sherman became a critical member of the U.S. foreign policy team during the second term of the Clinton administration.

I spoke with Ambassador Sherman about those years and about the important personal and professional events and opportunities leading up to that moment. Two themes emerged throughout that conversation. The first, she said repeatedly, is that for all of her accomplishments, she was never the only person responsible. She was always part of a team of people, passionate about their work and moving toward the same goal. The second is that the skills she has employed, whether as a high-ranking official in politics or as part of the negotiating team sent to North Korea to hammer out agreements with Kim Jong Il, are the skills she learned as a graduate student in social work and later as a practicing social worker. In other words, throughout her very eventful life, Wendy Sherman has remained a social worker.

The Early Years

Wendy Sherman was born in Baltimore into a family committed to social activism, and particularly to racial equality. Their commitment was unusual but not unheard of. Notably, Baltimore was one of the first places to desegregate public schools following the U.S. Supreme Court's *Brown v. Board of Education* decision. Furthermore, the rapidity with which the schools began to desegregate was a result of groundwork that was laid long before the case was decided: the city's Division of Colored Schools had been abolished in the 1940s and had been folded into a single school system (Crenson, 2006).

The relative tranquility with which schools became integrated, however, did not influence such efforts in other systems, such as housing and employment. Social change was coming, but it would require strong proponents.

Young Wendy's parents were at the vanguard of this change. As active members of the Baltimore Hebrew Congregation, they were stirred by the sermons of Rabbi Morris Lieberman. Throughout his professional life, Rabbi Lieberman spoke of social justice from the bimah (pulpit), but he also lived his principles. For example, in the summer of 1963, along with the Reverend William Sloane Coffin and twenty-five other members of the clergy, Rabbi Lieberman marched in an effort to integrate the Gwynn Oak Amusement Park, just outside the city. The march, sponsored by the Congress of Racial Equality, resulted in the arrest of all the religious leaders, thus fostering a growing awareness in religious communities across Baltimore that segregation was unjust and its days numbered (March on Gwynn Oak Park, 1963). At about the same time, Wendy's father, Malcolm Sherman, a successful residential realtor, heard Rabbi Lieberman's call for integration from the bimah and asked what he could do. Rabbi Lieberman responded that he could contribute significantly to the cause by advertising open housing.

Briefly, open housing refers to a housing market in which access to property is not restricted on the basis of race, religion, or ethnicity. In Baltimore, before the Civil Rights Act, the city was both racially and religiously segregated. Neighborhoods were often redlined (a practice in which home sales in certain neighborhoods were, by tacit agreement between lenders and real estate agents, restricted according to race or religion). Failure to participate in this system of business practices, aimed to keep neighborhoods homogeneous, would have put any business at risk.

Nevertheless, encouraged by Rabbi Lieberman, Wendy's father became the first realtor in the city of Baltimore to advertise open housing. Sherman noted that this was not a decision her father entered into lightly: he knew there was a strong possibility that his business would take a significant financial hit (it did). And he was not unaware of the potential for physical violence (there were death and bomb threats after the advertising began). But this seemed only to move the family forward in their desire to reshape their community.

As time went on, Wendy said, "my parents took us on civil rights marches and restaurant sit-ins, to try to help desegregate [Baltimore]. And it was a very powerful experience, very powerful. During that time, my father also brought me over to what was then the Sheraton Hotel in Washington to hear Eleanor Roosevelt speak. I was completely stunned by her presence, by her call to get done what needed to be done, and to bring the world together. So it was a time growing up, of enormous activism, and my parents' example of what it meant to be involved in your community, take risks and try to make a difference. And that got me interested in community development. It got me very interested in being an actor in my community and not just a citizen in a passive sense." Thus, the groundwork for a remarkable career was laid.

After graduating from high school, Wendy entered Smith College. It was her first choice: she had always wanted to go to a women's college. "I wanted to have the affirmation that it was OK for women to be leaders," she said. But after completing two years at Smith, she felt it was not activist enough, not engaged enough in the tumult and social change occurring all over the country but particularly in urban areas.

So she transferred from Smith and the relative quiet of Northampton, Massachusetts, to Boston University.

Her years in Boston are a bit of a blur: "I went to classes but I also worked in the local community center organizing teenagers in a housing project to try to get them activities. And so I sort of remember my last two years in college, but it was really about organizing, protesting, [and] activism. And I knew fairly early on that I wanted to be a community organizer and help to make a difference." She graduated with a degree in sociology in 1971.

Career Beginnings: Combining Vocation and Avocation

Following graduation, Wendy worked for a year at the Boston-area Middlesex County Hospital with patients suffering from chronic and terminal illnesses. County hospitals are extremely busy places, and they most often provide care for the indigent. Although Middlesex County had a higher median income than the rest of the United States, it was also home to many struggling families. Therefore, workers carried out the common tasks of (what is now called) case management and discharge planning with a highly diverse set of patients. The work was both interesting and rewarding, but after one year, Wendy moved to Savannah, Georgia.

In 1971, the country was less than a decade out from the legislation signed by President Kennedy in 1963 that shifted funding away from mental health institutions to the "least restrictive environments" for people with mental illness. Unfortunately, there was considerable lag time across the country between the exit of thousands of formerly institutionalized clients and the development of appropriate community services. Georgia, however, had a governor with considerable foresight, Jimmy Carter. As a result of his efforts, and because of the values he brought to the office, an infrastructure of community mental health services grew to accommodate the need, and Wendy was part of that new system. She took a position running a community hotline for a local mental health center.

The differences between the urban center of Boston, where she had been, and the Deep South in the early 1970s cannot be underestimated. To complicate matters, her work associate at the time was a young African American male professional. "And I was a white Jewish woman. We were a very strange pair to go into rural Georgia and only found out afterwards that everybody . . . really had been working quite assiduously to get us the heck out of there!"

It would be nice to be able to say that, after living in the South, Wendy and her professional colleague came to be accepted as part of the community. This never happened, though, and the reasons for that are lessons to all social workers who are outsiders to the communities in which they work. The most obvious reason was undoubtedly prejudice. The second was a kind of cultural nativism, a reflexive reaction to anyone whose roots are not in the community. As an example of this, while she was living there, Wendy read the obituary of a ninety-five-year-old woman that said that, although she was not a native of Savannah, she had lived there for the last ninety-three years!

The experience of living in Savannah and working in the surrounding rural area was an important lesson for Wendy ("It gave me an understanding of another part of America that I never would have known.") and an object lesson for the rest of us: if one wants to build an expansive view of humanity and a broad base from which to draw for empathic understanding, move to a place that is completely out of your comfort zone and keep your eyes and ears—and heart—open.

Graduate School: Acquiring a Social Work Frame of Reference

In 1974, Wendy entered the University of Maryland School of Social Work and Community Planning (as it was then called). The school offered a specific track for community organizing and social strategy, and the dean (Daniel Thursz) was highly regarded as both a scholar and a practitioner in this area. Thus, it was a great place to further her ambition of becoming a community organizer.

During her years as a graduate student, Wendy had many opportunities to engage in meaningful social change work and to take advantage of excellent mentors. One of the projects assigned to her, under the supervision of Dr. Stan Wenocur, was to enable public welfare workers to form empowerment support groups. As is often the case, public welfare workers are often asked to enable clients to change their circumstances but without the resources to do so. Wenocur and Wendy surmised that empowering these workers through a mutual support model might be helpful for both workers and their clients. Their assessment proved correct, but it took the skills of community organization and group work to make the groups successful. The experience and outcomes of developing the groups were later reported in a scholarly publication (Sherman & Wenocur, 1983). Those community-organizing and group-work skills, learned in graduate school and honed throughout her life, have served Wendy well in all of her subsequent work.

Another important social work mentor of Wendy's was Professor Arthur Naparstek, director of the Washington Public Affairs Center of the University of Southern California School of Public Administration (based in Washington, D.C.), who was her boss at the center, one of her first jobs following graduate school. It was through Naparstek's contacts with activists in the fight for livable, low-income housing that Wendy met Congresswoman Barbara Mikulski. A foray into electoral politics would soon follow, but not before she took the position of director of the Office of Child Welfare for the State of Maryland, where she supervised protective services, foster care, adoptions, and group homes.

A Turn toward Electoral Politics

In 1982, Wendy made the leap to Washington, D.C., which is both a short train ride and a world away from Baltimore, to work as chief of staff for Mikulski. They became (and still are) friends, a relationship that developed when Mikulski reached out to Wendy for assistance in developing new public policy models in domestic violence services. When Mikulski became a national cochair of the Democratic presidential campaign of Walter Mondale and Geraldine Ferraro, Wendy became a senior political adviser to the campaign and the liaison between the congresswoman's congressional office and the national campaign. Although the Mondale-Ferraro team lost the election, the excitement of electoral politics remained with Wendy. And undeniably, she brought something to the table that was valuable to the enterprise. The following year, she became the campaign manager for Mikulski's successful race to become the first Democratic woman elected to the Senate in her own right. Not coincidentally, the organization EMILY's List had provided Mikulski with valuable assistance. But apparently not just Mikulski earned the group's admiration: it clearly respected the skills and savvy of her campaign manager as well. Thus, after a brief stint as a political consultant, Wendy became executive director of EMILY's List.

EMILY's List is one of the most successful grassroots political organizations in history (EMILY is an acronym for Early Money Is Like Yeast— because it makes the dough rise). Founded in 1985, the primary mission of the organization is to elect pro-choice Democratic women to high political office. To that end, the organization recruits viable candidates, helps them build their campaign apparatuses, and then sends fundraising appeals to their membership of more than a hundred thousand men and women, each of whom pledges to provide at least $200 per year to one or more candidates. Many other advocacy groups have tried to replicate the EMILY's List model but have been unable to equal their success. During Wendy's tenure, EMILY's List broke the million-dollar mark in fund-raising for the first time: members contributed $1.5 million to fourteen candidates and helped elect two governors and seven members of Congress (EMILY's List, 2008).

At the same time that she was proving her bona fides as a political operative, Wendy was also building up a vast network of relationships in the world of Washington politics. This network, consisting of politicians she had assisted, other political operatives, and people in the media (she was a frequent commentator for the *MacNeil/Lehrer NewsHour*, CNN, and other outlets) was, in and of itself, a valuable resource. As experienced social workers know, it is relationships, built through time in the practice community with other social workers, allied professionals, clients, and so on, that are critical to our successes, both personally and professionally.

From Politics to Government

In 1993, Wendy Sherman was appointed assistant secretary of state for legislative affairs under Secretary of State Warren Christopher, a position she held until the end of President Clinton's first term in office. In this role, she guided a staff of fifty and coordinated the efforts of the State Department in dealing with the U.S. Congress and the executive branch. In 1994, the Republicans became the majority party in Congress and were often at odds with the Democratic president. The political environment was riven by ideology and not a little political gamesmanship. Despite this, Sherman was able to span these boundaries, and she and her staff actually got quite a bit done: they marshaled support for the Dayton Accords (a framework for peace in Bosnia and Herzegovina, and a signature foreign policy achievement for President Clinton), as well as intervention in Haiti and most-favored-nation status for China (both controversial foreign policy decisions).

In 1997, Sherman ascended to her high-level position in the State Department as counselor and ambassador under Secretary of State Albright. In this position, she was able to influence virtually every foreign policy decision, from the controversial return of a child (Elián González) to his father in Cuba to developing and directing policy toward North Korea and its dictator, Kim Jong Il.

We discussed many of the decisions she influenced, the agreements she helped broker, the difficulties of bringing together so many different cultures—and the continuing importance of her social work background.

"Well, I think that the things that I learned in social work school have helped me in every part of my life, going to presidential politics and then finding myself working as a political appointee by President Clinton, first with Warren Christopher and then with Madeleine Albright," she said. "I had learned community organizing and social strategy, [which require] you to understand the environment you're in, to scan it, to understand the power relationships, to understand the points of leverage, to make an analysis[,] and then to put a strategy together to meet a set of objectives. And . . . those skills have been useful wherever I have been. Social work also teaches you to start where the client is, not where you are. And in dealing with cultures around the world, it is most helpful to always remember to begin where those cultures are and not where you as an American are."

Continuing in this vein, she emphasized, "My skills as a social worker have helped me understand the conscious use of self, what my role is in any environment, . . . and how I can impact and use the skills and the person I am in that regard. I learned great group-work skills in social work. I can meet a delegation of Chinese or Koreans or Japanese and understand the group dynamics and figure out how to help the group move toward seeking a common goal and a common set of objectives. And along the way my social work background also gave me good, I think, management and decision-making skills, which have been quite crucial, as well as finely tuned political sensitivities. So I have said all of my life that my caseload changes but the set of skills that I learned as a social worker have stood me in good stead in whatever I have done."

I was particularly interested in Sherman's work in negotiating agreements with North Korea, and particularly with Kim Jong Il, whom many in the international community view as deeply eccentric, brutally authoritarian, and shrouded in mystery. The common wisdom in the diplomatic community is that Kim is a threat to the security of the United States, so I asked Sherman to expand on this particular part of her portfolio.

"Where North Korea was concerned," she said, "I was honored that President Clinton and Secretary Albright asked me to pay special attention to peace and security in northeast Asia, to ultimately become the North Korea policy coordinator and the senior person working to negotiate agreements with North Korea. It created a situation where I had to work very closely with Japan, with the Republic of Korea, with China, with Russia, with the European Union and many other countries, to lead a U.S. delegation on many, many trilateral meetings with Korea, Japan, and the United States, and then working with [former defense secretary] Dr. Bill Perry and then with Secretary Albright to actually try to gain some agreements, some of which we did with Chairman Kim."

I had referred to Chairman Kim as crazy, which brought about a gentle, but much-deserved correction: "I actually don't think he's crazy in the way we use those words," she said. "There is no question that he is a brutal authoritarian leader of his country, but that country is more like a cult than a country. He and his father, who preceded him, are the leaders of that cult. Undoubtedly he has some megalomania because there are monuments to him and his father all over North Korea and people wear a little pin with his picture on it every day to show their loyalty and fealty to him. But one can negotiate with him, and have a conversation with him, not because there's a great level of trust but because you can have those conversations and then one can make agreements and verify those agreements and make sure there are penalties if he does not follow through." It was that last sentence that allowed me to connect with the idea, expressed earlier, that social work skills remain the same, and can be applied, even in the most fraught situations with global implications.

A Postdiplomatic Career

A change in presidential administrations inevitably brought about a change in jobs for Sherman. In 2001, she became a founding principal of the Albright Group, a global strategy firm that works with companies to expand their business while making positive contributions to the larger global community. Today, the Albright Stonebridge Group works to leverage a diverse set of skills and experiences to the benefit of clients and markets around the world. So, for example, if a large conglomerate (or a start-up business) was contemplating an expansion into Asia, it might hire the Albright Stonebridge Group to analyze the legal and social implications of the move, to identify regulatory risks, and/or to help find private entities to partner with. The group has supported industry leaders in health care, telecommunications, insurance, entertainment, consumer products, water, information technology, energy, emergency response, and environmental protection, among others. Clients have included Fortune 50 companies, funded start-ups, foundations, labor unions, law firms, and not-for-profit organizations. In this capacity, Wendy continues her travels throughout the world, deploying the skills she has acquired over a lifetime: "I am very privileged and very honored to have been able to engage in diplomacy, to have been in virtually every Middle East peace set of talks, to have worked to try to make changes in Cuba policy, in Iran, in Iraq, and many other parts of the world. And I am very privileged to now have a set of great partners running a business trying to help businesses, groups, and organizations deal with the rest of the world. That, too, [harks] back to my social work skills because it's really about helping to build a middle class so that communities can have prosperity, send their kids to school, have a good job, and have a future. And investments in emerging markets are crucial to that happening and to ensuring peace and lack of conflict in the world. So I'm very privileged to be able to do that now."

But none of this means that Sherman has exited entirely from partisan politics. She was part of a foreign policy advisory team that shaped the positions of President Barack Obama in his candidacy, she acted as his surrogate on C-SPAN in 2008, and she wrote an op-ed piece on the futility of refusing to talk to one's enemies that used the relationship of the Bush administration and the government of North Korea as an example (Sherman, 2008). Following the election, she became part of the Obama-Biden transition team, serving as a team leader for national security. As to whether she might return to partisan politics in the future, Sherman said, "I have never had a five-year plan. What I have been, however, is open to the opportunities around me, to take risks, to remember who I am, what I can bring to the table, and then see if the opportunities that are around me are placed where I can make a difference and then present myself to see if I can have the opportunity to do so." And she emphasizes that this openness to a changing environment, coupled with profound self-awareness, is a model that aspiring social workers might want to consider.

This advice, she says, does not mean that people should not think ahead, but "if you're so intentional about your life and so planful about your life, you miss the enormous opportunities and the chance serendipitous happenings in life that can bring you great satisfaction and allow you to make enormous contributions. I didn't think when I graduated social work school that I would end up being the counselor of the Department of State, with the rank of ambassador, negotiating with the chairman of North Korea. One has to be open to what life brings you and then grab hold of it whenever you can."

I asked Sherman if she had any other words of advice for either students or new social workers who aspire to enable social change, either in their own communities or in the world. She said, "I would also urge students to have a heavy dose of humility about what you are and how important you are to what happens in the world. You do your part, but understand that it takes many people to accomplish things. All of the things that you mentioned [I had discussed with her some of the achievements of the other women to be profiled in this book] were very, very difficult. Sometimes I think the most difficult thing is exhaustion and just keeping your eye on the fact that many of the people that you're talking to for this book have done things in their own backyards, in their own communities in very difficult situations to make a profound difference. And trying to get water to your community where there is no water or to try to get health care when there is no health care is as vastly important and as difficult, if not more difficult, than trying to get Kim Jong Il to get rid of his nuclear weapons. So I think the other thing I say to the students is don't think [that] because something's on the evening news it's more important than what you might be doing in your neighborhood or in a community in a developing country. It's as, if not more, important even if no one knows that it's happened."

Conclusion

At the time this chapter was written, we were nearly one hundred days into a new administration, and Sherman might well find herself with another opportunity to engage in international diplomacy. Regardless, it was both thrilling and humbling to interview her, to consider the extraordinary responsibilities she was given, and to hear how her preparation for a career in social work equipped her to span cultural, national, and international boundaries. Undoubtedly, she is unique. But her gratitude to this profession, for the skills she learned and for the doors that opened because she possessed those skills, should energize all social workers to learn, to be open, to be humble, and to think big.

References

Albright, M. (2004). *Madame Secretary: A memoir.* New York: Pan Books.

Crenson, M. A. (2006, August). *Learning to lobby and litigate: Baltimore's contributions to the civil rights movement.* Paper presented at the annual meeting of the American Political Science Association, Philadelphia. Retrieved February 4, 2009, from http://www.allacademic.com/meta/p150935_index.html.

EMILY's List. (2008). Where we come from. Retrieved August 16, 2009, from http://www.emilyslist.org/about/where_we_come_from/.

March on Gwynn Oak Park. (1963, July 12). *Time.* Retrieved August 16, 2009, from http://www.time.com/time/magazine/article/0,9171,940281,00.html.

Sherman, W. (2008, July 2). Opinion: Talking isn't appeasement. *Los Angeles Times.*

Sherman, W., & Wenocur, S. (1983). Empowering public welfare workers through mutual support. *Social Work, 28*(5), 375–379.

CHAPTER TWO

The Honorable Barbara Mikulski

Fighting for Social Justice in the U.S. Senate

Kathryn Collins and Marceline Lazzari

Barbara Ann Mikulski was raised in an extended family in a close-knit, Polish-Catholic, working-class neighborhood in East Baltimore. Her early experiences in these environs, combined with sixteen years of Catholic education, were instrumental in shaping the philosophy that has guided her life. Recalling those years, she has said, "The neighborhood was really our extended family. . . . If Bethlehem Steel was on strike, my father extended credit to the guys. In the middle of a snowstorm, if he didn't see Miss Sophie, who was a diabetic, he called down there to see if she needed anything. I ran down the oranges" (Broder, 1980, p. 149). This was a living lesson in the moral obligations we each have to look out for our neighbors, a lesson Mikulski took very seriously. By the time

In researching and writing this chapter about Senator Barbara Mikulski, we were unable to schedule a face-to-face meeting. We were able, however, to correspond indirectly with her via e-mail. Special thanks to Cassie Harvey, Denise Nooe, and Melissa Schwartz in Senator Mikulski's Washington office for facilitating her responses to our questions. We thank Sara Davis and Jessica Cantley, MSW students at the University of Maryland's School of Social Work, for their assistance in conducting the research for this chapter.

she entered the University of Maryland School of Social Work, the match between her values and those of the profession was virtually seamless. As Whitney (2000) has noted, "By the time Mikulski graduated from the [school], she had earned a master's degree in community organization. She already understood that community organization wasn't just the title of a course she had taken or a subject she'd majored in. It was an attitude she exuded. It was the very ground of her being" (p. 28). And it is the ground that she has continued to stand on, through more than forty years of public service, including two decades in the U.S. Senate.

It's better to light one candle than to curse the darkness.

—The Christophers motto

Barbara Ann Mikulski is the most senior ranking female U.S. senator, a woman of numerous talents and many firsts: the first Democratic woman to be elected to the Senate in her own right, the first Democratic woman to serve in both houses of Congress, and the first woman to win a statewide election in Maryland. From the beginning of her political career, Mikulski has viewed her work through a social work lens: "I'm still a social worker," she has said, "but now my caseload is the citizens of the State of Maryland!" (Barbara Mikulski to Alice Lieberman, personal communication, Majority Council Conference, EMILY's List, Washington, D.C., June 9, 1994). Certainly she has carried out the principles of the profession of social work in her current and prior roles as an organizer, activist, advocate, and change agent. In an article published in *Maryland Social Worker*, Mikulski is quoted as saying, "Social workers are sworn to a Code of Ethics—and they live and work by this code. They can't turn their cheek to injustices—no matter their size or if they occur after work hours" (Powell, 2007, p. 19).

Growing Up in Baltimore

Barbara Ann Mikulski was born on July 20, 1936, the eldest of three daughters of Christine and William Mikulski. Mikulski's great-grandparents emigrated from Poland to the east side of Baltimore, Maryland, where the senator maintains strong ties to this day. She was raised in an environment that valued hard work and in which people supported their neighbors. Her commitment to public service took root in her family's store, where it was her job to deliver groceries to homebound individuals. Mikulski attended parochial schools in Baltimore and received her bachelor of arts degree in 1958 from Mount St. Agnes College (now Loyola College) (Mikulski, 2007).

From a young age, the Catholic Christophers movement motivated Mikulski. The founder, Maryknoll priest James Keller, was known as a "man of hope in action," and he often used the movement's motto, "It's better to light one candle than to curse the darkness," to urge social justice and advocacy among the faithful (Christophers, 2008). At the age of fifteen, this sentiment resonated with Mikulski, and she made it the central mission of her lifework. Answering the call from President John F. Kennedy to wage a war on poverty, Mikulski decided to earn her master's degree in social work. She was a student under the tutelage of Daniel Thursz, a leading professor of social and political organizing and action at the University of Maryland School of Social Work. Mikulski stated that Thursz saw the profession "as working with the power sources as well as the powerless to empower them. This sounded like what I wanted to do, so I signed up" (Mikulski, 2007). She graduated in 1965 and began her professional career as a social worker:

> I started out as a foster care worker at Catholic Charities where families had been so devastated they had been broken up. Then I went to work for the Department of Social Services as a child abuse worker. Boy, did I grow up. It really had a searing effect on me. As a result, some of the big issues I've been committed to working on in the Senate are violence against women and protection of children. (Barbara Mikulski, personal communication, May 13, 2009)

Entry into Local Politics

Her social work career took a twist during the late 1960s. Mikulski was planning to enter a postgraduate program in public health; instead, she took on her first political battle in what would become a long career in social activism:

> In 1968, I decided to go back to school. . . . I was all set to go when I got a call from a social worker friend of mine. She said, "You've got to come to a meeting tonight at the church." She told me about a plan for a sixteen-lane highway that would run through the neighborhood. So I went. Of course I stayed and fought. I figured it would take ninety days. It took two years. (Barbara Mikulski, personal communication, May 13, 2009)

Along with others, Mikulski organized a coalition of community members and residents called the Southeast Council against the Road (SCAR). African, Polish, Greek, Lithuanian, and Ukrainian Americans all came together to fight the development:

> I . . . told them "the first thing we need to do is give our-selves a militant name so they'll take us seriously." We went to a local bar on Thames Street, had a couple of beers, and called ourselves SCAR. Later at a rally site where the highway would come through, I was asked to speak. I jumped up on the table and exclaimed, "The British couldn't take Fells Point, the termites couldn't take Fells Point, and goddamn if we'll let the State Roads Commission take Fells Point!" (Barbara Mikulski, personal communication, May 13, 2009)

This effort was targeted at stopping plans to build the aforementioned highway through Fells Point and Baltimore's Inner Harbor, which would have destroyed parts of Fells Point as well as the first African American home ownership area in the city. For the area's residents, the effects would be devastating. "This was the new middle class, living the American dream. And it would be destroyed, just like that. . . . Imagine the impact! Complete neighborhoods would be lost forever. And the residents would get nothing. No relocation benefits, and only the assessed value of their homes . . . about one-third of what they were worth. They were going to destroy Baltimore so there would be a highway for people living in the suburbs—that was really stupid" (Whitney, 2000, p. 29). Under Mikulski's leadership, they began the hard work of fighting back:

> But we had to do our homework. We had to build coalitions that would increase our power. The first step was joining forces with the black community on the west side. This was the aftermath of the civil rights riots, and at that time it would have seemed impossible for the Polish neighborhoods on the east side and the black neighborhood on the west side to work together. . . . I knew differently. We were facing a common threat. I knew some of the leaders on the west side. (Barbara Mikulski, personal communication, May 13, 2009)

Senator Mikulski recalled a particularly important meeting that occurred in West Baltimore one evening when approximately four hundred African Americans and about sixty white residents from the east side met together. This was clearly a turning point in their efforts to stop the highway. A man from the East Side group got up:

[He said:] "My name is Frank Milkowsky and I fought in World War II to save America. And I fought to save the government of the United States. Now I'm here to join with the black community, and the veterans and their wives, to save the neighborhoods of Baltimore."

There was thunderous applause. We clapped, we sang, we cheered. The ice was broken.

We were together. Mutual need, mutual respect, mutual identification. (Barbara Mikulski, personal communication, May 13, 2009)

Thanks to those successful efforts to block construction of the highway some forty years ago, both areas were transformed into thriving commercial and residential communities. And Barbara Mikulski was transformed as well. Reflecting on the experience with the United Press International reporter Helen Thomas many years later, she said, "When I was growing up as a young girl in the fifties, I never thought about politics. Politics in my neighborhood was boss machine politics. It was older, white, pot-bellied guys who smoked cigars" (Mara, 2005, p. 75). But after the road fight, she told us, "I decided I'd rather be opening doors from the inside than knocking on doors from the outside. I realized that politics was social work with power" (Barbara Mikulski, personal communication, May 13, 2009).

Her successful election to the Baltimore City Council in 1971 provided Mikulski with a new venue from which to advocate for others' needs. She campaigned door-to-door, listening to potential constituents and forming relationships that would serve her well into the future. From repairing potholes to supporting public education, Mikulski got things done. She was exceptionally skillful at putting her values into action. To this day, congruency between her values and her actions is a central quality that has sustained her long service in Congress. Voters know whom they are electing and what they can expect.

In the same period that Mikulski served on the city council, she also worked as an adjunct professor of sociology at Loyola College in Baltimore. She wanted to stimulate students with her passion for social justice and community activism. One can just imagine the lively, thought-provoking discussions in her classroom.

Entry into the National Scene

In 1974, Mikulski ran for the U.S. Senate for the first time and lost to the Republican incumbent—the only election she has ever lost. Not allowing that defeat to stop her, she ran for a seat in the U.S. House of Representatives two years later. With an extensive network of volunteers fueled by her seemingly endless energy, she won the Democratic primary and defeated the Republican nominee in the general election.

Mikulski entered a political establishment that comprised primarily economically privileged white men as a self-described "klutzy and frumpy" woman, with a feisty voice that was far louder and more powerful than others had expected. However, because she is not naive to the influence of physical appearance and behavior, she has made adjustments over time, such as losing weight, changing eyeglasses frames, altering hem lengths, and toning down her volume.

Despite such alterations, Mikulski's career has not been devoid of attempts to smear her image by raising questions about her personal life. In fact, as early as 1971, when she was running for the Baltimore City Council, questions about her single status were surreptitiously raised. When finally she was confronted, in person, with the question of why she had never married, she said, "'Cause nobody ever asked me!" (Mandel, 1981, p. 67).

But it was in her first Senate race, against another woman, that she had to deal with this issue on a large scale. Her opponent was following the old (but very effective) tactic of trying to frame Mikulski's identity before she did. Mikulski's response to the issue is instructive for aspiring advocates. In 1986, framing your opponent's identity regarding sexual orientation could be extremely damaging. To this identity frame, delivered sub rosa through coded phrases, words, and images, Mikulski fought back. First, she emphasized her service to Marylanders in print and television ads, something her opponent, who had never held elective office, could not do. Second, she tied her candidacy to the popular Democratic candidate for governor; his endorsement held great sway with the electorate. Third, she heeded the advice of that gubernatorial candidate, who told her to adhere to the strategy her team had developed and to not be led off track. Finally, she reinterpreted her opponent's words and phrases, turning them against her opponent, thereby creating a backlash. All these things, combined with her natural sense of humor, enabled Mikulski to prevail. And though subsequent challenges have not been as difficult, the experience was an object lesson. Ever since, Mikulski has made a conscious decision not to engage in what she views as personal slander. Instead, she concentrates her energy on taking stands on issues of great importance to her through coalition building that crosses party lines.

A Legislative Record of Accomplishment

Mikulski's first ten years of national service in the House of Representatives were characterized by her ongoing commitment to the issues that affected the citizens of Maryland and concerns over the entire country and its future. Her accomplishments included passage of legislation to fund shelters for battered spouses, to dredge Baltimore Harbor to make it internationally competitive, and to amend an omnibus antiterrorism bill to improve passenger safety on the high seas. Mikulski's appointments to the Merchant Marine Fisheries Committee and the House Energy and Commerce Committee provided significant platforms for her legislative efforts. In addition, she was a major proponent of the equal rights amendment and a collaborator in the establishment of the Congressional Women's Caucus. Reflecting on her approach to work in Congress, Mikulski stated: "My own principles . . . are based on what I learned as a social worker: meet people where they are, not where you want them to be; organize on a felt need, not an abstract one; the people have a right to know, a right to be heard, and a right to be represented; the people who are the most affected should have the most say in a solution; and building coalitions is the best way to get things done" (Influencing State Policy, 2003).

Mikulski considers collaboration essential to facilitating social change. She is acutely aware that not all politicians share her commitment to meeting human needs, and she knows that tough decisions must be made when there are so many competing priorities and only so much money to fund them. But collaboration and respect remain essential ingredients. In Mikulski's (2007) contribution to *Tales from the Warehouse: The Class of '65 Remembers*, she recalls the efforts of SCAR and how they organized on intention rather than anger: "We didn't make the other side the enemy; we made the road the enemy" (p. 50).

To that end, she has reached across the aisle whenever possible. For example, in 1999, when the Senate was on the verge of making significant cuts to Medicare to balance the budget, Mikulski formed a coalition with Senator Susan Collins (R-ME). Together, they launched a successful petition drive to prevent the Senate from adjourning until the cuts were restored. In 2005, she cosponsored, with Senators Mel Martinez (R-FL) and Kit Bond (R-MO), among others, the reauthorization of HOPE VI, an innovative revitalization initiative through the Department of Housing and Urban Development. The law would create sustainable, mixed-income communities, ending the concentration of the poor in distressed areas and emphasizing high-performing schools. She has also successfully introduced legislation expanding funding for nursing programs, and she continues to work to increase the federal investment in social work through loan forgiveness. She also successfully cosponsored S.2, which raised the minimum wage, and she is a strong advocate for children. In 2007, the Children's Defense Fund Action Council noted her 100 percent voting record in favor of improving the lives of children. In the area of health care for women, Mikulski's ongoing support, in concert with others, has resulted in a 700 percent increase in funding for breast cancer since 1990. "We've [also] increased funding for the [Food and Drug Administration's] Office of Women's Health. We've secured funding for the Institute of Medicine to review the status and future of women's health research" (Barbara Mikulski, personal communication, May 13, 2009). Her voting record also reflects continued support for military families and progressive environmental legislation.

Recently, the senator's bipartisan collaborations facilitated the continuation and expansion of services to women victims of domestic violence: with Senators Richard Shelby (R-AL) and Patty Murray (D-WA), she sponsored an amendment to increase funding for Violence against Women Act programs. And it was Mikulski's leadership that resulted in the vote to strike the Vitter Amendment from that bill. The Vitter Amendment would have denied community-oriented policing services (COPS) grants to cities that would not ask about immigration status when people report crimes. Clearly, this would have had a very negative impact on immigrant victims of domestic and sexual violence, who likely would have been reluctant to call the police under such conditions (Northern Virginia Coalition, 2008).

In 2009, Mikulski is continuing to champion women, children, and the working class, most notably by taking a leadership role in the effort to pass a universal health-care law (Stein, 2009). She brings social work values and ethics to the Senate floor and remains faithful to her community-based public service roots (for a complete list of Mikulski's Senate activities in 2009, see http://www.thomas.gov/cgi-bin/bdquery).

The "Dean of Women"

As the longest-serving female senator, Mikulski has been dubbed the "dean of women." It is a role she takes seriously, mentoring female senators from both parties as soon as they come into the Senate and "proving that women are not solo acts, but work together to get things done" (Mikulski, 2007). In 1992, she launched a series of bipartisan workshops for four newly elected female senators to help them understand the sometimes-arcane rules and the culture of the Senate. It enabled them to assert themselves more quickly and to avoid potential pitfalls:

> When I got to the Senate, I did my homework. I established relationships with the old guard, starting with Senator Byrd, listening to him and watching him and other effective senators in action. In this way, I learned the rules, ways of

being effective. . . . And I continued to do my homework, going to all the hearings and traveling on Senate fact-finding trips, because homework impresses the Senate leadership. And the other thing I did was treat everybody fairly, including the Republicans, even when I was at war with them on something like the Anita Hill debacle. (Mikulski, 2007, p. 50)

Role Models

Senator Mikulski's role models include, among others, Jane Addams and Florence Kelley, who are acknowledged as foremothers of the social work profession. Both pioneers engaged in political processes to improve the lives of women and children in particular. Mikulski recalled their achievements in a 2003 question-and-answer session with the organization Influencing State Policy:

> The great names in social work . . . claimed the power they needed, and changed this nation forever. Jane Addams worked with her state legislature and with the federal government to create child labor laws. She got the state government to put expiration dates on milk so children wouldn't drink spoiled liquids. Florence Kelley founded the National Consumers League. Her name is synonymous with the fight to secure better wages for women. In 1909, social workers organized the first White House Conference on Children. This was the first time the government showed an interest in child welfare.

In addition, Senator Mikulski credits the nuns who taught her. They were her role models, and they had a tremendous impact on her: "The nuns taught the values of the Catholic faith: love your neighbor, care for the sick, worry about the poor. They placed an emphasis on leadership and development: putting values into action, speaking up and speaking out. They also taught us that we could be smart, womanly, and effective" (Barbara Mikulski, personal communication, May 13, 2009).

While Mikulski values community organizing and political action, she has always maintained respect for those who engage in direct practice and clinical work. This is evidenced in her attempts to secure resources for those in need of services such as drug interventions, legal aid, child protection, support for senior citizens, and domestic violence programs.

Beyond Bills: Being a Woman in Congress

The lack of gender balance in the Senate is troubling, and its impact on our country is significant. Reflecting on the 1996 election, when twelve women were elected to national office, in 2002 the professor and television news personality Steve Roberts spoke about the impact of women in Congress: "They bring life experiences to Congress—as mothers, caregivers, single parents, etc. They see the practical effects of legislation on women. They place [certain] issues higher on their agendas, saying, 'This is what I care about.' They vote in a way other women support, such as banning assault weapons. They civilize the Congress. They tend to be more reasonable, accommodating, and thoughtful" (Blais et al., 2002).

And yet, as of 2008, little progress has been made in this arena. According to the Center for American Women and Politics (2008), "Women hold 86, or 16.1%, of the 535 seats in the 109th US Congress—16, or 16.0%, of the 100 seats in the Senate and 70, or 16.1%, of the 435 seats in the House of Representatives."

Nevertheless, Mikulski believes that having women in Congress has made a positive difference despite the low numbers:

> As more women Senators joined me over the years, we've been able to make a real difference. Together, we've raised awareness. We raised our voices and got things done. For instance: funding for breast cancer research used to be skimpy and Spartan. We've changed that. . . . We've increased funding for the FDA's Office of Women's Health. We've secured funding for the Institute of Medicine to review the status and future of women's health research. Those are just a few examples. . . .
>
> We are in an institution where people love to work on the big picture and talk so much in empty abstractions that it was often women who are talking about how it works at the community level, at the family level and what it means, whether it's keeping our economy going, or it's women in the military and what that means in terms of the families, all the way through our domestic and our foreign policy. Because every issue is a women's issue. (Barbara Mikulski, personal communication, May 13, 2009)

In 1999, the nine female U.S. senators discussed the lessons they had learned and wanted to share with other women who might serve in public office. Their words of wisdom clearly reflect the words of Senator

Mikulski and offer advice for social workers who are considering careers in public office.

1. When someone says, "Why you?" think "Why not me?"
2. Remember who you are, and where you came from.
3. Create a team effort.
4. Don't take it personally—and don't make it personal.
5. Identify the felt need (have a cause or a principle).
6. Respect your losses.
7. Control your agenda.
8. Ignore the babble.
9. Pass it on. (Blais et al., 2002)

These points of advice describe how Mikulski has conducted herself throughout her public life. The motto from the Christophers movement, which has been her guiding light, is the message that she gives to others. Finally, in the senator's own words, "Senate women are not a caucus, we're a force. We're not solo acts, we build coalitions and zones of civility to get things done" (Barbara Mikulski, personal communication, May 13, 2009).

Ending on a Personal Note

Senator Mikulski is a role model for all social workers, especially for those who wish to engage in macro-level practice and public service. One author of this chapter (Collins) remembers hearing then representative Mikulski speak in the early 1980s at a national social work conference in Washington, D.C. Attending this conference and knowing no one, I stood in awe of the social work leaders whose books and articles I had read as a MSW student. However, the most moving session I attended was the talk by Representative Mikulski. At that point in her own career, she was uncertain about whether to remain in the social work field. It was Mikulski's speech that motivated her to stay in the profession and to earn her doctorate in social work. Mikulski's message was clear: it doesn't matter what you do, just do something and stay involved. Barbara Mikulski clearly has done just that during her lifetime. Although she is a strong fighter, she appears to engage in battle through collaboration whenever possible. This is good advice for all of us. At the same time, she speaks her mind and does not allow herself to take attacks from others personally. We need many more social workers to take the path of public engagement and to light candles, especially on behalf of those who have limited or no voice.

References

Blais, D., Farmer, S., Fauver, R. B., Fina, E., Gibber, J., Gordon, M. E., et al. (Eds.) (2002, March). The impact of women in office. In *League of Women Voters in the Fairfax Area Education Fund* (p. S-4). Fairfax, VA: The League of Women Voters of the Fairfax Area.

Broder, D. (1980). *Changing the guard.* New York: Simon & Schuster.

Center for American Women and Politics. (2008). *Facts and findings: Women officeholders fact sheets and summaries: Women in elective office 2008.* Retrieved May 6, 2008, from the Center for American Women and Politics, Eagleton Institute of Politics, Rutgers University Web site: http://www.cawp .rutgers.edu/Facts.html.

Christophers. (2008). Our mission statement. Retrieved February 1, 2008, from http://www.christophers.org/NETCOMMUNITY/Page.aspx?pid=266&srcid =192.

Influencing state policy. (2003). Retrieved February 1, 2008, from http://www.state policy.org/newsletter_archives/newsletter7-1.html.

Mandel, R. (1981). *In the running: The new woman candidate.* New Haven, CT: Ticknor & Fields.

Mara, M. (with interviews by Thomas, H.) (2005). *Changing the face of power: Women in the U.S. Senate.* Austin: University of Texas Press.

Mikulski, B. A. (2007). Barbara Mikulski: My life as a student. In H. Chaiklin and the Class of 1965 (Eds.), *Tales from the warehouse: The class of 1965 remembers.* Baltimore: H. Chaiklin and the Class of 1965, School of Social Work, University of Maryland.

Northern Virginia Coalition (2008). *In the NEWS.* Retrieved July 20, 2009, from http://www.novaco.org/news.html.

Powell, P. (2007, July/August). From social work to Capitol Hill: Senator Barbara Mikulski and social work staff keep social work in the forefront. *Maryland Social Worker, 1,* 19–20.

Stein, S. (2009, June 2). Obama, Senate Dems consider a public health care option with a trigger. *Huffington Post.* Retrieved July 18, 2009, from http://www .huffingtonpost.com/2009/06/02/obama-senate-dems-conside_n_210390.html.

Whitney, C. (with Mikulski, B., Hutchison, K., Feinstein, D., Boxer, B., Murray, P., Snowe, O., Collins, S., Landrieu, M., & Lincoln, B.) (2000). *Nine and counting: The women of the Senate.* New York: HarperCollins.

CHAPTER THREE

Alicia M. Kirchner

Minister of Social Development in Argentina

Irene Queiro-Tajalli

I flew to Buenos Aires, Argentina, to interview Dr. Alicia M. Kirchner because of her strong identification with social work and her extensive participation in macro-level social work. However, on my arrival in Buenos Aires, I realized that this would be a daunting project. On that day, President Cristina Fernández de Kirchner and her cabinet were dealing with grain-export taxes. To protest these taxes, farmers began to strike and to block roads, thereby preventing trucks from delivering produce to stores in Buenos Aires and other cities. The political climate was tense, and I was concerned that clashes would break out between those in favor and those against the government measures. Clearly, Minister Kirchner was extremely busy with cabinet meetings and negotiations.

Despite these developments, I felt confident that I would be able to conduct the interview and that it was important for me to be patient and relaxed. But as the time of my departure became imminent, my anxiety began to rise. Finally, five days before I was to return to the United States, the phone rang and I was told that the minister (the sister of ex-president

Néstor Kirchner) was ready to see me. Her story is an inspiration to me, and I hope to social work students and graduates
as well.

Background

With a population of 39.5 million people, Argentina is the world's
eighth-largest country, covering an area of 2.8 million square kilometers
(about 1.74 million square miles). It has diverse terrain with some of the
world's tallest mountains found in the Andes, the breathtaking Iguazú
Falls, extensive deserts, the vast cattle-grazing plains of the pampas, the
majestic beauty of the glaciers in Patagonia, and Ushuaia, the southern-
most city of the world. Argentina declared its independence from Spain
in 1816 and became a republic. It is considered one of South America's
largest economies, with a well-educated workforce, and it is one of the
main cereal-producing areas in the world. Throughout its history,
Argentina has had a mixture of democratic and military governments.
The last military government ruled the country from 1977 to 1983, a
period of terrible repression. Tens of thousands of people were
abducted, tortured, killed, or disappeared during the seven years of the
Dirty War (*guerra sucia*). These were cruel years that left open wounds
in the fabric of the Argentine society. "The paralyzing of the democratic
institutions in society gave the opportunity for the flourishing of the
most conservative perspectives within the [social work] profession"
(Queiro-Tajalli, 1995, p. 99) and a drastic reduction in the scope of social
work intervention. As many government programs were curtailed or
eliminated, practitioners and faculty who spoke up in opposition
placed themselves in great danger. Some left the country while others
continued the struggle against the military junta.

In 1983, the country returned to a democratic government. However,
freedom from the oppressive military government did not mean economic freedom from the institutions of global oppression. From the
Argentine point of view, organizations like the International Monetary
Fund and the World Bank began to shape harmful policies, albeit in a
subtle manner during the mid-1970s (Hintze, 2007). For example, as a
result of the structural adjustments imposed by both of these institutions as a condition for receiving foreign loans (including privatization
of many government functions, extremely high interest rates on the
national debt, and free trade), the country was left in a deep recession.
This resulted in the collapse of the Argentine economy in 2001.

The collapse engendered chaos and unrest. Widespread rioting
swept the country. When it was over, twenty-nine people were dead,
and thousands of families found themselves in poverty (Clemente &

Girolami, 2006). After the resignation of President Fernando de la Rúa in December 2001, three presidents took office in ten days. The country suffered debt defaults and currency devaluation. Amid all of these tragic events, one positive development was the rebirth of grassroots organizing and innovative projects created by citizens to survive the crisis.

In my view, Argentina in the new millennium is quite different from the country at the end of the previous millennium. It has moved from a government heavily guided by neoliberal policies to a populist government established by the election of Néstor Kirchner in 2003. He governed until 2007, when his wife, Cristina Fernández de Kirchner, was elected president. President Néstor Kirchner tried to distance the government from the repressive ways of the 1990s and emphasized transparency and social inclusion in social policies. It is worth noting that he moved his government away from a heavy dependence on the United States and Western Europe, reinforced alliances with Latin American countries, rejected the Free Trade Area of the Americas, and canceled the debt with the International Monetary Fund. President Cristina Fernández de Kirchner has, by and large, continued a similar national agenda away from neoliberal globalization.

With this brief snapshot of the country, I am delighted to present my interview with the minister of social development of Argentina, Dr. Alicia Kirchner. The Ministry of Social Development is one of the eleven ministries that work with the president in the area of social assistance and human development. Among other things, it manages the resources assigned to impoverished sectors of the population.

The Early Years

Dr. Alicia Kirchner realized early on that she had a great desire to help others and she thus began her passionate drive to change the world. She is a third-generation Argentine. Kirchner was born in Río Gallegos, the capital of Santa Cruz, a southern province of Argentina in the well-known Patagonia region. Her mother was a second-generation Croatian and her father was of Swiss-German ancestry.

As a child, Kirchner spent her summers with one of her aunts who lived near an indigenous community. She remembers the housing there, which lacked basic amenities. "The girls from that community were my friends in adventure and through them, I learned about their culture and their constraints. The girls were very respectful of their ancestral customs and I learned to respect those customs as well, even though I did not always agree with them."

Dr. Kirchner traced her interest in social work back to a secondary school project, when she had had the opportunity to participate in a community census as part of her studies. The experience of observing and surveying in a systematic manner gave her firsthand knowledge of the realities of her community that she otherwise might have missed: "More than likely, this school assignment gave me the motivation that, together with my temperament, oriented me toward social work." With the advantage of time, one can see that her school project from more than forty years ago provides us today with an excellent example of the importance of service learning as an educational tool for current-day students.

Kirchner spoke fondly of her father, remembering him as someone who had inspired her to take action and fight for justice and human rights. When she was very young, he taught her to be responsible for herself and to be true to her values and principles. Politically, he was a person who advocated for the common good and believed that any critique of social issues had to include possible responses or solutions.

When Kirchner entered high school, she studied to become a primary school teacher. By the time she entered college, the passion for social justice she had acquired in childhood moved her to pursue a career in social work.

Early on, her parents questioned her decision to pursue her chosen career path. As she thought back on it, she commented that they probably expected her to pursue law or medicine, two of the most valued career choices among Argentine parents at that time. She was, however, steadfast in her decision. So to pursue her dream, she moved to La Plata, the capital of the province of Buenos Aires. La Plata was more than 1,200 miles away from Río Gallegos, so at the age of sixteen, young Alicia was truly away from home: "I was the only female from my high school graduating class who was allowed to move away to attend the university in another province. My other classmates were not allowed to do so by their parents."

Kirchner stated that it was a true challenge (*desafío*) to a culture that viewed women as teachers or professors who were to stay with their families to be protected as long as they were single. However, Kirchner was determined to become a social worker. She had only the support of her father, who was still not convinced of the appropriateness of her career choice but respected her decision and decided to partner with her in the endeavor.

Entry to the Profession

Kirchner entered the university in the mid-1960s. The country was under military rule, and the times of great political repression led to, among other things, military occupation of the national universities. This open attack on the autonomy of higher education led to the elimination of student and faculty governance, which were replaced by a centralized military administration. With one declaration, universities that were once bubbling with new ideas and theories from Christian democracy to socialism and Marxism were suddenly silenced by the power of the gun. Faculty opposed to the military ideology were soon removed from their positions and expelled from academia.

Despite the trying times and the curtailment of the human rights of all students and faculty, Kirchner continued her studies. Her social work courses provided her with theoretical foundations, skills, and technical information that helped her understand the social realities of her country. Her vision developed out of her political commitment to democracy in a country that routinely violated the human and social rights of its citizens while under military rule. She saw firsthand the tremendous need for social change in her community and country: "As a student in social work, I had the opportunity to participate in the daily life of the disenfranchised that lived in the poor areas of La Plata City while doing my practicum at Caritas [an international organization that provides assistance to the most vulnerable on behalf of Catholics around the world]. This training, together with my passion for justice, helped me to generate new questions about societal conditions. It created a sense of purpose that I could put into action through a militant praxis within a social context." The praxis (or practical application of a theory) of the practitioners during military rule was questioned because they were in search of participation, social change, respect for civil liberties, and the promotion of human capacity, all concepts that the military detested. Although all aspects of her social work education have been important to her, social justice and respect for others have a special place in her professional makeup.

Kirchner worked diligently to fulfill her educational goals and received both her *licenciatura* (a baccalaureate) as well as a master's degree and doctoral degree in social work.

I asked whether she had mentors guiding her career choice. Kirchner responded that she did not have one particular mentor. When pressed to mention others, she said that her mentors were the citizens living in poverty in a society that considered those conditions natural: "Undoubtedly, those citizens helped me make my decision. It was based on a spirit of solidarity with vulnerable people and the need for the transformation of their precarious realities within a framework of respect for their human and social rights."

After graduation, Kirchner worked in various fields of social work, which gave her a more comprehensive view of the profession. Her initiation into the real world (*mundo real*) of practice was at the community level in neighborhood organizing. She worked in community centers and other civic societies in communities of high social vulnerability and poverty. Her work in the area of children and families, particularly child protection, later led her to coauthor the 1998 book (with Maria Elena Armas) *El arca de Noé, la familia, y el trabajo social* (Noah's Ark, the Family, and Social Work). Other areas of her practice portfolio include working with older adults, with inmates released from the penitentiary, and in schools for the physically challenged. Her contributions at the municipal and provincial levels include the empowerment of neighborhood groups and participation in the creation of day-care centers, community centers, senior citizen centers, and health clinics. Furthermore, Kirchner has a strong record organizing groups of parents with special-needs children and promoting interdisciplinary teams to work with the families and special education teachers.

She taught at the Universidad de la Patagonia Austral, the Universidad del Museo Social Argentino, and the Universidad Nacional de Lanus. In her role as an academic, Kirchner shared her conviction for interdisciplinary social work and for the praxis of the profession by proposing curriculum changes representative of those components. At the national level, she created the specialization in community practice for graduates from social work and related disciplines.

Reflecting on her experience, Kirchner recalled how difficult the practice of social work was during certain periods in the history of the country. She also has many good memories from working with communities, whose members taught her so much and challenged her to find answers to complex problems.

With respect to social work, a profession in which many social workers choose to work with individuals, groups, and families, I was curious to know why she decided to pursue macro-level practice. Kirchner mainly attributes her choice to her political involvement. Her inquisitive mind has always taken her beyond the individual issues and helped her address problems from a big-picture perspective. As she described her perspective, I saw that she was interested in understanding both the people involved in a particular situation and the larger environment that affects those people.

From Traditional Practice to the Political Arena

Kirchner's political career started much earlier than her present position. She served in different government positions in her native province, including undersecretary of social action, secretary of social promotion, and minister of social affairs. She was adviser to two national senate commissions, one on education and the other on the family. In 2003, she was appointed minister of social development by her brother, President Néstor Kirchner, but she has also served in positions to which she was duly elected: in 2005, for example, she was elected to the National Congress as senator from Santa Cruz Province. She returned to her previous position of minister of social development in August 2006.

Her life as minister is fast paced and ever changing, with constant challenges that call for creativity and vision. She works twelve- to thirteen-hour days and communicates constantly with her team members, engages herself in dialogue with others, and oversees the many projects in her portfolio. She reminded me that the country has approximately 40 million inhabitants and that her administration has to make sure that it understands all the different voices of the population: "I enjoy being in direct communication with the citizens. For me it is essential that I listen to their opinions and recommendations."

For the minister, change cannot be shaped in an office behind a desk. Instead, it needs to happen in each community, integrating experiences and actions, setting aside the attitude of "What's in it for me?" and developing a complete commitment to the cause of justice and equity. For this to happen, people and government need to work together: "We cannot be mere spectators; a country in development needs the active and energetic participation of all its citizens." Kirchner loves to travel across the country to meet and talk to people and to assess the impact of social policies and projects. This direct interaction with the citizens is fundamental in allowing her to learn about their opinions and suggestions. Her chief of staff told me that when Kirchner travels around the country by car, she makes a point to stop and talk with the farmers working the fields. By doing this, Kirchner learns firsthand about the accomplishments and challenges faced by the people she serves.

Because so much of her administrative philosophy rests on including the community voice into the national policy dialogue, I asked Kirchner what she considered a healthy community. She responded, "I define a healthy community as those communities that are continuously improving the physical and social environment, and developing community resources that allow people to carry on their daily activities and to achieve their maximum potential through mutual support. [It is] a place where all the institutions, public and private, involved in socioeconomic development in general, or in specific areas such as health, education, and transportation, work together with political, religious, and civic groups to . . . promote the well-being of all people."

The concept of social inclusion is also reflected in the creation of comprehensive community centers. The brainchild of Kirchner and sponsored by the national government, the centers are anchored in the concept of a civic society that promotes a democratic way of living from a local perspective. The goal is to stimulate resources and foster the full participation and development of all local potential. The centers convey at the local level the public policies designed to address the individual socioeconomic and sociocultural problems of different communities. They alleviate much of the fragmented policy implementation that so often alienates community residents and coordinate activities of the various national, provincial, and municipal agencies with those of local community organizations. According to Kirchner, the community centers are "the state [government] present in the community." Because the planning and implementation of programs vary on the basis of idiosyncratic community needs, it is almost impossible to enumerate the services that the centers provide. However, it is safe to say that they provide public health and social services, education, job training, cultural activities, sports, and a safe physical space "owned" by the community residents where they can engage in dialogue about common concerns and incubate projects leading to the progress of their communities. As Kirchner said, the community cannot be a passive receptor of programs. It is the people who must be participants in the solutions and the developers of projects.

In summary, the comprehensive community centers create and strengthen citizenship in some five hundred communities and socially vulnerable neighborhoods countrywide, and they greatly increase access to preventive social policies, comprehensive services, resources, and government opportunities. Indeed, the centers are in line with Kirchner's concept of social policies that need to contribute to the improvement of the individual, the family, and the environment. Kirchner added that she would like to take her experience of building communities through a participatory process to other parts of the world, all while acknowledging that there is still much to be done in Argentina.

When I asked about her personal accomplishments, Kirchner preferred to talk about collective gains achieved through shared leadership: "Undoubtedly, the achievements of our projects are part of a larger national project to which I have devoted my professional life." She seldom used the word *I* in our conversation.

Kirchner has faced many challenges. When she took office in 2003, the country was still suffering from the collapse of the economy in 2001. According to Kirchner, "The social welfare system was one of paternalism, yet we were able to gradually overcome this crisis based on the conviction that other realities are possible. In order to mitigate the results brought about by the destruction of the country, it was imperative to recover lost time and rebuild the country expeditiously."

Another challenge that Kirchner highlighted was that of a bureaucratic system that was not in line with her administrative philosophy. As she explained, her office had to deal with officials who were still trapped in old-style politics while working in an administration that was shifting away from such governance. For Kirchner, people deserved more than just temporary relief. For example, she believes that problems related to a nutritional safety net cannot be resolved simply with food kitchens but by discovering and developing people's unique abilities and skills to improve their human condition and by putting those to work in service to the problem. An example of this would be the introduction and subsequent proliferation of microcredit finance institutions to the economy (Mitchell, 2006). Conversely, people with immediate needs cannot be given only long-term solutions, as dependency might result.

Another example of the change in modus operandi that has taken place on her watch is illustrated by an incident that took place only a few hours after she took office. At that time, she was instructed to immediately sign a contract to approve that an international consulting firm take over one of the country's social programs. The message was clear: sign it now—there was no time to read or analyze the contract because there was a chance of losing the private funding arrangement. Kirchner resolutely refused to sign, convinced that the state would meet its obligation to its people: "We were no longer going to be trapped in policies of dependence, more often than not signed under pressure and without scrutiny." The main mission of her administration has been to ensure that social policies reflect the needs of the communities and are embraced by the government. In her view, it is imperative that social policies improve the quality of life of all individuals, through political, social, economic, and cultural transformation.

When Kirchner started her administration, there were few social workers in the ministry. One of her first foci was to increase the number of social workers and to ensure that social policies were framed in a social work perspective and with social work's professional values at the forefront. She further explained that the implementation of comprehensive and territorial social policies demanded an increase in the number of social workers employed by the Ministry of Social Development, workers who are trained in interdisciplinary work and share a similar professional view on the role of social policies in constructing a strong society. The goal, she added, is the institutionalization of a comprehensive network of social policies to improve the quality of life of all citizens. One of the many examples of this is the involvement of social workers in the national train project. This is a collaborative project between the Ministries of Social Development and Public Health to improve the social and public health indicators of the communities they visit (by train) through prevention, promotion, and direct assistance in the areas of social functioning and health. It promotes the rights of families, children, mothers, the elderly, and the physically and mentally challenged. The train does not operate in a vacuum but articulates its services in collaboration with the provincial governments, municipalities, nongovernmental organizations, local community groups, cooperatives, hospitals, health clinics, rural schools, and others. The train carries doctors, social workers, nurses, administrators, support staff, and technical personnel, all educated to respect the unique cultural and social characteristics of the communities and geographic areas they serve.

In summary, Kirchner is aware that her ministry is in need of a larger cadre of social workers and other human services providers, yet the increase has to be gradual and based on the economic realities of the country.

The profession of social work, she believes, builds on the precepts of a civil society and safeguards social participation. As she pointed out, "I would like to see a society that promotes freedom as well as citizens who are respectful of that freedom, with our profession being a key actor in the promotion of such a vision." Employment, education, and social development in a culturally sensitive framework are challenges to be faced in the evolution of contemporary social policy. Respect for regional characteristics and regional autonomy is required. Yet again, I realized that Kirchner is putting into practice what we learn in social work: to build a culturally sensitive practice based on the specific characteristics of the community in which we work.

Social Development in a Globalized Society

We could not finish the interview without talking about globalization and its impact on the people she serves. Kirchner addressed the question of globalization within the neoliberal economic model and its catastrophic worldwide consequences. In particular, her administration is faced with the elimination of sources of work and the exclusion of millions of citizens from the benefits of social welfare, an aftermath of the long years of devolution from the 1990s. She pointed out that, since 2003, to respond to the crisis, the government has worked to reinforce policies that create sources of employment. For her, there is a direct link between labor policies, the social economy, and social development. Of particular focus for her administration has been the creation of cooperatives, the support of access to microcredit (i.e., small business loans), the finding of ways to commercialize local products, and the development of networks for the distribution of their products. The central government has also become a buyer of some of those products. Furthermore, public assistance programs have been strengthened for female heads of household with seven or more children, for seniors seventy years old or older, and for the physically challenged. Although these are but some of the measures designed to counterbalance the effects of the financial global crisis, Kirchner is well aware of the extraordinary number of issues affecting social development in a global society. Clearly, her social work background and her many years of experience in the field of social work came out when she verbalized her own questions related to the praxis needed to address globalization and social development. These questions touch on how to achieve social integration in a globalized society, how to create new approaches to counterbalance the increasing global violence and addictions that impact the local communities, how to use informatics as a common denominator to improve people's well-being, how to protect millions of families worldwide from the rapid depletion of natural resources, how to develop technologies to protect the environment, how to integrate social research with the realities of diverse communities to bring about a social transformation that does not violate the characteristic of their people, and how to create a collective understanding that all citizens are responsible for the welfare of the country. Although the interview time did not allow us to go into deeper discussion about the extent to which she has dealt with some of these questions, a look at her administration's plans indicates her leadership, which has provided the principles and foundation for addressing some of those questions. The comprehensive community centers might just be a blueprint for social development in a globalized society.

Advice for New Social Workers

When asked to provide some advice for recent graduates, Kirchner replied that social workers should not fear change. Complacency is disastrous for the profession. Furthermore, social workers should not lose sight of the extreme need to act in defense of the voiceless. Social workers must also understand that they need professional autonomy if they are to devote their career to helping others. Kirchner feels so strongly that social work professionals should be equipped to become skilled social activists that she played a key role in the development of a social work master's degree program with a concentration in comprehensive community approaches. This specialization is now offered in a number of universities and emphasizes knowledge, reflection, and praxis.

When I asked Kirchner whether, at any point, she had thought of leaving the profession, she answered that the ongoing struggle for justice and the promotion of human rights have given her the impetus, even during trying times, to continue in the field of social welfare. She urged all social workers to find their passion in the profession and never abandon the cause.

In closing the interview, Kirchner said that she has felt privileged to have the opportunity to create public policies with the support and commitment of so many people. Furthermore, she is appreciative of being a part of a government that is people oriented and concerned for social welfare. As she notes, not many professionals have had such an opportunity. For a woman making so much change at this high level, I found Kirchner to be exceedingly modest. Throughout the interview, she emphasized teamwork. She gave herself little credit but continuously acknowledged the work of all the members of her team, both professionals and community members, working at the grassroots level. Most important, she applauded the citizens for their willingness to try new ways of thinking and doing. As our interview ended, I felt privileged to have met and spoken with a woman of her personal stature and commitment to social justice for all. If Alicia Kirchner will not acknowledge her many contributions to the Argentine people, my hope is that this interview will do so for her.

References

Clemente, A., & Girolami, M. (2006). *Territorio, emergencia, e intervención social: Un modelo para desarmar.* Buenos Aires: Espacio Editorial.

Hintze, S. (2007). *Políticas sociales argentinas en el cambio del siglo.* Buenos Aires: Espacio Editorial.

Mitchell, J. (2006, August 1). Americas: Argentina; Microcredit hits the big time—Banks are considering joining microcredit institutions in offering loans to Argentina's post-crisis generation of microentrepreneurs. *The Banker.* Retrieved August 21, 2009, from http://www.highbeam.com/doc/1G1-14908 9949.html.

Queiro-Tajalli, I. (1995). Argentina. In T. D. Watts, D. Elliott, and N. S. Mayadas (Eds.), *International handbook on social work education* (pp. 88–102). Westport, CT: Greenwood Press.

CHAPTER FOUR

Nazneen S. Mayadas

An Advocate for Refugees Worldwide

Uma A. Segal

Condensing the work of a social work exemplar par excellence, such as Dr. Nazneen Sada Mayadas, along with her work's antecedents, contexts, and consequences, into one chapter is challenging. Global advocate, practitioner, researcher, and academic, this social worker has practiced and taught social work across national boundaries for more than four decades. Her life's journey through social work in many nations has seen her contribute to the knowledge base of the discipline through her research and scholarship, inspire young professionals through her outstanding teaching, and traverse the globe as an advocate and practitioner seeking improvements for those in abject desolation. Nazneen is a truly bicultural individual, as at home watching a theater performance in Dallas as she is celebrating a birthday or family occasion in New Delhi with her many close friends. I interviewed her several times over the phone, by e-mail, and in person.

The Beginning: Childhood and Youth in Lucknow, India

Nazneen Sada Mayadas was born in India, the younger of two daughters of a renowned physician in Lucknow, in the Awadh region of India, who maintained a lucrative family practice. His patients were the city's elite and the nawabs of Awadh (*nawab* is the title of rulers who governed Awadh in the eighteenth and nineteenth centuries; as such, nawabs were central to the Awadh power structure, and their descendents continue to assert influence in the region to this day). He also had a parallel pro bono client base consisting of indigent patients, whom he supplied with food and medicine. Nazneen's mother, a homemaker, was always actively engaged in church and community service. Born fifteen years after her only sibling, Nazneen was dearly loved by her parents, sister, and the extended family; however, her childhood was bittersweet. Her mother contracted tuberculosis, for which there was then no cure, and she died at the age of forty-nine, after a three-year quarantine, leaving the ten-year-old in the care of a grieving father. Nazneen's sister had married and moved to Bombay two months before their mother's death. The next ten years necessitated the development of an independent and self-directed young person. In the absence of external controls, family expectations and values such as duty and integrity became Nazneen's modus operandi for survival and success.

The India of Nazneen's childhood was under British rule but well on its way, under Mahatma Gandhi's inspirational leadership, toward independence. The culture of Lucknow was, and still is, renowned for its graciousness, art, poetry, architecture, and finesse of its language and manners, which are derived from Shiite traditions. Imbued with this culture, Nazneen continues to enjoy the art, music, language, and cuisine of her native land. Many who know her recognize the Lucknowi graciousness in her manner and the elegance of the language of Lucknow is translated into her communication style in English. Privilege during this time was synonymous with a Western Weltanschauung and lifestyle, including access to English-language elementary and higher education and relatively equal access to life's opportunities for women. Belonging to a Christian minority in a Hindu nation, Nazneen might have experienced discrimination; however, her family's social status and the multicultural academic institutions she attended (schools founded by American and British missionaries greatly respected for the caliber of their education) opened up for her an appreciation of Hinduism and Islam. It was in these institutions that she established a group of primarily Hindu friends with whom she developed such deep bonds of friendship that they continue in close contact today.

The home in which Nazneen grew up reflected the architecture typical of the Lucknow of the nineteenth and early twentieth centuries. The property was surrounded by orchards and gardens and consisted of two complete household units: that of Nazneen's father and that of his sister, who was also a physician in practice with him. The two families maintained their separate kitchens and domestic servants but socialized and related as one extended family. Each family employed a cook, a bearer (or butler), a maid, an ayah (who was responsible for caring for the needs of the children), a sweeper, a driver, a gardener, a night watchman, and a messenger (*chaprasi*). Many of them lived on the premises in servants' quarters. Servants, in those days, were considered an integral part of the family, and although they were free to leave, they frequently served families for generations.

After the death of her mother, Nazneen had to assume the responsibility of the household. At the age of twelve, while she supervised the staff at home, in school she managed to rally her peers against what she perceived as administrative injustice toward teachers. Her father was asked to remove her from the campus when she was found standing on a table "instigating a rebellion" among students, but this incident foreshadowed her commitment to social justice. Nazneen completed high school and then received her bachelor's degree in English literature, history, and economics from the Isabella Thoburn College, which was affiliated with the University of Lucknow. (Thoburn had founded the school for girls in 1870 with five students, one of whom was Nazneen's maternal grandmother. The school developed into a high school and finally a college. It is now one of the best women's colleges in India.)

Ten years after her mother's death, while Nazneen was attending college, her father, too, passed away. It was not considered seemly or safe for a young woman to live alone in so large a home, so her sister returned to Lucknow and made arrangements to sell the house; Nazneen moved into a residence on campus. Following the completion of her undergraduate education and seeking an experience outside her hometown, Nazneen went to the University of Allahabad, where she completed a master's degree in medieval Indian history.

On graduating, Nazneen joined the executive staff of the national Young Women's Christian Association of India and was based in Calcutta. She was given a dual appointment as international guesthouse resident superintendent and director of education. This experience, in addition to helping her learn the skills of management and leadership on the job, allowed her to interact with international guests and take them on city tours to observe social welfare programs. A program of considerable interest was Mother Teresa's Nirmal Hriday (Pure Heart) facility for the indigent and dying, which at that time was in an early stage of development. Nazneen found herself well suited to the work; it allowed her to broaden her network of contacts outside the country and become familiar with international service organizations, an area of endeavor that she found of great interest.

The Early Days in North America

Nazneen's exposure since childhood to Western culture, her international experiences in Calcutta, and the influence of her sister, who had studied both in the United Kingdom and in the United States, suggested that it was only a matter of time and opportunity before she would travel abroad. Opportunity presented itself through a scholarship that the U.S. YWCA offered to study at Case Western Reserve University, in Cleveland, Ohio, in the graduate social work program. Nazneen arrived in Cleveland in the fall of 1959 to begin a second master's degree. She had $8 with her, as the Indian government's restrictions on currency allowed only that amount to be taken outside the country at the time. Consequently, as she struggled financially, she found that the cost of living and the size of her scholarship required that she completely rescale her lifestyle. She says that she often did not have sufficient money to eat out with other students and would make an excuse to return to the dorm, forgoing many meals and companionship in this way. It would have been antithetical to her culture and family pride to admit to poverty. While she was in her second year in the master of science in social administration program, she was privileged to study under social work educators who were pioneers in their areas. She studied under Grace Coyle, a pioneer in social group work, and John Turner, whose expertise was community organization. Margaret Hartford, another well-known name in social group work, was her academic adviser.

It is difficult to determine whether Nazneen chose social work or if social work chose her. Her childhood and early role models, including her mother, geared her toward an orientation to service to those with few advantages. Her Christian upbringing propelled her toward the YWCA, which was then more religiously oriented than the social service institution that it is today; however, her exposure to the poor and indigent in Calcutta brought her insight into the lives and experiences of marginalized, vulnerable, disadvantaged, and exploited individuals and families. Thus, when the opportunity to move to the United States dovetailed with her growing interest in human service, the roots of her career path took firm hold.

On graduating from Case Western, trained in social work, Nazneen accepted a position of neighborhood worker at the Friendly Inn Settlement in Cleveland. Thus, she began her post-master's degree in social work as did many other young graduates: as a worker in the community, helping individuals and families improve their lives and cope with the hurdles they encounter in their environments. It was not unusual to see her moving gracefully in her sari through the housing projects while working with the residents. After two years, because of visa restrictions, Nazneen had to leave the United States. She moved to Canada and was appointed to a social work position at the Family Service Agency in Vancouver, British Columbia. Thus, Nazneen immigrated to a foreign country for the second time. In Vancouver, she moved away from community practice and developed her skills in family practice and social group work. Having been reared and educated in a Christian environment, the values of social work were ingrained, and she moved into clinical practice with ease. Along with these professional changes came personal changes, too: Nazneen married a fellow Indian. When later divorce became inevitable, Nazneen decided to focus on advancing her career, and because there were no schools in Canada that offered Ph.D.'s in social work at the time, she decided to return to the United States. On admission to the doctoral program at the George Warren Brown School of Social Work at Washington University in St. Louis, she received funding from the school and from the Canada Teaching Fellowship Award, which helped finance her doctoral studies in the first year. Later she worked at the Catholic Family Service Agency as a clinical caseworker and supervised field students from St. Louis University's School of Social Service. On graduation, she was hired as an assistant professor at St. Louis University, where she taught courses in direct practice and social group work. The popularity of her classes was such that students were known to camp in sleeping bags outside the registrar's office the night before the registration lines opened to enroll in her classes—and then to complain of having caught a cold through the night. Nazneen's popularity as an educator continued through her academic career at the Graduate School of Social Work at the University of Texas at Arlington for more than thirty years.

Becoming Established as a Social Work Educator

Two years after she joined St. Louis University, Nazneen was offered the position at the University of Texas at Arlington, with a promotion to associate professor. The program there was a relatively new one with a strong research focus. Her teaching in the early years was in the areas of direct practice and group work but, from her additional midcareer experiences, it later came to focus on diversity, multiculturalism, refugee and immigrant issues, and international social work.

Nazneen's students would say she is knowledgeable, interesting, and very challenging and demanding. She was both an innovator and a pioneer in a number of areas as she began her education career in the early 1970s. In the days when education typically involved the lecture method, she used classroom discussion to engage students in their own learning (I regret that, as a graduate student in the School of Social Work from 1973 to 1975, I waited until my last semester to avail myself of the resources of this excellent educator). In addition to a tremendous enthusiasm for teaching, Nazneen evidenced a superior ability to present her depth of knowledge of the subject matter in a manner that was both interesting and inclusive. In her group dynamics class, she taught by example, modeling the skills she expected students to learn.

While working on her doctorate at Washington University's George Warren Brown School, and later as a teacher at St. Louis University, Nazneen became convinced of the efficacy of video feedback for teaching, training, and practice. When she arrived at the University of Texas, she integrated this into her coursework for direct practice and to teach interviewing skills as well as group process. The use of video feedback enabled students (including myself) to immediately evaluate the group process, understand the dynamics among group members, and critically assess the effects of our individual actions. Her ability to constructively address areas that needed improvement increased students' willingness to internalize recommendations. Therefore, as students reviewed classroom role-playing activities and received both video and verbal feedback, they were able to closely scrutinize their own performance and the performance of others, which provided them with immediate feedback, a powerful tool for education and behavior change and for developing the critical ability to recognize and evaluate clinical skills. Furthermore, for Nazneen, it was not sufficient that the skills students learned be limited to the classroom; she required that they transfer their newly acquired knowledge to the field and teach practitioners in agencies. Students' final grade was based on agency presentations delivered to practitioners in the Dallas–Fort Worth area. For many students who were afraid of speaking in public (including, again, myself), the exercise was difficult. However, besides allowing the instructor to assess our knowledge of the subject matter, the experience was a major step for students to self-identify as professional social workers with the skills to impart knowledge to their colleagues who were already practicing in the profession.

This video feedback Nazneen had integrated into her courses was beginning to be used in psychology at the time but was still rare in the field of social work. Nazneen began developing a series of demonstration audiovisual materials, with associated instructor manuals (another innovation in the field of social work education), from the mid-1970s to the early 1990s. These materials modeled not only the basic skills of interviewing but also the more advanced skills of conducting interviews with specific client groups, working with marital dyads, group process and therapy, and assertiveness training, to name a few. I have used the tapes myself in classroom teaching and have found them highly effective—I'm not surprised that the tapes have been in such high demand and are so timeless. Even after thirty-five years, Nazneen continues to receive requests for them. The tapes are tremendous and lasting contributions, and even when and if they do become dated, the utility of such tools in educating for practice will persist. A consummate academic (for her it was not adequate merely to use the materials and to make them available for distribution), many of her journal articles during those three decades focused on the empirical validation of the use of video feedback, video-modeling, and stimulus videos in the education of social work students and practitioners. Before it was fashionable to do so, Nazneen was developing empirically based skill models and evaluating their effectiveness.

In the 1970s and 1980s, the young Graduate School of Social Work at Arlington was open to creativity and alternative modes of education, and it supported faculty who sought to implement new ideas, such as the integration of extension programs and distance learning into the teaching process. Nazneen enthusiastically participated in these, traveling to rural areas of Texas, such as the Rio Grande Valley, Amarillo, Abilene, and Nacogdoches to bring her distinctive brand of teaching to students in these outlying areas. As the curricula progressed and the programs became more advanced, she was among the first to teach in the distance education programs that provided video connections between the faculty member in one location and students in another. At that time, there were few models of teaching social work in this format, and Nazneen had to develop them herself while also integrating the video-feedback process into them. In these early days, her pioneering service to the profession was already evident: she cochaired, with Paul Glasser, then dean of Arlington's School of Social Work, the second international conference of the Association for the Advancement of Social Work with Groups. This was an important conference for the development of the organization and for the relatively new School of Social Work where the conference was held. After the conference, scholarship was never far away, and Glasser and Mayadas coedited a book of readings arising from the conference.

The triadic responsibilities of educators are research, teaching, and service. Nazneen's long record of publication, with books, book chapters, articles in peer-reviewed journals, and countless presentations locally, nationally, and in close to twenty countries outside the United States speak to her research capabilities.

The caliber of her teaching and supervision of students at the graduate and doctoral levels have earned her much recognition. Because of her known excellence in teaching and research, she was invited back to teach as a visiting professor at the George Warren Brown School of Social Work. She taught short, intensive one- to two-week courses for almost as long as she was a professor at the University of Texas at Arlington. At that time, she was also a visiting professor at Smith College School of Social Work in Northampton, Massachusetts, and an exchange professor at the South Glamorgan Institute of Higher Education in Cardiff, Wales.

The UN High Commissioner for Refugees Experience

In 1980, Nazneen was appointed chief of social services to the office of the UN High Commissioner for Refugees (UNHCR) based in Geneva, Switzerland. Once again, leaving all that had become familiar and taking a one-year leave of absence from the University of Texas (which then expanded to four years), Nazneen crossed international borders to live and work in another country. As chief of social services, she found herself in an international and multicultural environment that was demanding and challenging. She was the chief advocate for social work and social services in a working environment where the value of the profession was not always fully appreciated. Although Nazneen's office was at UN headquarters in Geneva, her work was primarily in refugee camps and UNHCR field offices in Africa, South America, and South and Southeast Asia. The majority of the world's countries, at that time, were signatories to the 1951 convention relating to the status of refugees and the 1967 protocol, which expanded the UNHCR mission to include African refugees. Signatory countries each had a UNHCR presence with a social service unit that was responsible to the head office through the social service section, of which Nazneen was chief. Consequently, Nazneen made mission trips to most of these countries, traveling at least once and often several times to fifteen countries in Africa, seven in Asia, ten in Europe, and another seven in Central and South America.

Local service providers, who were not trained in social work, staffed most social service units. If they had MSW degrees, they were immediately placed in regional, national, or international positions. The traditional role for the social service section in UNHCR disaster services had been in recovery and development rather than in the earlier stages of preventative planning and relief services. To extend and engage social work to its capacity in the full range of services that the situation demanded, Nazneen felt, was a challenge, especially as the expectations for social services to effect change were high.

Nazneen was responsible for overseeing the type and quality of all social services in the refugee camps but not for the administration of the camp itself. Thus, all services for children and adults that were identified as being of a social work nature (e.g., counseling, education, recreation, fund-raising programs, self-employment opportunities outside and inside the camp, vocational training, family adoption, psychosocial assessments, therapeutic services, language training) all came within the purview of social services. "The day is very long in the camp, and there is nothing to do," Nazneen said in our interview. Social services provided survival and adaptation tools to refugees. To some extent, these activities also served to prevent problems that could emerge from feelings of listlessness and uselessness. Nazneen provided an anecdote of a visit to a kitchen in a refugee camp in Africa that reflects this well. As the staff cooked a stew in an enormous pot in the center of the kitchen, the refugee women waited despondently with their children, and with sudden insight, Nazneen asked them if they would prefer to cook the food themselves for their families. Their affirmative response resulted in Nazneen's support of the reorganization of food distribution, allowing camp staff to redirect its efforts and empowering the women to resume a familiar role in their families.

In addition, all educational programs, including schooling for students and for urban refugees who were attending schools in the host country outside the camps, were under the auspices of a subdepartment of the Office of Social Services. Staff in this department were also responsible for advocating for refugee students in the school system and ensuring that they had equal access to support and scholarships as did children of nationals.

As chief of social services, Nazneen was introduced to a range of peoples and cultures, and she was received with the diplomatic protocol attached to the position. She was responsible for negotiating with government officials in host countries for refugees' needs both in the camp and in the community. In 1980, she recognized that the life of the refugee movement was at a point where countries had experienced the influx of refugees over a long period of time. Host countries had lost enthusiasm for the influx of families seeking freedom that was evident in the 1950s when refugees of World War II were being resettled. The countries were beginning to evidence compassion fatigue. In her observation, countries such as the United States, Canada, Australia, the United Kingdom, and nations in Western Europe that had admitted the white refugees (World War II) were finding that the newer refugees were nonwhite and culturally different from them—soon a resentment began building. The desire to accommodate such refugees declined, but because the receiving countries were signatories to the 1951 convention and the 1967 protocol, they were obligated to admit them. The outcome was that interaction with the host community became more difficult, and conditions in the camps began to be oppressive. Policies to control refugee flow were termed *humane deterrent*; for example, refugees in camps were forced to write exaggerated accounts of suffering to their families to discourage them from leaving also. Boats that were carrying refugees were turned around while still in international waters.

Nazneen's task was to negotiate policies to open opportunities for refugees who, because of the color of their skin and their countries of origin, were not welcomed. Compassion revival required that Nazneen negotiate with the departments that represented welfare in the host countries. These were usually ministries of welfare, although, in smaller countries, she would meet with people higher in the governmental hierarchy. Negotiations increased awareness of the plight of refugees to whom these countries had committed to provide refuge and revolved around the possibility of adding new programs for refugees, expanding programs, increasing the budget for services, and doing whatever they could to improve opportunities for the refugees. On one occasion, as she attempted to open a dialogue about additional programs for refugees that would permit them to work in the city while living in the camps, Nazneen was struck by the challenge of the discussions when one minister of welfare looked at her directly and blatantly said, "We are not running a Hilton Hotel; we are running a refugee camp here." Therefore, when there was any concession and the host country agreed to give the refugees more than it had thus far, Nazneen said that that was the "most rewarding, personally." "Now, of course," she said, "those camps have gone, and things have changed."

In Geneva, keeping abreast of what was going on in the world was overwhelming. Each morning, the desk in Nazneen's office was covered with files a foot high with reports from numerous parts of the world. Her responsibility was to assess how social services could intervene in particular situations, but frequently, social services had neither the authority nor the resources to intervene. In the UNHCR, social services were perceived either as consultants by country desks or as technical staff whose role was to implement decisions taken by the field office or the country desk. Hence, an unspoken and hidden task of social services was to bring about a cognitive shift regarding its role.

A major, tangible, and long-lasting product of Nazneen's tenure was the development of a manual, a handbook of social services. At the beginning of her tenure at the UNHCR, Nazneen was surprised to find that there were handbooks providing guidelines for the operation of other departments, such as protection and emergency departments, but none for social services. She hired an officer to prepare the social service handbook and oversaw its development. It was tested in the field as a pilot project and distributed globally to all field offices where there was a social services unit with the aim of standardizing social work interventions. Most important, it provided written standard operating procedures for social work units, thus lowering ambiguity and anxiety for the staff so that each situation did not have to be approached as novel. To standardize behaviors across the globe, taking into account the multicultural and multidimensional nature of social work practice in different countries requires sophisticated negotiation and a high level of sensitivity.

Finally, as chief of social services, Nazneen was responsible for coordinating social service activities with other UNHCR assistance department functions. She served as coordinator for women's programs, representing the UNHCR in all intra- and inter-UN and nongovernmental organization meetings. She was also responsible for services to special groups and refugees with physical and psychological disabilities.

The UNHCR and the Nobel Peace Prize

In 1981, the Nobel Peace Prize was awarded to the Office of the UNHCR, and all employees were given a personalized copy for their dedicated and effective service. The high commissioner invited interested departments to write a proposal suggesting how the money attached to the Nobel Peace Prize should be spent. Social Services developed a strong and compelling case for women, children, and refugees with physical disabilities, and they were awarded the money to start new projects for this clientele. It is not unusual for refugees to lose their limbs when land mines explode. The funds were used to purchase prostheses and to serve as seed money to generate funds from other sources for programs for handicapped women and children.

With her social work skills, her personal attributes, and her professional empathy, Nazneen was vigilant in identifying refugee needs, raising awareness of the role of social services in the UNHCR, and bringing to the forefront projects that would otherwise receive little attention. Her advocacy on behalf of those with disabilities, an oppressed minority in an already-destitute community, is laudable, reinforcing the merit recognized by the copy of the certificate awarded her. She continues to proudly display the certificate in her personal study at home.

The Return to Texas

As her fourth year at the UNHCR came to an end, so did her leave of absence from the University of Texas at Arlington. She had to make a hard choice: either to return to the university or to resign and continue with the UNHCR. The security of a hard-earned tenured position is difficult for anyone to forgo, but particularly so for a single woman and an immigrant, so she returned to the familiar academic life.

The experience in the UNHCR had dramatically changed Nazneen's attitudes and worldview. Her perceptions of social work and what was important had also altered by the time she returned. She found she was no longer at ease teaching her popular course on interviewing. Having experienced problems of world refugees, she felt that curricula should be more cognizant of global issues. It ought to be preparing social workers to deal with disasters and issues of a macro nature. Nazneen said: "As you will see in my publications after my return from Geneva, there is now a much broader world orientation. Much of my later work is focused on social work and social development."

As her focus turned to a broader world orientation, the substance of Nazneen's teaching, research, and service changed. They began to more emphatically include topics of oppression, human diversity, and the role of social capital in human life. She assumed leadership roles in social work's major professional organizations, the Council on Social Work Education (CSWE) and the National Association of Social Workers (NASW), and advocated for the inclusion of an international dimension in the profession's understanding of its responsibilities. Once again, she became the macro-level social worker that she had been before her move to Canada.

Recognition for Contributions to Social Work Education

Nazneen's many contributions have not gone unnoticed. She has lent her expertise to the profession at the local and international levels. She has been a member of and has assumed leadership roles in the NASW, the CSWE, the Association for the Advancement of Social Work with Groups, the Inter-University Consortium for International Social Development (IUCISD; now the International Consortium for Social Development), and the CSWE's International Commission. Her work related to international service resulted in her winning CSWE's Partners in International Education for Social Work, awarded by the Global Commission in 2007. Nazneen also coedited the IUCISD's *Social Development Issues* journal for six years, receiving an award recognizing "inspired and dedicated leadership" at the end of her editorial role in 2003. Bridging the distance between academia and practice, Nazneen has always remained engaged with the profession at the local and the national levels. From the early years of her tenure, she provided in-service training programs for social workers across the state of Texas, and she served the NASW as chair of its Book Committee for two years, followed by four years as chair of its Publications Committee. For her high level of service commitment to the profession, Nazneen was awarded the Distinguished Alumni Award of the George Warren Brown School of Social Work (2000), the Lifetime Achievement Award by the NASW of Tarrant County, Texas (2005), and the Lifetime Achievement Award by the NASW of the State of Texas (2005). When she retired from the University of Texas at Arlington in 2006, she was awarded the rank of professor emerita, an honor recognizing her extensive academic contributions and pledging to her lifelong university status.

An Individual of the East and the West

Nazneen has practiced international social work; she has taught social work internationally; she has lived in four countries on three continents; she has traveled to more than seventy nations; she is truly a global social worker, educator, and citizen. This woman of the East has always maintained her Indian identity: she values and enjoys the language, history, food, music, art, poetry, dance, and drama of her natal land. At the same time, she appreciates and participates in the culture of the West. She can quote and enjoy English literature and poetry as well as the poetry of her native language, Urdu. In Geneva, she taught herself to communicate in French. She equally enjoys Hollywood and Bollywood. Her diversity of intercultural and international experience is extensive indeed. Nazneen is a woman of both East and West: the sari that she always wears in her professional life is a statement of her cultural identity. Of her attire, she says:

> In my academic career, I'm sure students must have initially looked a little askance, but I think I related to students in such a way that the sari did not, to the best of my knowledge, act as a barrier. Perhaps clothes and race make a cursory difference at the beginning, but if one relates genuinely to people, then one is generally accepted. If I had adopted Western clothes, I would have been uncomfortable, and that would have evidenced itself in my behavior and made others uncomfortable too.

She did not feel that being an Indian woman in a sari negotiating on behalf of refugees was particularly problematic for her because the United Nations is, naturally, a multicultural and international group. Nazneen has enjoyed travel throughout her life, as presented through

UN missions, opportunities to present papers, or merely for the experience.

Nazneen's advice to young people seeking to enter the profession of social work is to develop a much greater awareness of diversity and to have a working knowledge of one or two other languages. They should have a better sense of the world outside the borders of the United States, know more of the world's geography, understand where other countries are located and their geographic relations to one another, and recognize the issues facing disparate nations. According to Nazneen, the profession speaks of international social work but does not prepare its graduates for it. It is not only multiculturalism within a country that is important; it is essential to also comprehend the functioning of other countries, including their political and economic systems and social and value structures.

The Person and the Character

Throughout her life, Nazneen Mayadas has retained the grace, elegance, and dignity for which the Lucknow of her youth was renowned. Family values are very important to her, and she maintains close links with family members. Blessed with a large circle of friends in many different countries, a testimony to her loyalty in friendship and her ability to relate to others, she has maintained close friendships in India over a lifetime while living on another continent for most of that time. Nazneen has a strength of character and determination that has enabled her to not only survive and succeed but also to excel in a foreign country, initially with little economic or social support. She is fiercely loyal and thankful to her country of adoption, the United States, for the opportunities it has offered her. Her love of academia and the United States came into play in her decision to return from Geneva to Arlington, Texas. Nazneen has a wonderful and often impious sense of humor, and an ability to cut to the core when others are searching for the right way to express an idea. Through her career, Nazneen has used her innate abilities and empathy, heightened by her education and her life experiences, to help enhance the quality of life of others without thought of recognition. In retirement, her penchant for travel and Hindi movies are just reward for a long and productive working life in the service of others.

In her career, Nazneen has traveled many paths, touched many lives, and in the words of her University of Texas colleague Thomas D. Watts, she has been "an early pioneer in the field of international and global social welfare . . . [and] contributed to and advanced the field at a time when it was in its relative infancy. She did so from both an academic perspective as well as a practice perspective." Nazneen Mayadas's career represents the highest standards in social work scholarship, research, teaching, practice, and service. It is rare that an individual excels in all areas to the extent that Nazneen has. She has served the social work profession and its constituencies and stakeholders with consistency and skill, representing the profession with expertise, sensitivity, professionalism, dignity, and elegance. Nazneen is, indeed, a social worker and educator exemplar par excellence.

CHAPTER FIVE

Ada Deer

From a One-Room Cabin to the Highest Levels of Government

Hilary Weaver

Tenacious, spirited, a force to be reckoned with—these are the words on my mind after my interview with Ada Deer. An optimist with love and compassion for people who has triumphed over the isms of racism, sexism, and elitism—this is how she described herself. In this chapter, I share a glimpse into Ada's life and career. Although many other pieces have been written about her, this is one of the few that specifically focuses on her as a social worker, a career that she continues to embrace with passion and enthusiasm, even into her retirement. In addition, as an American Indian woman and a social worker myself, I both hear her story differently and tell her story differently than another author, which makes this chapter distinct. Although we are very different people, Ada's life and work stand as a remarkable example to me and to other social workers. With the utmost respect and considerable awe, I tell her story here.

Growing Up on the Reservation

Knowing about Ada Deer's childhood is essential to understanding the driving forces in her life. So we will begin her story at the beginning. Ada Deer was born August 7, 1935, on the Menominee Indian Reservation in Wisconsin. She was the eldest of five children and grew up in a one-room log cabin with no electricity or running water. The reservation's beautiful setting along the Wolf River made a lasting impression on her. Ada absorbed a love of the land and an appreciation of the outdoors. The forest that surrounded her childhood home continues to be a primary element in the identity of the Menominee people.

Ada's mother, Constance, was the most central person in shaping her daughter's development. Constance was born into a wealthy family of English ancestry in Philadelphia. She was determined not to be relegated solely to the role of wife. Finding few career opportunities open to women, she became a nurse, initially working in Appalachia and then on the Rosebud Reservation in South Dakota, and she eventually moved to the Menominee Reservation in Wisconsin, where she met Ada's father. The life choices that Constance made did not go along with the tide of the times, and her family felt that she had rejected them and their way of life. Constance always had shown an adventuresome spirit, and she passed this characteristic along to Ada.

Ada's father was a Menominee man, fluent in his language, who had attended the local Catholic-mission boarding school. The school left him with significant resentment toward all things Catholic and negative feelings about his own culture. He chose not to teach any of his children the Menominee language in the hope that they would assimilate and not suffer racism and oppression the way that he had. Ada and her siblings grew up with little knowledge of their tribal culture. Ada's father worked in the local tribal lumber mill. He drank a lot, sometimes spending much of his paycheck on alcohol and leaving the family with little money for food or other necessities.

Ada lived on the Menominee Reservation until she was five or six years old. By the time she was old enough to attend school, her family had moved to Milwaukee, where she completed the first through fifth grades in an excellent public school system. After she completed the fifth grade, her family returned to the reservation. Constance was determined that Ada and her siblings would get the best education possible, which meant going beyond the boundaries of the reservation to attend the Shawano Public School in a small town nearby. The school also provided a high-quality education, unlike schools found in many other border towns. Ada recounted that her family were some of the first American Indians to attend school there. The tribal officials refused to allow Ada and her siblings to ride the school bus, but in Constance's relentless determination to be the best parent that she could be, she drove the children back and forth to school herself for a few years. Eventually, the tribal officials relented and the Deer children were allowed to ride the school bus. Ada attended the public school from the sixth through the twelfth grades. She was very fortunate to have attained an excellent public education in both Milwaukee and Shawano.

Ada recalls her school days with pride and enthusiasm. She recalls that, in Milwaukee, the "teachers loved being teachers." She still remembers the names of her teachers from the first through the fourth grades. Ada always enjoyed interacting with her teachers. This was the beginning of her lifelong love of learning. Her classmates, however, didn't know what to think of Ada. The other American Indian children were mystified that Ada often raised her hand and liked to talk in class. This surprised the white children, too. They all expected Ada to be like other American Indian children, who were quiet and reserved.

The Path to Social Work

As it came time to choose a career path, Ada found herself greatly influenced by her mother's experience as a nurse. She liked the idea of helping people. This was part of her core being, and she found much joy in it. As the eldest of five children, Ada cannot remember a time when she was not helping people. She enjoyed helping her mother with household duties and caring for her siblings, almost becoming a coparent at times. Although she was interested in following in her mother's footsteps as a helping professional, she was keenly aware that doctors had more power than nurses. After living under her father's domination, in which his drinking often left the family vulnerable, Ada had no intention of choosing a career in which a man would tell her what to do. The power that went along with being a doctor was much more appealing to her than was the subservient role of nurse.

As Ada approached her high school graduation, she knew that she wanted to continue with the best education possible. She asked her guidance counselor what the best school was, and she was told the University of Wisconsin, Madison. Wanting nothing but the best, Ada applied, was accepted, and enrolled.

To pay for her education, Ada applied for funding from the Menominee Tribe and received the only tribal scholarship. The funding was crucial in making her dreams possible. She was determined to someday repay the tribe. Indeed, Ada not only benefited from receiving support for her education but ultimately the tribe also benefited when Ada was able to assist in the restoration process after the tribe was legally terminated.

Once she began her studies at the University of Wisconsin, Ada found that she had difficulty keeping up with the other students in math and chemistry. Within a few weeks, she recognized that a career in math or science was not for her. She was, however, enjoying her studies in liberal arts. This area of strength was to become not only her niche but also her passion. By her senior year, she had to decide on a major and her adviser recommended social work. She recalled her early interactions with social workers on the reservation who had opened up opportunities for her like going to camp. It seemed like a reasonable career for her to pursue. Helen Clarke, one of her early social work professors, was a big influence and inspiration. Clarke introduced Ada to the conceptual and intellectual foundations of the social work profession. She had written a book on her own experiences in shaping legislation, which Ada found inspiring. From that point, Ada was clearly on the path to becoming a social worker.

Her career choice fit well with her mother's aspirations for her. As her mother had said to her earlier, "Ada Deer, you are an Indian. You were put on this earth for a purpose. You should help your people." As time went on, Ada began to think more about American Indians and their life circumstances. As a teenager, Ada looked around and wondered, "Why are Indians poor?" She had some vague ideas about how the land had been taken and how life had changed for American Indians. She saw around her oppression, injustice, and suffering. What she saw made her angry and motivated her to try to make a difference.

In 1955, Ada was introduced to international issues through the American Friends Service Committee. This spurred her to think about large-scale social change. As an undergraduate student in 1956, she was afforded the opportunity to attend the Encampment for Citizenship in New York City. This six-week program grew out of a recognition of the atrocities of World War II. Its founders believed that something needed to be done to educate the youth of the world to promote understanding and to prevent future atrocities.

At the Encampment for Citizenship, Ada participated in a six-week workshop on segregation, a topic to which she had little previous exposure. This workshop gave her an opportunity to hear Kenneth Clark speak about his experiments offering children the choice of playing with black or white dolls—and his findings that self-consciousness about skin color and resulting low self-esteem were by-products of racial segregation. He discussed how the then lawyer Thurgood Marshall had used his findings in arguing *Brown v. Board of Education* to the U.S. Supreme Court. Clark's significant work inspired Ada and clearly demonstrated the importance of social action.

Ada's passion for social change deepened as she learned more about the civil rights movement and the *Brown* case. She wanted to do something equally significant for American Indians.

The Encampment for Citizenship program also gave Ada the opportunity to meet Eleanor Roosevelt, whom she found to be truly inspirational. She clearly remembers Roosevelt's remarks that violence is not the answer to society's injustices; rather, education is the way to bring about social change. This powerful seminar reinforced the philosophy that Ada has followed all her life: we must learn, listen, and take advantage of the opportunities offered to us.

As Ada neared completion of her undergraduate degree, she gave thoughtful consideration to continuing her studies. Still focused on seeking out nothing but the best, she asked her college adviser about the best graduate school. When she was told that the New York School of Social Work was the top graduate program in the country, she applied, was accepted, and enrolled.

At the age of twenty-two, Ada moved to New York City to attend the New York School of Social Work (later the Columbia University School of Social Work). She was exposed to tremendous teachers who were among the leaders in the field. Ada's educational experiences, however, were not without their challenges. New York City presented a very different cultural milieu than that which she was used to. Ada remembers being treated like a "hick from the sticks." She found too many faculty members to be steeped in elitism. However, Ada was fascinated with the various cultural groups that populated New York City. Everyone seemed to converge in the city, including groups that she had had little or no contact with before, such as African Americans, Jews, and Puerto Ricans. This exposure to diversity greatly expanded her knowledge and appreciation of the peoples of the world.

Although things did not always go smoothly at the New York School of Social Work, Ada did find herself studying at the best school with the best teachers. She still recalls the course on race and class taught by Richard Cloward. The class gave her the opportunity to distill some of her thoughts about inequality in American society and about moving toward social change. She has found that the concepts she learned in the course are still relevant today. Likewise, she was afforded the opportunity to study with Alfred Kahn, who taught about the history and foundations of social work. Kahn instilled in Ada a true love of the profession.

Ada did, however, clash with some of her professors as she tried to select learning experiences that would be meaningful for her. The school initially tried to place her in an internship in a mental health setting, but she fought for an internship more suited to her interests. Even at a young age, she knew that she wanted to focus her work on social policies and social change rather than work with individuals. Later she would view this tension as a result of her being a "macro social worker trapped in a micro world." Ada received her first-year field placement on the Lower East Side of New York City, under the sponsorship of Henry Street Settlement House in cooperation with the New York City Housing Authority and the New York City Youth Board. She lived at the settlement for a semester and worked throughout the school year in local housing projects in work that she found meaningful. Her responsibilities included going door-to-door to identify the needs of the tenants and to refer them to appropriate services, as well as to facilitate regular tenants' meetings so that they could get to know one another and form a sense of community. This pilot project, conducted cooperatively through the school and the settlement, was later featured in an article in the *New York Times* (Four students cited in housing study, 1958).

For her second-year field placement, Ada worked at the New York Foundling Hospital, in the area of adoptive placements. Although this was not a placement that she particularly wanted, she did find it preferable to a site that focused on mental health issues, and she acquiesced. By that time, she was tired of fighting and just wanted to finish the program and move on to a career in which she would have more choices about the type of work she would do.

In the second year of the graduate curriculum, students were given the choice of doing a group project or research paper. Ada proposed a project working with the American Indians living in Brooklyn, but the school was not responsive. In the late 1950s, when Ada began her MSW program, the curricula of many social work schools focused heavily on clinical issues and working with individuals or small systems like groups. Her interests in change and macro-level issues were out of step with the primary focus of social work at that time.

Ada never had academic problems in graduate school, but the New York School of Social Work was not a good fit for her. Students were expected to take courses in either a casework or a group-work track. By her second year, Ada felt she had good exposure to groups from her first-year field placement and wanted to take courses related to working with individuals. When she wanted to learn about casework, she was told that it wasn't possible because it didn't fit her academic track. She was persistent in asking for what she needed. She had to "barge her way through" to get internships and courses that were meaningful.

In 1998, many years after her earlier educational struggles, Ada became one of the first people inducted into the Columbia University School of Social Work Hall of Fame. The honor was a far cry from her treatment as a graduate student. As part of her induction into the hall of fame, Ada attended a banquet at which she was seated next to her old professor Alfred Kahn. While Ada was being honored as the first American Indian to graduate from Columbia University School of Social Work, Kahn was honored as its first doctoral graduate. The banquet provided an opportunity to reflect on both the positive aspects and the struggles of her graduate education. Ada did, indeed, learn a lot in her graduate studies, but the school could not prepare her for how to go about helping American Indians, and it was not prepared for dealing with such an assertive and focused student.

After she earned her MSW degree, Ada naturally gravitated toward work with American Indians. She moved to Minnesota, where she was the program director for a neighborhood house. In this capacity, she supervised four people, including one who provided services specifically targeting American Indians. While program director, Ada helped form a local urban Indian council to respond to the needs of that population. At the time, the urban American Indian population was growing, and many such agencies were beginning to spring up to provide a variety of social services to the population, with a particular focus on work-related programs. She was driven by her own desire to escape poverty and to help other American Indian people do so as well. Her early work set the stage for the large-scale work she was destined to do: empowering American Indians.

Federal Indian Policy: Sovereignty, Termination, and Restoration

One of Ada's most notable accomplishments is her work with the Menominee Restoration Act, which returned federally recognized sovereignty to the tribe. She was a catalyst that ignited and focused the efforts of many people to bring about the significant policy change. Ada helped facilitate a grassroots movement that resulted in a historic reversal of American Indian policy and ultimately set a precedent for other tribes. In the 1960s and early 1970s, there were many Menominee people suffering ever-increasing poverty and its associated social ills, yet the Menominee people were uncertain about what they wanted to do or how they could initiate change. Ada stepped in to this difficult context and respectfully involved and empowered people for this social change effort. Her passion for justice and knack for leadership made her well suited for the role, but significant social change would not have been achieved without the involvement of many people. To understand the significance of Ada's work empowering American Indians and her involvement in shaping federal policy, it is important to provide a bit of background information on federal Indian policy and what is known as the termination era.

When European colonial powers first came to North America, they recognized indigenous people as belonging to distinct sovereign nations; thus, legally binding agreements were made between European countries and American Indian nations on a government-to-government basis. The U.S. Constitution affirms that treaties are the supreme law of the land. As the United States grew in power, it no longer made treaties with American Indian nations and began chipping away at American Indian sovereignty. The federal government began to assume jurisdiction over major crimes on American Indian land and, in many ways, assumed trusteeship over American Indian people. American Indian nations, however, still retained their own governments and sometimes operated their own schools, social services, and legal systems. By the late 1940s, many federal policy makers believed that the vestiges of sovereignty, including reservations and tribal governments, should be completely abolished and American Indians incorporated into the larger American society. The legal vehicle for accomplishing these tasks was called termination.

In 1953, House Concurrent Resolution 108 was passed, making termination ongoing federal policy (Indian Country Wisconsin, 2008). At the same time, Public Law 280 conferred civil and criminal jurisdiction over Indian reservations to states that adopted it. These provided the legal structure for dismantling tribal entities in the United States. Resolution 108 provided the authority to end all federal supervision and trust responsibilities for American Indian nations and to end all tribal governments, thus leaving American Indian people no means of governing their internal affairs. After passage of the resolution, specific legislation was required to terminate each tribe individually. The Bureau of Indian Affairs assembled a list of tribes deemed ready for termination. Because of their economic prosperity, the Menominee were the first chosen for termination. Congress set the process in motion by Congress in 1954 (Indian Country Wisconsin, 2008).

As part of termination, a plan had to be developed to deal with tribal assets and federally protected reservation lands. Eventually, all tribal property was transferred to a state corporation, Menominee Enterprises Inc. (Indian Country Wisconsin, 2008). Originally, the reservation was supposed to be divided and the land allocated to three existing counties. The plan was changed, however, and the reservation became a county in and of itself. The newly designated Menominee County became the only American Indian county in the state. Termination of the Menominee Tribe was effective April 30, 1961.

Termination was an unqualified disaster from the beginning. The hospital had to close, as the Menominee people were no longer self-sufficient and had no financial means to support the hospital and comply with state standards. Schools, utilities, and various services either closed or experienced dramatic cuts. The Menominee's assets, valued at more than $10 million before termination in 1961, dwindled to

$300,000 by 1964, quickly resulting in a significant onset of poverty and social disruption for the Menominee people (Indian Country Wisconsin, 2008).

The Struggle for Restoration

By the 1960s, the financially stricken Menominee Enterprises proposed the sale of some tribal lands to real estate developers who planned to create an artificial lake and then sell the surrounding property to non-Indian people (Indian Country Wisconsin, 2008). When the details of the proposed deal became known, they created an immediate backlash and led to the formation of the grassroots organization Determination of Rights and Unity for Menominee Stockholders (DRUMS), first led by James White and then by Ada Deer. Ada helped DRUMS develop an organized platform focused on stopping the sale. She facilitated the development of DRUMS as a grassroots effort, striving to include as many people as possible.

The DRUMS organization was a powerful vehicle for social change. With Ada's leadership, the group sought to reverse the tribe's termination. Ada was the right person, at the right place and at the right time, to provide leadership to the broad, grassroots effort. As she researched resources and sought legal services, her efforts began a synergy that involved others in taking on key roles.

The work of DRUMS was done in partnership with lawyers with a passion for justice and dedication for helping American Indian people. Joseph F. Preloznik, an attorney with Wisconsin Judicare, provided the legal services work associated with fighting for restoration. The restoration cause also garnered national attention. The Native American Rights Fund, established in 1970, took on the issue of Menominee restoration as one of its first legal cases. The attorneys Yvonne Knight and Charles Wilkinson worked tirelessly as part of this powerful alliance. With Ada as the chief lobbyist, the coalition lobbied Congress and then the staff of President Richard Nixon. Other Menominees also joined the efforts to lobby for change. Through a combination of creativity and advocacy, Ada and the other DRUMS activists persuaded Congressmen Manuel Lujan (R-NM) and Lloyd Means (D-WA) to hold hearings about restoration on Menominee territory so that more Menominee people could participate in the process. Ultimately, their efforts led to the passage of a bill, the Menominee Restoration Act, which restored the Menominee's status as a federally recognized tribe, on December 22, 1973 (Indian Country Wisconsin, 2008). Their successful battle led to a historic reversal of American Indian policy, thus setting an important precedent and bringing the termination era to an end for all American Indians.

Once the Menominee Restoration Act was passed, the long road to reestablishing the tribal government, infrastructure, and services began. The process commenced with the Menominee tribe electing the Restoration Committee and the committee members electing a chair. Ada had been very active in efforts leading up to the passage of the restoration act, but she then had plans to invest her energies in other arenas, including the pursuit of a law degree. She requested that they keep her informed and involved, and she agreed to serve on the Restoration Committee, but she did not plan for the restoration to be the ongoing centerpiece of her work.

Despite her reluctance to lead restoration efforts, Ada not only was elected to the Restoration Committee but also subsequently elected as its chair. She realized that few others could bring a comparable involvement and knowledge of the issues to this task, and so she agreed to serve. Although she had strong support to take on these roles, some members of the Menominee tribe were reluctant to see a woman fill this position. Men had always led the tribe, and some members thought that this practice should continue. Ada's success in overcoming this resistance and sexism represented a breakthrough for other women interested in leadership positions in the Menominee tribe. Today, men continue to fill most key leadership positions, but the precedent Ada set holds the door open for women leaders of the future.

The Menominee Restoration Committee, led by Ada Deer, took on the enormous task of reorganizing the tribe, re-creating the tribal government, and reinstating tribal assets. This involved many different organizational meetings both on and off the reservation. At these meetings, people came together, shared their ideas, and were empowered by their assumption of roles that would result in a significantly different, and better, life for the tribe. Both the restoration efforts and subsequent work on developing a constitution were cooperative efforts involving many people, not just a few key leaders. Ada used the basic organizing techniques she had learned as a social work student. She wanted as many Menominee people as possible to participate in the process so that they would know that it was their act and constitution rather than something a few had imposed on them. In particular, Ada appointed people to serve in key roles on the Enrollment and Constitution committees. Through this participatory process, she was able to express the communal value inherent in the nature of American Indian tribes. As Ada put it, "It's not me, it's we." This process presented many challenges and was fraught with dissension among tribal members with varying opinions of how they should proceed. Ada brought to bear her strong leadership skills and social work background to shepherd her tribe through these monumental tasks. Facilitating an inclusive process can be very difficult, but ultimately it was the only way to move forward.

Rising as a Political Leader

Ada has broken barriers in both the American Indian world and the white world. Neither racism nor sexism has stopped her from advocating for social change. In times when she has faced a barrier, she has repeatedly found a way to "go through it, go over it, or go around it."

After her work with the restoration, Ada was recruited to run for election for tribal chair of her own Menominee people. Although her supporters included both men and women, she again struggled to break gender barriers in the tribe. Ultimately, she was elected as the first woman tribal chair of the Menominee people, serving from 1974 to 1976. Other women have subsequently followed in her footsteps and have taken on various leadership roles in the tribe.

In 1976, during her tenure as tribal chair, Ada was recruited by the chancellor of the University of Wisconsin, Madison, to join the faculty as a lecturer with a joint appointment in social work and American Indian studies. This gave her an opportunity to instill her passion for social action in the students and to teach social work skills, values, and knowledge and ways to apply them to bring about social change for American Indians and other oppressed people. In particular, Ada is proud of her work to develop a field unit on advocacy in multicultural settings. She continued to serve on the social work faculty at the University of Wisconsin until her retirement in 2007.

Ada's convictions and passion for social change led her to seek other elected leadership positions. She ran, though unsuccessfully, for secretary of state in Wisconsin in 1978 and again in 1982. White people in the northern part of the state had some negative reactions to her candidacy. But although she lost the elections, she was not easily discouraged.

Ada ran for Congress in 1992 because of her belief that bringing a social work perspective to elected leadership positions is a powerful way to effect social change. Ada won the Democratic primary, despite her refusal to take money from political action committees. Her election gave her the long-awaited chance to stand up and say, with her own brand of humor, "Me Nominee." Ada ultimately lost the race to her Republican adversary, but she continued to look for venues in which she can assert her strong leadership skills.

Under the Clinton administration, Ada saw an opportunity to take her passion for social justice to a position of greater power. President Bill Clinton claimed that he wanted a government that "looked like

America." This was all that Ada needed to hear, and she began to position herself for a federal appointment. With her strong credentials and leadership experience, she felt that she would be a good candidate for an assistant secretary position in the federal government. She was qualified and competent for appointments in several areas, including education and housing. She had strong backing from a number of constituencies, including women and American Indians. In 1993, she was appointed assistant secretary for Indian affairs in the Department of the Interior. She was the first woman to hold the position. Although Ada made a lasting impact in her appointment, it is noteworthy that despite her qualifications for a range of federal appointments, she was chosen only for a position specifically dealing with American Indians. Although the talents and skills that she could have brought to other aspects of the federal government went unrecognized, she put her considerable energies to work on behalf of American Indian peoples.

Being in Washington, D.C., with the power of the federal government behind her, gave Ada an opportunity to push forward her agenda for social change. As assistant secretary for Indian affairs, she left her mark on federal policy through acts that granted federal recognition to various American Indian nations and affirmed the sovereignty of 224 Alaska native villages. Having experienced termination and its aftermath, Ada brought a unique wisdom to her job. She had a clear understanding of the importance of indigenous sovereignty and how it must be affirmed at the federal level.

Shaping Influences and Key Accomplishments

Ada became a forceful advocate for social justice in large part because of the key role models in her life, most notably her mother. Her family members have always been supportive of her work and proud of Ada (with the exception of her father, who was mired in his own problems).

When asked to identify her most notable accomplishments, she speaks of her family and of her work shaping federal policy. Although it is difficult to equate large-scale social change with family relationships, the fact that she speaks of both as important accomplishments reflects her balanced priorities. Her efforts in assisting three of her four siblings in obtaining college degrees and her extensive involvement with her nieces and nephews may be on a scale different from that of her federal work, but they reflect the same values of empowerment and striving for a better life. Ada counts her impact on her siblings and extended family as among her biggest successes. Although she is justifiably proud of her accomplishments with the Menominee Restoration Act, affirming the sovereignty of Alaska native villages, and establishing the Advocacy in

Multicultural Settings unit at the University of Wisconsin, she rates her family connections as equally important.

Ada counts John Gardner as a key mentor. Gardner had been secretary of health, education, and welfare in the Johnson administration. He was the founder of many national civic organizations, but best known as the founder of the Common Cause watchdog organization, and was committed to promoting better government in the wake of the Watergate scandal. Gardner's work in creating Common Cause with a critical consciousness around issues of oppression fit well with Ada's own sense of the social change that needed to happen in the United States. Ada refers to Gardner as "a true public intellectual and a phenomenal man."

These people and others encouraged, supported, and opened doors for Ada. In her long and productive career, Ada now finds herself in the position of influencing others and serving as a role model. Still, though, she has never outgrown the need for communication with, and advice from, those with wisdom.

Longevity and the Future

Ada's social work career spans several decades, and she recently retired from teaching in the School of Social Work at the University of Wisconsin, Madison. Despite having retired, she says, "once a social worker, always a social worker." Her extensive energy, sense of responsibility, and anger at injustice will always keep her involved in social issues. Her interest in the human condition is deeply ingrained. She is, however, thoughtful about how she spends her time.

She does not plan to go back to work on her reservation. The challenges that she faced with her tribe while working on the restoration reveal the factions and divisiveness found in many American Indian communities. She was able to function as an effective leader despite the many challenges she faced, but that type of work can be very draining. She does not want to return to all that negativity in facing the struggles that plague so many tribal governments.

As she looks toward the future, Ada notes two particular issues of concern for American Indians: funding and leadership. Funding is, and has always been, a problem in addressing the concerns of American Indians. (If the federal government were able to reach a bipartisan agreement to triple the Bureau of Indian Affairs and the Indian Health Service budgets for the following twenty years, then it would be possible to make a significant difference.) In addition, there is a continuing need for good leadership at all levels. Ada notes that we must cultivate leadership among American Indians, including by mentoring college-age people.

In addition to American Indian concerns, Ada has always been interested in greater societal interests. When she sought federal appointments or ran for Congress, she based her campaign on concern for all people in American society, particularly those facing oppression or marginalization. Ada is particularly concerned about big issues that need attention, such as health care and prison reform—and she cannot just sit home and do nothing. She is currently shifting some of her considerable energies to focus on these issues.

At the time of this writing, the United States was in the midst of a presidential campaign. Ada expressed her continuing interest in actively shaping the direction of the country, and the presidential election was a crucial component of this endeavor. As Ada emphasized, we cannot continue to put all of our money into war, because doing so neglects so many pressing social issues. Instead, each of us must do what we can to move the country toward a positive future. The underpinning of Ada's work continues to be struggles for social justice. She does this work on many different levels, from nurturing and empowering individual family members and friends to be the best that they can be to shaping federal policy through community advocacy.

Ada plans to continue working on many different levels: making a positive difference through her involvement with family and friends, staying involved with her tribe, and investing her time and skills in other projects as they come along. The struggle for social justice will always continue.

Reflecting on Her Work

Although Ada has faced many challenges and inequities in her life, including racism and sexism, she finds the greatest challenges to be human ignorance and apathy. She firmly believes that it is important to lead the charge, or at least be part of the effort, to bring about change. There will always be people who say that change isn't possible, but they need not discourage people who believe in making a difference. Ada encountered many such naysayers in the battle for Menominee restoration, but ultimately positive change was possible.

As Ada says, "We are all people on this planet. We must all pay rent every day." In other words, we must each accept responsibility for our actions and inactions. We must all work toward positive change in our society and in the world. Ada has certainly paid her share of the rent and has successfully brought about social change. As she put it, she "has become accustomed to succeeding." She is able to do this, in large part, because of the strong, loving, and nurturing foundation she received as a child, coupled with a strong educational background. The expectation that she could and would succeed was always present. Ada recognizes that many people in this country do not have a comparable foundation. They may not see that change is possible, or they may have encountered multiple barriers, such as poverty and racism, that inhibit them from striving for change. These barriers take their toll. We must get past the inequities that prevent American Indians and women from succeeding in order to encourage a positive mind-set not only that change is possible but also that socially just change is mandatory and, indeed, the ultimate goal of the social work profession.

References

Four students cited in housing study; city commends them for fostering neighborliness at La Guardia project. (1958, June 2). *New York Times*, p. 48. Retrieved August 22, 2009, from http://select.nytimes.com/gst/abstract.html?res=FB0611F8345B117B93C0A9178DD85F4C8585F9&scp=6&sq=%22Ada+Deer%22&st=p.

Indian Country Wisconsin. (2008). Menominee termination and restoration. Retrieved March 17, 2008, from http://www.mpm.edu/wirp/ICW-97.html.

PART II

Women at the Grass Roots
Social Change from the Ground Up

There are few things more difficult to achieve than taking a concept that exists only in the mind and turning it into something real, something essential, something that would not happen if not for the vision of that individual. The second part of the book tells the story of seven women, all of whom saw a vacuum in the web of social need that existed in their communities and, through conscious use of self (an encompassing social work skill), created structures that filled that vacuum for people all over the world. In the United States, Aida Giachello (chapter 7), Sr. Patricia Schlosser (chapter 10), Rev. Debra Trakel (chapter 11), and Sr. Jean Abbott (chapter 12) all took their understanding of grassroots organization and applied it in ways that have benefited populations that don't always receive our attention. Quratulain Bakhteari (chapter 6) practices what might be called extreme social work from her home base in Balochistan, in Pakistan, currently one of the most desolate places on earth. Finally, Theresa Kaijage (chapter 8) and Mulu Haile (chapter 9), both from the African continent, have achieved what outside observers might have thought impossible in their respective countries: they pioneered social service organizations that provided services and advocated for Africa's most stigmatized citizens.

CHAPTER SIX

Quratulain Bakhteari

A Community Development Pioneer in Pakistan

Alice Lieberman

I first learned of Quratulain Bakhteari from the noted Pakistani journalist, human rights advocate, and documentary film-maker Beena Sarwar, who directed me to Dr. Shahla Haeri, the director of the women's studies program at Boston University. Haeri's book, *No Shame for the Sun: Lives of Professional Women in Pakistan* (2004) details the struggles of seven women who risk shame, separation from their families, and social isolation because they exercise power and authority, and because they dare to seek societal change. Quratulain Bakhteari was one of those women. She is currently the founder and director of the Institute for Development Studies and Practices in Quetta, Pakistan, one of a series of major achievements in a remarkable life. The institute's mission is to develop a cadre of indigenous community-development thinkers, planners, and practitioners who can effectively cultivate community participation in social

The author is grateful to Dr. Vicki Mattice, of the Ontario Institute for Studies in Education at the University of Toronto. For her dissertation, Mattice studied the work of the Institute for Development Studies and Practices in Quetta and the work of Quratulain Bakhteari. In the course of her work, she came to be a great admirer of both.

problem-solving processes in their own communities. Over the decade of its existence, the institute has educated more than 1,200 community development experts who have used their skills to further social progress.

I initially contacted Dr. Quratulain Bakhteari (hereinafter Qurat) via e-mail and arranged to interview her in person at the home of her son and daughter-in-law when she came to visit them in Irvine, California. However, the imposition of martial law by Pervez Musharraf's government and violence in the city made travel impossible for her. Although she eventually made it to California, I was unable to return. This interview, then, was conducted on Skype. I could see her, but she was unable to see me.

The Early Years

Qurat was born on December 25, 1949, and came of age in a time of political unrest. Barely two years earlier, her grandparents, as Muslims in a largely Hindu country, along with more than 7 million of their fellow Muslims, had moved from Uttar Pradesh, in India, to the western coastal city of Karachi, now part of Pakistan. This mass movement of people was the result of what is known as the partition of India, a political movement to accommodate both Hindu and Muslim populations in the region.

Leaving India was extremely difficult for everyone. A once-comfortable life became very hard, as families in the refugee settlements lived in very close quarters, with only the most primitive facilities for cooking and hygiene. When Qurat's parents married, they moved in with her mother's family, making a bad situation worse. But when she was a toddler, her parents moved their family to a one-room house in a refugee settlement at the far end of the Karachi desert. It did not have water or electricity, but for her mother, it was preferable to their previous arrangements.

It also turned out to be a wonderful childhood experience for Qurat. "I was fortunate that my parents had not much means, and that meant that they were out of the home during the day, working and earning. That gave me freedom to be out of home." It was a freedom that she took full advantage of, exploring the neighborhood with the boys, playing in the streets, riding donkeys, and going to the nearby air force base to watch planes take off and land. But it was not all play: as the oldest child, she also helped her parents build the mud structure that became their home. To this day, Qurat looks back on these days as her real education, and she is grateful that her parents could not afford the luxury of treating her differently than the boys: she never wore a head scarf, and her parents did not ask her to behave demurely or modestly.

It is not surprising to hear accomplished people speak of their parents' influence on their early lives. But one incident involving her mother remains sharply in Qurat's mind: on returning from school with her mother one day, they saw a young widow crying outside the door of her home, surrounded by her belongings, her small children clinging to her. A group of men were blocking the door. Qurat and her mother hurried up to find out what was going on and quickly learned that the men had evicted the woman from her home (because she no longer had a man to support and protect her from such harassment). That was too much for Qurat's mother. Calling the men "useless," she picked up a rock, bashed the door in, put the woman's belongings back in the home, and then stood in the doorway and dared the men to try it again. This behavior was unheard of in a traditional Muslim community, with a highly patriarchal culture. And it made quite an impression on Qurat. She said, "This demonstration was my first lesson in being fearless and standing up for others, to take a position when it comes to justice."

Education was deeply important to Qurat's parents, and they sent their children to a Christian missionary school, St. Agnes, where they could learn English. It was strict, but the values of honesty, discipline, tolerance, and responsibility were central themes of the school. In my conversation with her, there was a clear sense that Qurat was somewhat wistful for the days when religion (both Islam and Christianity) stressed what she called "utmost tolerance."

Once she reached puberty, Qurat's world began to change. Her parents, particularly her mother, tried to enforce the traditional rules of conduct that applied to women throughout the Indian subcontinent, be they Hindu or Muslim. After such a free childhood, this effort was no more likely to be successful than putting toothpaste back in a tube: to an adolescent girl, the curtailing of freedoms that she had theretofore enjoyed felt like punishment. She grew resentful of her parents and alienated from them. For their part, her parents, vexed by her willfulness, believed that the best solution was to arrange a marriage for her forthwith. In 1966, after completing the tenth grade, Qurat was married to a young dentist, and over the following six years, she gave birth to three sons while also earning her BA in humanities from the University of Karachi.

Shaping Identity and Destiny

Qurat's husband, it is fair to say, did not know what he was getting into when he married her. Of course, he did not know her very well, so both needed a period of adjustment. Although she remained estranged from her family, she tried to settle in with her husband and his parents. She loved her three children very much and was a doting mother.

She traces the shift in her priorities from family to country to December 16, 1971, the day that East Pakistan (now the independent nation of Bangladesh) declared independence from West Pakistan, an event that brought about a bloody civil war. The Pakistan that Qurat had loved so much was no more, and she did not understand why. She had no idea what West Pakistan had done to East Pakistan to warrant secession as an independent country, but she was also concerned about the people. The East Pakistanis had been Pakistanis, and now they needed to move. Unwelcome in their own homeland, victimized by the extreme violence of war, they became refugees once again. Her heart went out to them.

At first, she ventured out to the refugee camps in eastern India, organized for the new East Pakistani refugees, meeting families as they crossed into the newly redrawn country. Qurat and her family took in one family with eight children that had lost many members, including the father and breadwinner, and supported them for six years. But this deeply generous action could not stem the tide of despair of the thousands of others who were similarly displaced and disenfranchised.

Eventually, she began visiting a refugee camp that sprang up near Karachi. The horrifying stories of rape, violence, and torture, perpetrated by the armies on women, fed her insecurity about the safety of all Pakistanis, including her own family. Although she had received training in the Montessori method of education and could have worked as a teacher, she wanted to do more. It was time, she felt, to begin working for change on a larger scale.

In 1977, Qurat enrolled in the MSW program at the University of Karachi. She loved the work and the classes, but her education carried a huge cost: estrangement from her husband and beloved children (because women were not supposed to be independent), and many years of financial insecurity.

A Life's Work Begins

The core of any social work education enterprise is field experience. It is here that social work students practice applying all that they have learned in the classroom to the real world beyond. And it was in her field placement that Qurat began to change the world.

Her first field assignment was to develop infrastructures to support life in a refugee settlement in Karachi. Specifically, she was to assist the community in building a school for girls and in constructing houses. Qurat accomplished these objectives, organizing the community and raising money from business owners. The university was so proud of her work that they trumpeted the accomplishments in the newspapers. The United Nation's Children's Fund (UNICEF) took note of the work and offered to collaborate with the school's social work department to build pit latrines in the settlements. Qurat took on this work, at a salary of twenty-four rupees (less than a dollar) a day.

The pit-latrine project was widely believed to be unfeasible because of the lack of water to flush the pits. But working in concert with the design teams from UNICEF and with residents, Qurat led an effort that resulted in sixty latrines being built in one year. As a result, she was hired as a community organizer to continue her sanitation work. She believed in what she was doing, and she derived great satisfaction from her work.

Between 1978 (when she was still a student) and 1982, Qurat worked as a volunteer, organizer, and researcher in the squatter settlements in and around Karachi. She made major contributions both to public health and sanitation. A total of five thousand soak-pit latrines were ultimately installed under her supervision. As a consequence, she became affectionately known as Gutter Wali Baji ("Elder Sister of the Gutters"). The initiative not only vastly improved the health of females in the settlements, who were forbidden during daylight hours from using the public latrines that were installed in open ditches known as lane open sewers, but also allowed them to claim dignity, as they could now exercise their bodily functions in privacy and at will. The pit latrines now are part of the official water and sanitation policy of Pakistan.

This very valuable but time-consuming effort did not sit well with Qurat's husband or her in-laws. Starting with her earliest days as a student, and continuing through her early work in the refugee camps, her absorption in her job engendered a great deal of anger. Her husband's insistence that she stay at home and take care of the children grew. A class system that reinforced negative ideas about women who work undoubtedly influenced his position. Qurat rejected such ideas. So, forced to choose between her family and her work, and considering all other options closed, she made the wrenching choice to separate herself from her family, although she remained very much involved with her children. And yet, when I asked her near the end of the interview if she had any regrets about the path she chose for her life, she said that even now, with the children grown and her relationships with them strong, she continues to regret the time she lost with them.

Qurat endured more than a decade of separation from her husband and children, and her once-comfortable life as the wife of a dentist became financially precarious. But after more than a decade of separation, she and her husband came to an understanding of and respect for the positions of the other. They reconciled and remained so until his death in 2006.

The Evolution of Education for Young Women

As each latrine was built throughout the camps, Qurat would painstakingly write out instructions for their cleaning and maintenance. It was very important to use the correct procedures because there was so little water. But the women were illiterate and thus unable to follow the written instructions.

For three years, Qurat worked only with the men, instructing them on latrine maintenance. Her hope was that they would see how handicapped their women were and that the drive to educate them would come from their own observations of the need. Eventually, there was a breakthrough, and the men began meeting to discuss and plan for the basic education of women.

The exemplary community developer that she was, Qurat worked with the people to develop a system of home schools for girls in which the community would have pride of ownership. This system combined the tradition of teaching the Koran in private homes, with additional secular education. Qurat developed a teacher-training model that originally attracted ten young women whose own educations stopped between the eighth and tenth grades. They went out and started the first ten schools, called HomeSchools. Slowly, the movement took on a life of its own. Today, the trademarked term *HomeSchools* is recognized all over Pakistan, and the schools are managed by the Sindh Education Foundation and other national education foundations as a component of Pakistan's nonformal education systems. It is not common knowledge that the nationwide movement started with Qurat. Yet because of her initial efforts to educate young girls, the literacy rate of women and girls in all of the rural areas of Pakistan has quadrupled in the past twenty-five years (Choudhry, 2005).

Taking Stock and Establishing New Goals

By the late 1980s, Qurat was still in her thirties and had already accomplished more than most women. Thousands of the poorest, most disenfranchised people on earth, particularly girls and women, were living lives of dignity and hope because of her. Her reputation as a change agent was growing, and UNICEF hired her, once again, this time as a regular budget officer who would train and orient other UNICEF officers in Pakistan. She made considerably more money this time, too. She also enrolled in the University of Loughborough and earned a Ph.D.

under a distance-education model. Then UNICEF offered her a promotion, this time to program officer for Sindh Province, in the southeastern corner of the country, at a higher salary, with excellent benefits, and a large travel allowance.

But Qurat soon discovered that the demands of the job would not allow her to work directly with communities. Her life, she knew, was with people, working to solve real-life problems on the ground.

Although they tried to persuade her to reconsider, Qurat resigned from her position at UNICEF and spent the following decade continuing her sanitation and public health work in the province of Balochistan, Pakistan. She assisted in the construction of three thousand pit latrines in Quetta, the provincial capital, and then joined the Girl's Primary Education Project, in rural Balochistan. It should be noted that Balochistan had a strict tribal and feudal moral code that made female education taboo. But in the five years that Qurat worked on that effort, girls' participation in school went from less than 22 percent in 1981 (Nazli, 2001) to 27 percent in 1986, a significant increase considering that the population of Balochistan is about 7 million.

Throughout her life as an organizer, Qurat had lived many of the principles that the social work education system in the United States tries to promote. She had learned to operate on the cardinal principles that understanding the culture you work in and starting where the client is are keys to a successful endeavor. With respect to the formation of schools in Balochistan, she noted, "We tried to reach families by first learning about the community culture and tradition. Then we undertook a process of identifying people who could effectively take on key roles. This was very, very difficult. In our education program, the parents had to demonstrate commitment to the project by contributing their own funds. There was then a probationary period as the teachers were trained, and the program established. Once this happened, then the government came in, conducted its own assessment, and approved the operation as a government school. At this point, resources for teacher pay and building materials became available."

Thus it was that the community owned the schools from the start. Although the work was difficult and sometimes slow, the payoff came when Balochistan's provincial government tried to shift priority in education from girls to boys, and the community, using community organization skills and an effective appeal strategy, successfully fought back.

Qurat's Third Act: The Institute for Development Standards and Practices

By the mid-1990s, there were very few professional social workers like Qurat working in community development, despite the presence of social work schools in Peshawar, Bahawalpur, Karachi, Dhaka, Lahore, and Quetta, and despite the obviously enormous need. She therefore decided to launch a course of study, the Institute for Development Standards and Practices (IDSP) aimed at the education and training of community development workers.

Since its inception, Qurat has inspired, developed, established, and led the IDSP from its location in Quetta. It is now the leading citizen-based organization in Pakistan; approximately 1,200 community-based outreach learners (both college graduates and dropouts, ranging from twenty to thirty-five years old) and faculty currently conduct projects that serve the residents of more than 50 of Pakistan's 139 districts. Since 2002, Qurat has included courses on feminism and women's studies (relevant to the specific sociocultural contexts of such traditional cultures as that of Balochistan) as part of the IDSP curriculum "Mainstreaming Gender and Development." All courses of study link the theory and practice of community development to a firm commitment by the students to return to their communities for two years and to conduct their own development projects as part of their education.

An exhaustive list of the projects undertaken by Qurat, the "learners" (as the undergraduates are called), and the IDSP faculty is beyond the scope of this chapter, and readers are encouraged to access resource material listed in the references (see also the institute's Web site, at http://www.idsp.org.pk/). However, it is important to describe some of them, to convey a sense of the scale of social change under the IDSP that, for them, is really all in a day's work.

The first example is the institute's work in supportive partnership, formed in 1999, with the Aurat Foundation. This nonprofit national nongovernmental organization mobilized more than 350,000 women to cast their votes in the 1999 provincial elections in Balochistan. Many of the women were first-time voters.

In 2000 and 2001 in Balochistan, under Qurat's leadership, the IDSP designed and implemented the Pakistan Participatory Poverty Assessment, the aim of which was to reduce poverty among Pakistani women. This initiative informed and reinforced both the government of Pakistan and the government of Balochistan's poverty reduction interventions across Pakistan. The institute led the research in nine of Balochistan's twenty-six districts.

Yet another example is a community mobilization project established in an Afghan refugee village. Using IDSP's established community development methods, a program was established to aim to enhance women's participation in the education process, decrease the dropout rate in schools, and activate a parent-teacher association in the camps to increase parents' involvement in the education of their children.

Another project was established in the city of Khuzdar, where IDSP graduates have set up their own prototype of the IDSP that offers similar courses and hopes to generate similar outcomes: increased educational and civic opportunities for women.

Finally, the Tawana Pakistan Project is one of IDSP's largest efforts to date. Begun in 2001 in collaboration with the government and other nongovernmental organizations, the project's goal is to increase educational opportunity for more than five hundred million children (mostly girls) between the ages of five and twelve in targeted high-poverty districts. A particular emphasis is placed on nutrition and health (many of the girls and women in the targeted high-poverty districts suffer from serious malnutrition). Their goal is not only to reduce the gender gap in education but also to enable community members to empower themselves to sustain the project beyond its initial funding.

The Future

For all of the initial focus that Qurat placed on the daughters of poor families living in the settlements, she has found that she is thinking a lot more these days about their sons. She plans to create public forums across Balochistan that would educate male youths to resist the lethal attractions of religious extremism, communal violence, drug abuse, and trafficking in drugs and arms, all of which, both directly and indirectly, negatively affect the welfare and rights of women and girls. Her insights concerning the need to address the underlying systemic causes responsible for the oppression of women and girls demonstrate, once again, her ability to see problems holistically (i.e. from a systems perspective) and to attack root causes.

Conclusion

Qurat continues to work with IDSP to considerable international notice. In 1989, the Japanese government honored her for her work in the settlements. In 1998, the organization Ashoka selected her as one of the world's leading social entrepreneurs, and she received the Ashoka fellowship. In 2005, she was nominated for the Nobel Peace Prize. In 2006, she received the prestigious Skoll Award for Social Entrepreneurship, with prize money of US$450,000. In 2007, she was nominated for the Gruber Foundation Award for Women's Rights, which honors individuals who have made significant contributions to human rights that advance the rights of women and girls around the world. Although IDSP pays for her living expenses and a travel allowance for work done under its auspices, she reinvests all other funding that she receives in the organization. She takes no money home. Although her parents now live in California (her mother teaches Urdu to a new generation of Pakistani children), and her children are spread out across the United States, she remains committed to her work with the people of Pakistan.

About a month after I interviewed with Qurat, Benazir Bhutto, the former (and, many believed, future) Pakistani prime minister was assassinated. As it happened, Qurat was still in the United States, heartsick over this latest milestone in Pakistan's turbulent history. Bhutto's widower, Asif Ali Zardari, is now Pakistan's eleventh president and cochair of the Pakistan People's Party. It remains to be seen how these events will affect the geopolitical situation in the future. But of one thing there is no doubt: Quratulain Bakhteari, mother, educator, advocate, community developer, social worker, will continue her life's work: to bring resources, education, dignity, hope, and a better standard of living to the most disenfranchised people in her beloved country.

References

Choudhry, M. A. (2005). Where and who are the world's illiterates? Background paper prepared for EFA Global Monitoring Report, 2006. New York: UNESCO.

Haeri, S. (2004). *No shame for the sun: Lives of professional Pakistani women.* Syracuse, NY: Syracuse University Press.

Nazli, S. (2001). Literacy without formal education: The case of Pakistan. *Journal of International Development, 13*(5), 535–548.

Pakistan is far from Bangladesh. (2006, September 3). *Acorn.* Retrieved June 20, 2008, from http://acorn.nationalinterest.in/2006/09/03/balochistan-is-far-from-bangladesh/.

CHAPTER SEVEN

Aida Luz Maisonet Giachello

Improving Health in the Latino Community

Margaret S. Sherraden

If you have faith even as tiny as a mustard seed, all things are possible.

—Biblical quote in a tiny frame atop a
bookshelf in Aida Giachello's office

On a frigid and windy Chicago morning, Aida Luz Maisonet Giachello pulled over in her old black Mercedes to pick me up for our breakfast interview. After driving back and forth on North Avenue several times looking for Nellie's, a popular Puerto Rican restaurant, Aida turned to me and smiled. "I'm a little absent-minded," she admitted. Her mind was not on details. Like most other mornings, her mind was on work.

Aida Luz Maisonet Giachello's work—prodding and pushing the health care system to respond to Hispanics/ Latinos and other underserved groups—has filled most of her

In researching this chapter, it was a pleasure to have the opportunity to talk with Aida Giachello's colleagues and friends, each of whom gave freely of their time and shared far more insights and stories than I could include in this chapter: Jeannette Noltenius, Jorge Girotti, Silvia Pedraza, Mildred Hunter, Jose Arrom, Aida McCammon, Gwen Stern, and Omayra Giachello. Natalie Meza, Giachello's assistant, provided helpful assistance in locating key contacts and in coordinating interviews. Above all, I am grateful to Aida Giachello for the assistance she gave me early in my academic career and, above all, for her unremitting commitment and boundless energy and efforts to improve the people's health and access to quality health care.

days and evenings for the past thirty years.[1] As Giachello talks about her research, facts fly about disparities in health and access to health services for ethnic and racial minorities in the United States. Her unwavering focus and success in drawing attention to widespread inequities attracted the attention of editors at *Time* magazine when they named her a health crusader and one of the twenty-five most influential Hispanics in the United States (Cole, 2005), and more recently the attention of the editors of *People en español*, who named her one of the hundred most influential Hispanics (Cepeda, 2007).

Growing Up

Aida Luz Maisonet Giachello's biography suggests a strong link between early life experiences and later career decisions. When she was three years old, she and her three brothers stayed with relatives in Puerto Rico for several months while her parents moved to New York City for better opportunities. Once reunited with their parents, they joined the growing exodus of migrants leaving for New York and other U.S. mainland destinations. Loss of agricultural and home-based employment in Puerto Rico fueled the massive migration that swept up the young family (Ayala & Bernabe, 2007). Giachello's parents hoped to make enough money to return to Puerto Rico and open a restaurant.

In New York, young Aida became aware of poverty and gangs in Spanish Harlem, where she and her family lived for seven years. For a time, the family had to turn to public assistance. Because welfare rules at the time prohibited a "man in the house," as Giachello says, her father moved out of their walk-up apartment. Giachello recalled, "The social worker would come out in the middle of the night" to check whether her father lived with them. "If you had a radio or something, you needed to hide it because they would come and check whether or not you had an appliance of any sort and, if so, they'd disqualify you for further assistance." Although her father was gone for only one year, the treatment the family received at the hands of the welfare department made a deep impression on Giachello and began to stir her sense of social justice: "I remember those fears and all those concerns . . .

---

1. *Hispanic* and *Latino* or *Latina* are terms used interchangeably in this chapter to refer to people who identify as Mexican, Mexican American, Puerto Rican, Cuban American, of other Spanish-speaking Caribbean nations, or as a person born or raised in Central or South America.

becoming aware of poverty, unequal treatment, and the sense of help-lessness when people are in those kinds of systems, and the impact that it has on your family."

When Aida was ten years old, the family had saved enough to open a small restaurant and returned to Puerto Rico. Back on the island, Aida's interest in social justice continued to grow: "I remember being inter-ested, always, in issues-doing surveys in high school, trying to find out [about] problems. I was interested in research since I was very young. I remember talking in political meetings when I was thirteen, fourteen years of age, in the public housing, and wherever there was an election, getting involved in whatever way I could."

After high school, Giachello entered the University of Puerto Rico to study social science. She was one of the few students from her public high school to pass the required college entrance examination and the first person in her family to attend college. Although her mother was proud, her father hesitated to help her finance her education, saying, "It's not going to be in my best interest to invest in your education, because your husband will be the one taking advantage of it." But Gia-chello prevailed, walking the twenty blocks to school from her house instead of asking her parents for the ten-cent bus fare. This experience offered her greater insight into poverty: "I remember one time I was really tired and I really needed to take the bus. I was looking [for some-one] with a friendly face, that I could approach, to ask them for ten cents for the bus. It was so difficult. . . . I followed an older lady for almost a block until I was finally able to ask her, 'Do you mind giving me ten cents for the bus?' And she did. . . . I don't know why it was so difficult, but it was."

Reflecting on that experience, Giachello noted, "It has really helped me to understand how difficult it is to ask for help. That's why I'm very sensitive about anybody who approaches me for anything. Just to be able to ask for help takes . . . tremendous . . . courage." After college, Aida met and married Stelvio Giachello, an immigrant of Italian descent from Uruguay. Before she met Stelvio, she had not been interested in marriage. "I didn't want to get married, because I always had a percep-tion that Latino men would mistreat me. My father ended up being a womanizer. . . . [H]e used to fool around. And my mom—there was some domestic violence whenever he got involved with some woman. So I was scared to death that I would be involved in that kind of situa-tion when I married."

Adjusting to marriage during the first year was "traumatic," accord-ing to Giachello. It began on their honeymoon. Her boss called and asked her to go on a last-minute fund-raising trip. She recalled with a slightly self-conscious look that she was already packing when her incredulous husband asked her where she was going. She explained the project to him and that they needed the money. Stelvio said, "Either you call them and tell them you're not going to go, or I'm going to call them and tell them you're not going." Her first reaction was swift. "How can a man tell me what to do?" In the end, she reconsidered and explained to her boss (who wondered why she had agreed to go in the first place) that she hadn't discussed it with her husband first and that he was "very much upset, because we are on our honeymoon." It was an object lesson in how to balance one's passion to change the world with one's love, devotion, and commitment to husband and family.

Returning to the U.S. Mainland

Giachello's research career was launched in 1966, when she completed her university studies and landed a job conducting research in Puerto Rico and nearby islands. One project, led by researchers at Northwestern University, was a ten-year study of social change in Puerto Rican society. The researchers soon realized that their young colleague had scholarly potential, and they invited her to move to Northwestern's campus in Evanston, Illinois, to help with data analysis.

Giachello's husband was lukewarm about the idea. Stelvio did not speak English very well and didn't care for cold weather. Giachello was undeterred: "I was very convinced that I was going to leave if he wouldn't come with me. I knew in my heart that it was a big opportunity."

Ironically, following the move to Evanston, their marriage grew steadier and stronger. They rented a tiny apartment and joked that it was so small "you could open the refrigerator with your toe from the bed." Giachello recalled, "That time was the best thing that could happen to us because it allowed me to really develop a close relationship with Stelvio that I hadn't developed up to that point. . . . I was expecting a baby. The weather was cold. We didn't know anybody. But he was extremely caring and loving. And so it really helped us to work through some of the many issues . . . in our relationship."

While in Evanston, a lakeside suburb on the northern edge of the city, Aida became acquainted with Silvia Herrera de Fox, executive director of Aspira, a program that promotes education and leadership among youths of Puerto Rican descent. Silvia encouraged Giachello to return to school, but she was trying to be a more traditional wife and mother, learning how to cook and sew. Ultimately, the new sewing machine never made it out of the box and Giachello never learned how to cook well, but she entered graduate studies in social work, the profession that most closely matched her values and aspirations. Along with nine other Latino students, she entered the School of Social Service Administration at the University of Chicago on full scholarship. She remembers that "it was a wonderful experience. . . . Our instructor nurtured our group of ten people. We had monthly meetings in one of our homes. . . . Students from previous years would help us navigate, tell us how we should deal with different professors, how we should organize in terms of studying. You know, they gave us a lot of tools, in addition to giving support. It's not just the students, but our spouses were part of this. They were able to hear the challenges that we were going through. My husband became more supportive of me as a result."

Initially, her focus on community organization was an accident—all the other specializations had closed by the time Giachello was admitted. As luck would have it, community organization suited her interests and temperament. She is also grateful, though, for the direct practice experience from her first placement, "because it helps you the rest of your life, in everything you do about understanding group dynamics and individual behavior and understanding yourself." Nonetheless, her heart was in community organizing. It helped her understand and frame the concerns she brought from childhood about poverty and social injustice.

At first, she struggled academically. Studying in English was difficult, but with support from peers and professors, the Cs she earned in the first year became As by the second year. Giachello completed her master's degree in social work. On graduating, she took a job at a community mental health center as a psychiatric social worker: "As a result of that experience, I [knew] I didn't want to do direct work with individuals and families. I wanted to move into policy and community work, because the problems that people were bringing to my attention . . . the roots of the problems were poverty, unemployment, immigration issues. Helping one individual, you are not really addressing the bigger picture."

A few years after graduation, her husband decided it was time to move the family back to Puerto Rico. There, Giachello worked in human services directing a youth program in a poor barrio of Santurce, a district of San Juan. After a year or two, and pregnant with their third child, she was invited to take a faculty position at the Interamerican University in Río Piedras. She loved her work; she had come to believe that research, teaching, and policy were the keys to improving life chances in the Latino community.

To be truly effective, however, Giachello believed she needed a doctoral degree, and she thought immediately of the University of Chicago. Although the admission deadline had passed for a doctorate in social work there, she applied for and was admitted to the sociology program, requiring a move back to the U.S. mainland for her family. While she was pursuing her doctoral degree, Giachello worked as a public health social worker in a nearby Chicago Department of Health neighborhood clinic: "Once you're in social work you are always a social worker. Your heart is in the right place, and you're doing very concrete things of helping communities and families, you immediately connect your effort with impact. [In contrast] in sociology, it was a group of people that traditionally would go to Notre Dame and then would come to the University of Chicago or Harvard or whatever. And many of them were elite . . . talking about issues of poverty. But none of them had experienced poverty."

Through her public health work, Giachello became increasingly interested in health care. She found two professors at Chicago with similar interests, Ronald M. Andersen and Lu Ann Aday, whose seminal work continues to guide health services research to this day. They immediately "embraced me, mentored me, [and] got me into their Center for Health Administration Studies," where she explored health access among Latinos and other minority groups.

Giachello's job at the research center at the University of Chicago ended when federal funding became scarce under Ronald Reagan's presidency. At the same time, however, the political winds in Chicago were also shifting. Harold Washington was seeking election as one of the first viable mayoral candidates in many years not beholden to Mayor Richard J. Daley's machine politics. Giachello worked "around the clock" as a volunteer on Washington's campaign, "doing his speechwriting and research." In collaboration with Hispanics and women's groups, she wrote proposals for the establishment of the Mayor's Office of Hispanic Affairs and the Mayor's Office of Women's Affairs. "It was an opportunity to really think about policies, ideas, building a broader coalition of diverse racial and ethnic groups. It was a really fun time . . . I really enjoyed that experience."

After Washington's election, Giachello testified in citywide public hearings on the health-care needs and access of Latinos. Afterward, the newly appointed health commissioner, who had been present during the hearings, called to offer Giachello a position as special assistant for Hispanic affairs in the Chicago Department of Public Health. It was a heady time, and Washington's supporters were excited to change the way business was done. Giachello and her staff recommended and began to implement comprehensive health policies and to call for wholesale reorganization and allocation of resources for Latino health, including "comprehensive needs assessments to determine the health needs of Latinos, recruitment of bilingual/bicultural staff, and community education to reach the Latino community." Giachello believes that this was "the most comprehensive initiative for addressing Latino health to date."

In three years, the political leadership ramped up for Mayor Washington's reelection. They moved Giachello to city hall to begin mobilizing. She soon grew tired of the political maelstrom. She left city hall, having realized that she wanted to work at the nexus of research, teaching, policy, and community service. Moreover, she had abandoned her Ph.D. dissertation and had been told that she had to finish it or forfeit her doctoral degree. In 1986, Giachello joined the faculty of the Jane Addams College of Social Work at the University of Illinois at Chicago. She focused on her studies of health in the growing Midwest Latino population and completed her doctoral degree on time.

Leading the Way in Improving Health Care in the Latino Community

Although the nature of her work became less political, in direct terms, when she joined the faculty at the Jane Addams College of Social Work, Giachello never stopped working with grassroots groups, community organizations, political leaders, and others. At one point, for example, she joined a demonstration against the university's plans to merge with (and close) the university's medical hospital. Local community leaders asked her to join their efforts in voicing concern to university officials. The social work dean found out about the meeting and came to her: "I just heard that you were confronting the [university] president. What do you think you're doing? You're never going to be able get tenure here." Giachello believed it was "more important to sleep well at night knowing that you are doing what you think is right in speaking out." Nonetheless, she later reengaged with her research "until things got a little bit more calm." Through this experience, she learned that she would be more effective if she voiced concerns in a strategic and less "confrontational way." "I learned not to be Don Quixote, to try to work with others, and work within the system . . . to get changes made."

By the mid-1980s, Giachello and other health activists had founded the Midwest Hispanic AIDS Coalition. Among its first accomplishments was to compel the Centers for Disease Control (CDC) to begin a grant program to help community groups engage in HIV prevention. Not long after, Giachello acquired CDC funding for the creation of the Midwest Hispanic AIDS Coalition, and she spent the next few years building the organization (now called Salud Latina).

During that time, Giachello also worked with other public health scholars to create the Latino Caucus of the American Public Health Association to focus attention on Latino health issues. In its work with Jeannette Noltenius and other public health colleagues, the caucus focused attention on an understudied group, Latinos in the Midwest.

As Noltenius observed, "Giachello filled an enormous void by doing research in Michigan, Kansas, Illinois, Nebraska, Indiana, and the rest of the Midwest." Early on, she understood the need to create a health action network, which led to the creation of Redes en Acción, a National Cancer Institute–funded approach to cancer prevention and control that included community-based organizations, research institutions, government health agencies, and the public (for more information about Redes en Acción, see http://redesenaccion.org/about_us.htm).

The Midwest Latino Health Research, Training, and Policy Center

In 1993, armed with social work values, skills, education, experience, and unremitting drive, Giachello established what would become the center of her professional life, the Midwest Latino Health Research, Training, and Policy Center at the University of Illinois at Chicago. The center has since become the organizational hub for her relentless efforts to improve health care in the Latino community. Since its founding, Giachello has raised many millions of dollars to fund research and community partnerships. In particular, she has dedicated the center's work to health promotion, disease prevention and management, and control of chronic illnesses, including type 2 diabetes, asthma, cancer, and cardiovascular diseases—all of which take a steep toll on Latino lives and budgets.

The center's work built on the applied social research tradition pioneered by the women of Hull House, whose founder, Jane Addams, is the namesake of the College of Social Work where Giachello is on the faculty (today, Hull House is a museum on the university's campus). Like Addams, Giachello combines data collection with education, community empowerment, and policy change (Giachello, 1996). Her work has been published widely, appearing in journals such as *Cancer, Public Health Reports, Diabetes Educator,* and *Journal of Medical Systems,* as well as in books on health care, Latinos, minority health access, and women's health. She regularly speaks at social work, medical, mental health, education, and policy conferences, and local and national community and professional meetings. Like an early associate of Hull House, Alice Hamilton, who was a major influence in the founding of the field of public health, Giachello focuses her efforts on health promotion and disease prevention among the poor and vulnerable in society.

Giachello's frustration with the health-care system stemmed from her work as a medical social worker in a public health clinic in the 1970s, where she grew increasingly aware of the financial, cultural, and institutional barriers to health and mental health services. Through the center,

Giachello breathed life into the idea of expanding access to health care in Latino communities, beginning in the Midwest, and increasingly in national and international contexts. Giachello's research shows that the health-care system has limited ability to meet the health needs of populations with different health beliefs and practices, and that multiple barriers prevail in service delivery. These dynamics affect quality of care and ultimately health outcomes.

Giachello and her colleagues at the center generate understanding of the socioeconomic and political forces underlying health disparities. They balance research with community mobilization, coalition and capacity building, training of leaders in research methods, instrument development, data collection, analysis, and social action. They use data to stimulate community and system change and to inform program and policy design. Changes may focus on increasing linguistic and cultural competence in the health-care delivery system at the institutional level (e.g., changing norms, policies, and practices) and at the individual level (e.g., improving patient-provider communication). Giachello was an early proponent of providers who understand cultural influences on health and health care, including "folk healing" or traditional health practices (Giachello, 1995).

Giachello is committed to changing stereotypes and helping people understand the heterogeneity of the Latino population and their health and social needs. As a colleague noted, "People think that when immigrants cross the international border they get a lobotomy, and Aida is determined to counter this stereotype." This includes making sure there are more Hispanics doing research. According to Giachello, "Research can be scientific, but also sexist, racist, and political. Research in this country has often been used to reinforce stereotypes and keep minorities in subordinate positions. Therefore, there is a need to change the research paradigm from research on minorities to research by and for minorities. This requires training minority researchers who can collect and analyze data based on social and community norms, and with deep sensitivity and understanding of the realities of Latino and other minority communities."

According to a colleague, "Giachello is driven by the importance of bringing Latinos to the table in academia." In an admirer's words, "she has paved the way for others that follow."

Innovations in Community Health Research

With an ear to the grass roots, Giachello and her collaborators at the center have developed several innovative and effective models for health-care delivery. One is based on the popular-education ideas of

Paulo Freire (1972). This model, community participatory action research (CPAR), combines reflective thinking about circumstances and root causes of health problems with principles of adult education and community organizing (Giachello et al., 2003). The CPAR model includes six key steps:

1. Community engagement through partnership and coalition building using health and social issues as tools for community mobilization and organization
2. Community capacity building, in which community leaders learn about key health issues in the community, as well as the sociopolitical and economic contexts
3. Participatory data collection and analysis, in which community members engage in needs and asset assessments, such as community mapping, focus groups, community surveys, and PhotoVoice (the technique of using photos to document a grassroots issue)
4. Information dissemination, during which community researchers provide evidence and offer directions for community action through town-hall meetings and community forums
5. Action planning, in which a broader group of community members develop strategic community action plans for changing health conditions
6. Community social action, in which community members implement the action plan

In some of their work, staff have trained communities in PhotoVoice. In the case of diabetes, for example, residents may document a dearth of grocery stores that carry fruits and vegetables and other healthy food or lack of secure places where residents can exercise safely. In this way, community residents "tell the story from their photos, documenting and educating policy makers." Community residents also help develop health assessment surveys: "In this way, community input plays a key role in determining what they want to study, the types of questions that will be included, how the questions will be formulated, and how study participants are adequately protected from any research risks. In order to encourage community involvement, we simplify and avoid the jargon, make the research fun and useful, and use it to teach research methods (e.g., sampling, evaluation), and at the same time providing job opportunities (e.g., training and recruiting community interviewers or providing subcontracts to community-based organizations). Throughout the process, we facilitate leadership development."

"The whole idea" of CPAR, according to Giachello, "is to build leadership, so you displace yourself gradually and let the new leaders take over . . . as they emerge and feel comfortable. This is important because people tend to get scared if they have not been in these types of roles before. You tell them to be a chair of a committee and they get scared to death."

Since the beginning, the center's CPAR model has been used to address issues ranging from environmental health to tobacco control, type 2 diabetes and other chronic diseases, and injury prevention (Giachello, 1985; Giachello et al., 2003; Ramírez et al., 2005). When the center began this work, CPAR was relatively unknown, and funders were skeptical about an approach that focused on community and system change (Giachello & Belgrave, 1997). Nonetheless, the center prevailed and the CPAR model contributed to establishment of the National Center of Excellence for the Elimination of Disparities, an initiative of the CDC and its Racial and Ethnic Approaches to Community Health (REACH) 2010 plan.

The center has also developed promising approaches for direct work with individuals and families. Perhaps best known is the Diabetes Empowerment Education Program (DEEP). This bilingual diabetes education program consists of a three-day train-the-trainer curriculum for community health workers and health professionals, and an eight-module curriculum that addresses essential aspects of diabetes management and control. The program's success is measured in positive clinical outcomes and behavioral assessments, such as healthy eating and increases in physical activity. The DEEP program has been implemented in partnership with diabetes prevention and control programs in public health departments across the United States and in community-based organizations and neighborhood health facilities in United States–Mexico border areas, Puerto Rico, Mexico, Peru, and Colombia.

Another innovation is creation of diabetes learning centers, or self-care wellness centers, in Chicago's Latino communities. Community members, including community health workers (*promotores*) manage the centers, which offer direct services (e.g., case management, health education, advocacy, policy) and provide internships for high school, undergraduate, and graduate students in public health and human services.

Currently, the center is involved in perhaps its most ambitious project to date. The Hispanic Community Health Study is perhaps the largest longitudinal epidemiological study of Hispanic chronic health issues. It will identify the prevalence of risk factors among sixteen thousand people of Mexican, Puerto Rican, Cuban, and Central and South American descent, and aims to educate participating communities about a variety of chronic diseases. The center's role in the study is to reach and maintain contact with four thousand study participants in the Chicago area. As a colleague pointed out, government funders turned to Giachello's center because of its long-standing connections to the community and its reputation for getting things done.

Mentoring a New Generation of Researchers and Community Organizers

One of Giachello's legacies is the many gifted people who have received training or have worked with center staff. Since its inception, staff estimate that the center has trained more than five hundred undergraduate and graduate students, postdoctoral fellows, and faculty. Occasionally, staff find Giachello's optimism daunting, but they respect her profound belief in people's potential. They say she always chooses to offer each person an opportunity to demonstrate what she or he can do.

This faith extends far beyond her professional associates. While on a recent sabbatical and in between research trips to Latin America, Giachello responded to an e-mail from a high school student in Los Angeles. The student, David, had written that he needed information from Giachello for a class assignment as soon as possible: "i need to have information on when you were a child, where you grew up, what universities u went 2, and when and where u were born." Many busy people would ignore such a request—not Giachello. She responded with a two-page story of her upbringing and education. She concluded her e-mail with this comment: "Thank you for wanting to write about me. I am just an ordinary person like you. I am not smarter. I had to work hard to overcome many barriers as I had low self-esteem, and I thought I was not able to achieve much. I have surprised myself." For Giachello, overcoming the odds in her own life has fueled a desire to extend opportunities to others, including a high school student doing his homework at the last minute.

One of her personal goals is to create a "trampoline" for others, launching them toward future opportunities. Whether she's mentoring a high school student or a young professional, teaching social work students, training community health workers, or organizing community leaders, Giachello uses an empowerment and participatory approach. She does not draw lines between research, community organizing, teaching, and policy. As a longtime colleague explained, Giachello believes in action—it is her "signature." She firmly believes that the process has empowered more than a few to become researchers themselves, which is illustrative of that trampoline effect.

In her teaching, Giachello engages social work students in the same way as she does the community. For social workers to develop effective community organizing skills, she is convinced that they must get involved with the grass roots and become competent researchers.

"Most social workers don't like research or are scared to engage in research." She doesn't blame them, because research is often taught "out of context." Giachello describes her teaching: "I immediately merge them into the community. The first thing you have to learn about is how to work in a community, get to know gatekeepers, build partnerships and trust, and make the research process participatory. It's not about your needs and what you want. It's about getting them to connect with the community. This way students can develop understanding, and consequently a passion for what they're doing . . . [and] see that research is fun, that it's an opportunity to not only increase their body of knowledge, it also presents an opportunity to impact the community. Too often social work education is disjointed and doesn't examine the environment or conditions that are really leading to a problem."

In the past, the center's successes resulted from the sheer force of Aida's personality, hard work, and the relationships she built across communities and disciplines. Now, say her colleagues, much of the center's work—the numerous studies, training, and advocacy projects—is well beyond her personal reach. Other scholars and activists, facilitated by a dedicated and talented staff, carry on the center's work, both through direct partnerships and independently, supported by federal and state governments, international organizations, philanthropic foundations, and professional groups.

Leader and Organizer

Giachello's office in a former manufacturing building on the periphery of the University of Illinois at Chicago campus is overflowing with photographs, posters, awards, degrees, and certificates displayed haphazardly atop bookcases and on the walls. Interspersed among family photos, including ones with Aida alongside her husband, Stelvio, at three presidential inaugural balls, are others of Giachello with a host of community leaders and luminaries, including Mayor Washington, Chicago's first African American mayor, and former first lady and now secretary of state Hillary Clinton. Her academic degrees are surrounded by dozens of testimonials, certificates of appreciation, awards, and certificates of recognition and appreciation, including ones from the Puerto Rican Senate, the U.S. Senate, and the U.S. House of Representatives.

Like the arrangement of the photographs in her office, bringing everyone to the table is central to Giachello's approach to her work. As a colleague observes, "She is a masterful networker; she always tries to link her work to other groups or people, and to seek their input and participation." This pays off repeatedly, say her collaborators; people are willing to work with the center because they know and trust her. In the Latino community, says one observer, "she is a star."

The center has brought people from all over the Midwest to Chicago for training, introduced leaders to one another, and created a community of support among researchers, students, community leaders, practitioners, and policy makers. In this way, Giachello has built considerable political capital. Public officials, for example, know from experience that they can count on her for information and advice about thorny issues. According to a medical school colleague, changes in funding for chronic disease management are due, in part, to Giachello's influence with policy makers: "Her policy-oriented focus benefits the community without us always knowing her precise role." According to another person who has worked closely with Giachello in the American Public Health Association, "She has been one of the most outspoken people on the need to change policy."

Giachello routinely invites public and elected officials to speak at forums and workshops. They attend, a colleague explained, because of Giachello's nearly universal appeal: "At every event, the press is there, especially the Spanish-speaking press. And because the press is there, legislators are also there." When the center celebrated its tenth anniversary, for example, U.S. senator Richard Durbin; Dr. Quentin Young, a health activist, advocate of single-payer health coverage, and former president of the American Public Health Association; and other public officials and leaders came to pay tribute to Giachello and the center's work. As a colleague explained, "It's because they see that she can bring the common folk to the table. Her message is about social change, social justice, and spending our lives making this a better place for everyone."

Faith and Inner Strength

To really understand Aida Giachello, say her friends and colleagues, requires understanding the depth of her faith. They say this is something that might surprise people, because, although faith drives her optimism and resolve, she never wears religion on her sleeve. But, said a good friend, "Aida is a profoundly religious person. She goes to Mass every day early in the morning. It's a daily spiritual motivation." Giachello puts her faith into action through her work and her commitment to making life better for ordinary people. In this way, they say, she does not think about her work as a career. "It's more like God has put her in this place for a reason," says a friend. According to another, Giachello is an "eternal optimist, someone who believes there is nothing that can't be done, and she inspires others to also feel that things can be done as well." This includes her staff at the center, to whom she "gives free rein and an opportunity to grow."

Another source of Giachello's strength has always been her family, including her husband, her children, and her mother. In 2004, her husband, Stelvio, died of lung cancer. It was a huge loss. According to her friends, Stelvio "was the mainstay, the oak." He was extremely supportive of Aida's work and, for many years, took much of the day-to-day responsibility for raising their children. Her friends and coworkers said that Aida showed great resolve throughout Stelvio's illness. One colleague recalled a wonderful birthday party that she organized for her husband with all of his closest friends: "That day stands in my mind as a testament to her strength."

Perhaps because her motivation comes from deep within, and because she knows the job is enormous, Giachello drives herself hard. "She has never in all these years," says a friend, "lost sight of her focus on the common person. She is never afraid to speak up. She always looks for ways to improve herself so she can work for the community." Another friend noted, "Aida is one of the most unselfish people I know. She helps everybody as much as she can even though she is always a busy lady." This level of commitment takes its toll: "I have seen her overstretched and sleep little," reports a female colleague. "I have seen her done in, exhausted."

Her years of hard work and significant achievement have brought Giachello long-overdue recognition. Hanging on the wall of her office is a framed cover of the 2005 *Time* magazine issue that recognized Giachello as one of the twenty-five most influential Hispanics in America. The award is affirmation of a lifetime of inspiration and hard work to place Latino health and access to health services on the research and policy agenda.

Going Global

Perhaps in part because of the *Time* magazine recognition and related events of 2005, Giachello began to think about new ways to move the Latino health agenda forward. Like others driven toward social change, she has increasingly shifted her sights to the international stage. With increasing human migration across North, Central, and South America, she understands the imperative of learning about health issues across borders and the potential for exploring new approaches based on other countries' health policies and programs.

When the opportunity arose for a sabbatical, Giachello obtained a research fellowship to spend time in Latin America learning about promising practices and innovations in health access, affordability, and quality of services. Her goal is to facilitate transfer of policies and skills in both directions. Beginning with the perspectives of health leaders in Chicago immigrant communities, she has traveled to Mexico, Puerto Rico, Guatemala, Chile, Brazil, and other countries to build relationships with university faculty and health leaders. She is, according to a colleague, building a "two-way street," aimed to develop ongoing links that will bring health leaders together across international borders.

Giachello has many questions: How is Brazil using the model of empowerment developed by Paolo Freire to improve patient care? How have some Latin American nations, such as Chile, Brazil, Colombia, Mexico, Argentina, and Cuba, incorporated the idea of the right to health in their constitutions, and how have they translated this into policy and services? How well do models of cultural competency in Afro and indigenous communities in Bolivia and Peru function? How are promising models of primary care, including the use of *promotores de salud* (community health promoters) implemented in various countries?

During visits back to Chicago, Giachello engages in discussions with Univision and Telemundo/NBC television (the largest Spanish-speaking media outlets in the Chicago area), and with the top public health officials in the state about making health care universal. As of this writing, she and her staff plan to hold workshops and to collaborate with other organizations to disseminate what she is learning from Latin American countries about the vexing challenges of health-care delivery for the poor and minority communities. Furthermore, Aida Giachello shows no signs of slowing down. As a colleague pointed out, "She could retire, but she just wants to keep working." Much work remains for this scholar and crusader. Giachello has frontiers to push for Latinos in social work, health, and medicine, and new milestones to achieve in public health.

In closing, it is perhaps not surprising that all of the people who reflected on Giachello's life and career in this chapter are leaders in their own right, and this says a great deal about Aida. She not only seeks out talented people of all ages and professional disciplines but also promotes them through her work. They help one another achieve significant milestones in social work and public health. Working with people in the community, academia, and government, Giachello has pushed the frontiers for Latinos in social work, health, and medicine. In the generative applied research traditions of Jane Addams and Paulo Freire, Giachello is a scholar and crusader for her people and all people.

References

Ayala, C. J., & Bernabe, R. (2007). *Puerto Rico in the American century: A history since 1898*. Chapel Hill: University of North Carolina Press.

Cepeda, E. J. (2007, January 31). Suburban doctor makes Hispanic "influential 100" list: From humble roots in Puerto Rico, she leads UIC center's Latino health study. *Chicago Sun-Times*, 7.

Cole, W. (2005, August 13). Aida Giachello. *Time*. Retrieved February 1, 2009, from http://www.time.com/time/nation/article/0,8599,1093646,00.html?promoid =flashLink.

Freire, P. (1972). *Pedagogy of the oppressed*. New York: Herder and Herder.

Giachello, A. L. (1985). Prevention: A Hispanic perspective. *Journal of Health and Medicine, 3*(2–3), 24–25.

Giachello, A. L. (1995). Cultural diversity and institutional inequality. In D. L. Adams (Ed.), *Health issues for women of color: A cultural diversity perspective* (pp. 5–26). Thousand Oaks, CA: Sage.

Giachello, A. L. (1996). Challenges and opportunities in establishing a Latino health research center in a majority academic institution. *Journal of Medical Systems, 20*(5), 351–376.

Giachello, A. L., Arrom, J. O., Davis, M., Sayad, J. V., Ramirez, D., Chandana, N., et al. (2003). Reducing diabetes health disparities through community-based participatory action research: The Chicago Southeast Diabetes Community Action Coalition. *Public Health Reports, 118*(4), 309–323.

Giachello, A. L., & Belgrave, F. (1997). Task group VI: Health care systems and behavior. *Journal of Gender, Culture and Health, 2*(2), 163–174.

Ramírez, A., Gallion, K., Suarez, L., Giachello, A. L., Marti, J., Medrano, M., et al. (2005). A national agenda for Latino cancer prevention and control. *Cancer, 103*(11), 2209–2215.

CHAPTER EIGHT

Theresa J. Kaijage

The "Mama Teresa" of Tanzania

Dorie J. Gilbert

The opportunity to write this chapter has only reinforced my high regard for Theresa Kaijage. I met her years ago and have followed her work closely because of our shared interest in HIV/AIDS work among African-descent people in the diaspora. To interview her for this book was a great opportunity to sit down with her and hear about how her life and career path led her to a leadership role in the social work field. And so it was, on her recent trip to the United States to give an invited talk and to visit family, friends, and colleagues, that I was able to sit down with her at my home in Austin, Texas, to discuss

So many friends and colleagues of Theresa Kaijage's have been instrumental in assisting with this chapter. I would like to thank my colleague, Cal Streeter, for introducing me to this remarkable woman years ago. Streeter also facilitated Kaijage's most recent visit to Austin, which made this in-person interview possible. Several other friends and colleagues of Theresa's have provided details and comments to this chapter, including Nathan Linsk, who has worked closely with Theresa in the American International Health Alliance's HIV/AIDS twinning center program, and Sandy Wexler, Theresa's dissertation chair at the University of Pittsburgh. Finally, I appreciate the comments from Floyd M. Patterson, executive director of the Seven Project in Pittsburgh, and Anna Mukami of WAMATA U.S. Inc.

her extraordinary contributions to those suffering from the most misunderstood illness in Africa today.

Introduction

Theresa J. Kaijage, Ph.D., MSW, is the founder and guiding force of WAMATA (an acronym for the Swahili phrase "Walio katika Mapambano na AIDS Tanzania," which means "Those in the Struggle against AIDS in Tanzania"), a national nongovernmental organization (NGO), based in Tanzania, that provides counseling, testing, education, social care, and economic support to individuals living with HIV/AIDS, and to the orphans, widows, and family members of those so affected. Established in 1989, WAMATA started as a community-based support organization for families affected by HIV/AIDS in Tanzania and developed into an NGO with branches in villages and towns in several regions of the country. Because of Kaijage's leadership, the country was mobilized early on in the fight against the AIDS pandemic, and she has remained committed to the battle for the past twenty years while, since 1980, also serving on the faculty of the National Institute for Social Work in Tanzania.

Described by many who know her as a Tanzanian "Mama Teresa," Theresa has a powerful impact wherever she goes and on whatever goal she is pursuing in international social work. Many who have worked with Theresa think of her as a "human magnet," drawing a wide variety of people to her, from the most to the least powerful. I am among the many people who count Theresa not only as an inspiration in international social work but more specifically as a pioneer in AIDS activism. Her devotion and commitment to healing her own little corner of the world seems to have been part of her destiny and was clearly influenced by her experiences as a child growing up in Tanzania.

Childhood Village Life in Tanzania

Theresa (her birth name was Kajumilo) was born on September 30, 1947, in Bukoba, Tanzania, a small village located in the northwestern part of the country, seven hours from Dar es Salaam, the largest, wealthiest city in the country. The first of three girls and one boy, gender and birth order were two key factors that shaped Theresa's early experiences. In a time when it was unusual for fathers to prioritize the education of their daughters, Theresa's father was clear about his commitment to her education. She admirably described her father as a peasant farmer with a progressive political mind, and she remembers his words: "A girl

I have and a girl I will send to school!" Theresa credits a great deal of her motivation and inspiration to her father's ability to see beyond gender.

From an early age, schooling and education placed Theresa in a position to create unity and action around a cause. Her earliest memories are of having to transcend religious separatism in her village. Originally placed in the Omurugando Catholic preschool, Theresa later changed to the Kikomero Lutheran preschool because she could walk the long distance with kids from her neighborhood. Having to bridge friendships and manage the rivalry between the Lutheran and Catholic peers are what Theresa describes as her grounding in nonsectarianism and humanitarianism. Eventually, because of the long distance her family lived from both the Lutheran and the Catholic primary schools, Theresa's father negotiated for her to go and live with the nuns in the Rutabo Catholic convent in 1955. The experience of being away from home was difficult for Theresa; she remembers leaving home crying and her father saying, "Someday you will thank me for this!" Today, Theresa has nothing but sweet admiration and praise for her father's insight. After the initial shock, Theresa came to love the convent and her formative experiences there. In January 1956, she was baptized in the Catholic Church, and it was then that she chose the name Theresa for herself.

Later, Theresa would go on to middle school and then secondary school, but she recalls with much regret those days when so many of the family's resources were funneled into her education, given her status as the eldest child. When it was time for her next sister to attend middle school, her father could not manage school fees for both Theresa and her sister, so her sister had to lose a year, which affected her so much that she never made it to secondary school. This was a devastating experience for Theresa. The saying "To those who are given much, much is expected" has always resonated with her. Having received so much of the family's resources, she knew she needed to give back to her siblings. Giving was also a lesson she learned from her mother, whom Theresa describes as humble but profoundly thoughtful, unassuming, and loving, a woman who would share her last piece of bread (*ugali*) with a passerby. "We were poor," Theresa recalls, "but we were never hungry," and her mother would share whatever they had with anyone in need.

Early Career in Teaching

After secondary school, Theresa attended Teacher's Training School in Dar es Salaam. She was committed and driven in her goals not only because of her love for teaching but also because she realized that she needed to gain sufficient education and work to go back and support her sisters and brother before continuing with her higher education. In January 1970, then twenty-three years old, Theresa started teaching at the secondary school in Bukoba, her birthplace, on the shores of Lake Victoria. Theresa loved and cherished her experience of teaching the children, some of whom were older than she was. Also important was her ability to give back to her siblings, but Theresa's spirit of giving extended far beyond her siblings. In general, Theresa's spirit of giving and caring reflects the African adage "It takes a whole village to raise a child."

Children have always been at the center of Theresa's heart, and it was children who gave her the best gift she has ever received. When Theresa married Frederick Kaijage in Bukoba, on August 26, 1972, the schoolchildren whom she had taught over the years came together from across religious traditions to join in a nonsectarian celebration. It was a great show of religious unity (all sects were involved in the wedding mass: Muslim, Seventh Day Adventist, and a joint Lutheran-Catholic choir!). She valued those years of teaching and the lessons she learned from the youths, but she feels that her greatest contribution was reflected in the cooperation that those children practiced at her wedding.

Immediately after their wedding, the couple left for Coventry, England, where Fred was already studying for a Ph.D. in social and economic history at the University of Warwick. Their first daughter, Milembe Ana, was born in Coventry in October 1973. In 1975, the couple returned to Tanzania, where Fred began a career as a professor of history at the University of Dar es Salaam. Theresa returned to secondary school teaching. Still driven by a need to give back, Theresa went on to complete her bachelor's degree and then taught at Lugalo Secondary School until 1980, when she left to teach at the Institute of Social Work (ISW), where she still teaches today. At the ISW, Theresa began her career by teaching psychology and communication skills, but she quickly acknowledged that she needed to acquire skills and experiences related to social work. It was that desire for social work education that led her to the United States.

U.S. Social Work Education

Theresa applied for the MSW program at the George Warren Brown School of Social Work at Washington University in St. Louis and was accepted as a Fulbright scholar. By the time she was ready to leave Tanzania to study in the United States, she had given birth to all three of her children. Her sons, Karumuna Augustine and Mukurasi Michaelangelo, were both born in Dar es Salaam, in 1978 and 1981, respectively. Because Mukurasi was two at the time of her departure, she never intended to stay long in the United States. Theresa describes the time as a "hard two years without her children," but she persevered, giving 100 percent to her studies. She was getting the education not only for herself but also for all those whom she wanted to go back to, to be with, and to support—her husband, her children, her siblings, and her community. She focused on finding the most challenging of field placements—an experience that would provide her a solid background in family and community practice work in different settings to enhance her clinical experiences. She had no idea at the time, though, how or why these experiences would be relevant to her future back home.

Ironically, it was not news from home or a special program on Africa that first alerted Theresa to the emerging crisis of AIDS. Rather, Theresa remarks, "The first I heard of AIDS was in St. Louis." Colleagues at her placement were rather incredulous. They asked, "Do you mean you haven't heard about AIDS? But it came from Africa, your continent!" This was interesting news to Theresa at the time, and she remembers thinking, "Not in my country!" However, by the time Theresa returned to Tanzania, she learned that the very city where she had come from, Bukoba, a town on the border with Uganda, already had a high incidence of AIDS and in fact was the town of the first reported case of AIDS in Tanzania and the epicenter of the early epidemic.

Founding WAMATA: Changing the Lives of People Living with HIV/AIDS in Tanzania

Back home in Tanzania, Theresa started working at the medical school psychiatric unit at the National Hospital in October 1985, as an honorary lecturer in family therapy. She also started working with AIDS patients and talking with doctors about the epidemic. She was frustrated that nearly all the services revolved around individual therapy or death and dying, without a social focus on families or on the context of social support and coping. At a time when confronting HIV/AIDS in Tanzania clearly called for more than individual therapy, Theresa stepped in to advocate for the necessary next steps of supportive therapy and social activism.

Theresa's work to mobilize the communities around HIV/AIDS support groups started in the years before 1989, but it was not until she attended her first HIV/AIDS conference that year, the Third International AIDS Conference, held in Montreal, Canada, that Theresa started to craft a plan for action. At that conference, she recalls that the activist organization AIDS Coalition to Unleash Power (ACT UP), a New

York–based advocacy group, was present. ACT UP was known for its nonviolent civil disobedience activities, which included dramatic protests and demonstrations to call attention to the rights and needs of people living with HIV. Theresa recalls that, while ACT UP put on an impressive show of activism, Africans living with HIV/AIDS were conspicuously absent from any dialogue. Apart from President Kaunda of Zambia (who was the keynote speaker), the voice of grieving African families was not heard. Theresa remembers saying to herself, "The next time I attend an AIDS conference, I will be the voice or I will be busy raising funds." Theresa left that conference with a strong sense of courage. She had been especially inspired by the work of ACT UP, and that inspiration fueled her next steps toward building an organizational structure to empower families back in Tanzania.

When she returned to Tanzania, Theresa was more shaken than ever by the deafening silence around the AIDS epidemic, a silence that she could not tolerate. So it was that, in 1989, soon after the AIDS conference, she decided to go to the people in Dar es Salaam. She went out into the community and knocked on doors of the homes of those who had been friends of someone who had died of AIDS, those who had lost family members to AIDS, anyone she could reach who had been touched by the disease. Once she had enough people who agreed that they would come if she started an AIDS/HIV support group, she called the first meeting to be held at ISW. The time for the first meeting came, and no one showed up. Undaunted by the no-shows, Theresa went back into the community, encouraging all those who wanted to come but felt paralyzed by the stigma. She rescheduled the meeting for the same time the following week. At the next meeting, five people showed up. She recalls:

> So, five people came. . . . And we decided from that day that we would go ahead and start the support group. . . . The next week, each person brought five more people and before I knew it the room wasn't big enough. So, we moved into town. The YMCA gave us a room but soon that room wasn't big enough. So, they gave us an outside space and that was great because each week we could see how the crowds were growing out under the tree and out in the open. But then it wasn't too long before the day came when it rained. So, we had to look for a large indoor space and more formal meeting arrangements.

And so in 1989, Theresa founded WAMATA. Her ISW students served as the volunteer counselors until funds were raised to hire some of those volunteers as staff. Every week, the group would leave about ten to fifteen minutes to work on rules and bylaws. By March 1990, WAMATA was fully registered as the first AIDS service organization in Tanzania. The group began to develop strategic plans and funding proposals. The Danish International Development Agency, DANIDA, made the first significant charitable contribution to WAMATA. The U.S. Agency for International Development (USAID), a government agency that provides humanitarian assistance worldwide, funded WAMATA's first vehicle, and it received funds from the Norwegian Agency for Development Cooperation (NORAD), whose mission is to assist developing countries, to rent office space. Years later, NORAD provided the funds to purchase two buildings in Dar es Salaam that became WAMATA's current headquarters. As additional funding came in, many organizations insisted that Theresa assume the position of chief executive officer, but she resisted. Her philosophy is, "When you start something as a volunteer, it's best to remain a volunteer." And she did. Thus, to this day, Theresa remains on an equal footing with all the other volunteers who were or are part of WAMATA. She continues her paid work at ISW.

Theresa's conscious choice to remain a volunteer meant that she could accomplish one of her goals: to give volunteerism visibility, respect, and honor, which was crucial because all of WAMATA's first responders were volunteers. These were affected family members. Without the courage they demonstrated in those early days, WAMATA would not exist. But from those initial meetings a movement emerged that has changed the face of HIV/AIDS-supportive intervention in Tanzania.

Gradually, Theresa came to believe that she needed to further her education still. Because of her volunteer status, and because the institute allows for unpaid leaves, Theresa was able to pursue advanced study outside the country. In 2000, she returned to the United States to pursue a master's degree in public health and a Ph.D. in social work, at the University of Pittsburgh. She finished the latter in 2004. Her doctoral work focused on factors influencing adherence to HIV/AIDS treatment and prevention among people living with the disease in Dar es Salaam. Her choice of topic was very purposeful; she wanted to study something that would have practical implications for the people she served. She approached the study with enormous sensitivity, realizing that those who would be interviewed had experienced so much already and that she couldn't just come in and "take" from them. Her whole approach was premised on the idea of how to give back, whether to the individual respondent, to the students helping with the interviews, to the agencies that were providing contact information, or to the field in general. Theresa was determined to complete the dissertation, and finish it she did, just in time for her oldest son's wedding, which coincided with her final dissertation defense.

During her doctoral work, Theresa had an enormous impact on her peers and colleagues. She is described as having been "at the center" of her student cohort. This group of students supported one another in coursework, the dissertation process, and beyond. Although the group was highly diverse in its characteristics—U.S. and international students, men and women, younger and older—and interests, it was clearly a tightly knit whole. And Theresa was the "mother," offering (and receiving) warmth, support, and encouragement.

In 2005, Theresa became involved with the American International Health Alliance's (AIHA) HIV/AIDS twinning program, which is operated through the U.S. President's Emergency Plan for AIDS Relief. Twinning partnerships are peer-to-peer relationships between organizations working to improve services for people living with or affected by HIV/AIDS. The partnerships create an effective framework for building sustainable institutional and human-resource capacity through the open exchange of knowledge, information, and professional experience. Expanding on her work both at the ISW and at WAMATA, Theresa has been instrumental in the establishment and management of the AIHA's twinning program. She has spent the past three years developing a para–social worker workforce for her country and assisting the AIHA in enhancing and developing educational programs. She is the heart and conscience of this large social work education center (with more than two thousand students), and she continues to teach and to push for improvements, recognition, and continuing human rights and social work values.

Challenges for WAMATA, Today and Tomorrow

WAMATA was the first AIDS service organization in the country, and one of the first in Africa. Today, Tanzania has many more such organizations, but that doesn't necessarily translate to more or better funding or services. WAMATA is competing now for funding, from both within and outside the country, and as long as grassroots organizations have no stable funding sources, there will be challenges. According to Theresa, African organizations have had a history of supporting one another but mostly informally. And local communities often lack the financial ability to sustain highly structured programs. Furthermore, AIDS is a very complex problem—one that is embedded in poverty and intertwined with many other social ills and issues that play out in unique ways in Africa. To demonstrate this, I offer specific examples of service for families with HIV/AIDS in Tanzania that WAMATA provides.

When WAMATA first began offering services in the late 1980s, there was a significant gender difference in participation, with women much more likely to participate because the stigma of the disease was far greater for men. The stigma has since been reduced somewhat, and there has been growing equality in the participation of men and of whole families. It continues to be the case, however, that women with children are especially disadvantaged when HIV/AIDS strikes the family. When a man dies, the prospects for his widow to remarry are slim. Thus, these women, who relied on husbands for income, are in particular need of material support, which WAMATA offers to the extent that its resources allow. Furthermore, if a mother subsequently becomes ill and requires hospitalization, she may have no one to care for the children. In this case, WAMATA secures a place for the children if there are no relatives to take them in. WAMATA also provides consultation on legal questions that the families may face. For example, if the mother remarries or moves into another family, property rights and inheritance rights of her children to their father's estate may require protection. WAMATA personnel act as mediators between families in this instance, and lawyers assist in the process. When both parents die, issues of orphan status and custody must be worked out as well, and WAMATA helps with this also.

But for all of these fundamental services that WAMATA provides, it has lagged in attracting funds from outside, especially when competing with faith-based organizations (WAMATA is nonsectarian). Further, reducing the impact of AIDS requires a holistic view of the client that includes medical, social, nutritional, and other aspects of living, a view that is sometimes lost on funding sources. It is not uncommon, for example, for a funder to provide money for a building but to leave the agency to find other sources of support for services. Theresa described the frustration of having funds to open a new office but no funds for the services and the disappointment of having more people on antiretroviral medications when some of those same people don't have food. Children live with AIDS in orphanages, but there is no money to help them with education. There are times when WAMATA cannot provide food for clients who come for meetings; the agency also lacks the ability to provide subsidized housing for clients who are homeless or provisions for private hospital care when patients are likely to die without it. This is a problem not only for WAMATA but throughout the country's social service network. It is a struggle of competing needs. In Theresa's words:

> WAMATA used to be able to provide many supportive services, but because of structures imposed around how funding can be used, this is less the case today, which leaves the

staff with a sense of inadequacy. Donor fatigue is another huge challenge in a world with many problems and challenges—money must go to tsunamis, earthquakes, wars, famine—all these compete with a never-ending crisis like HIV/AIDS. Donors were not used to having a problem that doesn't go away; they were used to a crisis that has an end—AIDS is an ongoing crisis! Also, government policies change over time; new governments come in with new mandates and issues of importance change with time as well as the fact that often new funding has different, very specific mandates. In some ways, AIDS is no [longer] fashionable. One has to constantly compete with the new crisis of the day.

Theresa always finds it difficult to talk about the successes in HIV/AIDS because there is so much more to do. But she says, "Each time I go somewhere and I run into someone who was a client of WAMATA's when the agency was first started and that person is still alive, I say 'God is good!'" Theresa recalls those disappointing moments in the beginning when people would ask, "What difference do you think you can make? AIDS is a terminal disease, people will die, what good is the counseling going to do?" Those times have passed, and Theresa counts as successes the small milestones, the bits and pieces of help that have given clients a reason to stay the course. When asked about what else she looks for, Theresa replied that she has one very important indicator of success: "If I see any teenage pregnancy, then I know the AIDS message is not getting there. I believe in that indicator more than any statistics."

"To give you have to have received"

There is a long list of people whom Theresa says she could never repay. It starts with her father, an inspiring "peasant intellectual" who never went to school. Growing up under colonial rule in Tanzania, Theresa recalls his comment, "You can't fight colonialism unless you speak their language, write like they write, think like they think. Come rain or shine, at least one of my kids will get a high education." She says, "[He] and the priests and nuns were my role models," and she is grateful for the emphasis they placed on education. Her mother (who died at the age of ninety-three) and her mother-in-law were also influential, serving as examples of women who did not have the opportunities she did but who did everything they could to give other women a chance. It is because of them, she feels, that she has been able to inspire other women.

Her husband, Fred, has always been her "rock." Theresa cannot say enough about his support, and she believes that he has earned his own social work designation through his supportive role. When Theresa was overwhelmed from visiting patients or organizing support groups, Fred would pitch in. He would visit patients when Theresa was unavailable and drove her to every funeral. "It wasn't easy," she recalls. "At times we were using our own salary, and our pickup truck was the only car WAMATA had. That truck was the delivery vehicle, the taxi, the ambulance."

Of her children, Theresa says, "All my kids were wonderful! They were so patient with me!" She has a niece, Stella, who now lives in Oregon, and a nephew, Joeffry, both of whom Theresa and Fred raised. They are older than her own children, but they are like siblings to them, and they were also behind Theresa in every way. All have spent some time at WAMATA volunteering.

Theresa also has a great deal of gratitude for Marywood University, in Scranton, Pennsylvania, which, in 2000, gave her an opportunity to be a visiting professor, even before she had her Ph.D. She credits that opportunity as her springboard into the Ph.D. program. She recalls the support of Sandy Wexler, the chair of her dissertation committee at the University of Pittsburgh, and Shanti Khinduka and Michael Sherraden, a former dean and distinguished scholar, respectively, from Washington University, where she received her MSW. She also voiced her gratitude to the many people in her MSW and Ph.D. programs who provided housing and transportation when she needed it, assisted her in getting to conferences, and otherwise generously responded to the needs of an international student.

During the time she spent in Pittsburgh working toward her Ph.D., Theresa embedded herself in the Pittsburgh HIV-services community, applying lessons in community mobilization and support that she had learned by trial and error in Tanzania. The evidence of her impact is reflected in the different forms of recognition she received during her time in the United States: in 2002, the Shepherd Wellness Community honored her as a pioneer in the fight against HIV/AIDS. In 2004, Theresa was the recipient of the James E. Dixon Humanitarian Award for Education in the area of HIV, granted by the Seven Project, a nonprofit AIDS service organization. As part of her recognition for that award, Theresa was praised for her work in Pittsburgh's black community and was described as helping to "create and set the standard for people reaching out to one another." Finally, the *Pittsburgh Gazette* published a feature story on Theresa, and although she considered it a great personal honor, she was happiest that it helped raise WAMATA's visibility and increase its donor base.

Words of Wisdom on International Social Work

"Where you are is where WAMATA is—it's the people with the tears like you who I have invited to join me in WAMATA"—these are the words Theresa shared with people like Anna Mukami, the founding director of WAMATA United States Inc. (registered in Maryland in 2001), a forum for Africans affected by HIV/AIDS at home and abroad. Clearly, then, Theresa's work has had an international impact. The WAMATA model has been replicated in several countries, from the United States to villages in Uganda and the townships of Soweto, South Africa.

Theresa's words of wisdom to students of social work are these: "AIDS work—social work in general—is an honorable profession. Whether you concentrate on the community where you were born or you choose to go outside your community or country, the principles are the same." The central principle, articulated in the National Association of Social Workers' Code of Ethics, is the intrinsic value of every human being. If social workers really believe this, then they must be prepared to work anywhere. They also must be willing to change and grow as they change the world. A case in point is the students who have been placed at WAMATA as international social work interns. Through the program, Theresa continues to have a direct impact on the international social work education of students in the United States.

For Theresa, her efforts in HIV/AIDS in Tanzania were similar to her own struggles against the effects of HIV/AIDS in the African American community. Recognizing the global effects of AIDS on people of African descent everywhere is part of the work I share with Theresa. In our interview, we paused to reflect on a panel we had spoken on together at an international conference on women in Africa and the African diaspora. We imagined how much progress we could make by drawing on ancestral strengths for working with people of African descent, specifically those strengths inherent in the Nguzu Saba ("the Seven Principles of Blackness"): *umoja* (unity), *kujichagulia* (self-determination), *ujima* (collective work and responsibility), *ujamaa* (cooperative economics), *nia* (purpose), *kuumba* (creativity), and *imani* (faith). All of those elements are part of the healing forces that need to take place for work with people of African descent.

Finally, Theresa's powerful impact on others has been attributed to the "seamlessness of her being"—who she is as a person and how she practices social work are deeply interwoven. I asked Theresa to discuss this sense of interconnectedness and her special approach to social work. She thought for a moment and then spoke of how it all goes back to the fact that she grew up in a family that never had much but always shared whatever they had with neighbors and friends. She spoke of being raised in a home that many people considered their own. She commented, "I was loved and therefore loving back is a duty. I was the apple of my parents' eyes and therefore I have been privileged to have an opportunity to give back."

Theresa's attitude is that all the people who helped her along the way and those who recognized her ultimately are the ones who brought significance to WAMATA. She reminded me that, when we all look back, even the most privileged have had someone holding their hand at some point. At that point, she remembered the lyrics to the once-popular song "Up with People!" and started to sing, "If more people were for people, all people everywhere, there'd be a lot less people to worry about, and a lot more people who'd care." And on that note, we ended the interview.

CHAPTER NINE

Mulu Haile

An Advocate for Ethiopian Women

Alice K. Butterfield and Tigest K. Abye

The primary author of this chapter has a long-standing interest in international social work and in Ethiopia in particular. In the course of her research, she met Mulu Haile and the second author, a native of Ethiopia, who was able to conduct the interview in their native language. As a young woman starting out, Mulu had some rather unconventional life goals for a woman in Ethiopia. In this chapter, you will see that many female-headed families in Ethiopia's poorest communities are better off for her success in attaining those goals.

Introduction to Ethiopia: The Practice Context

Ethiopia is one of the most populous states in Africa, with 85.2 million people occupying its approximately 438,000 square miles. Heavily dependent on agriculture (coffee is a major export), it is also susceptible to periods of severe drought. For this reason and others, it is one of Africa's poorest states. Nearly two-thirds of the country is illiterate. According to UNICEF, life expectancy for an Ethiopian child born in

2007 was fifty-three years. As with the rest of Africa, HIV is a significant problem: more than 2 percent of the population is estimated to be HIV positive (in the United States, this figure is less than 0.45 percent), making the disease a contributor to the country's relatively low life expectancy. With an average annual per capita income of about 1,138 birr (about US$100), the United Nations has classified Ethiopia a least developed country.

Because so many families live on the brink of subsistence, child labor is the rule rather than the exception: approximately 70 percent of children between the ages of eight and fifteen are working, rather than in school, and the majority of these are girls. Obviously, the inability of so many families to allow their children to be educated means that the cycle of poverty is perpetuated. But it is girls who suffer most in this regard, because of the prevalence of patriarchal culture.

It is in the context of these demographics that Mulu Haile's work must be seen and appreciated.

Mulu Haile: Dreaming of a New Ethiopia

Mulu Haile is the founder and executive director of the Multipurpose Community Development Project (MCDP), a development-oriented nongovernmental organization (NGO) located in one of the poorest slum areas of Addis Ababa, Ethiopia. She was interviewed using a narrative approach to compile her life history. Throughout her life, Mulu has benefited from the support of significant men in her life. Her father, a social work professor, and her husband guided, mentored, and encouraged her to break through the traditional boundaries set for women in Ethiopia. But the backbone of her success is her own. Her determination to do more, become more, and give her life to helping others is formed through her own decisions. As a young mother, her pluck in pursuing social work education at a time when her husband was imprisoned for participating in a student democratic movement became the bedrock of her future as a woman leader and manager. Mulu Haile is a program developer at heart. She has an exceptional ability to learn from practice and then use her lifelong learning experiences to create new programs that address unmet needs. The energy that she exhibits in telling her life story can be described as coming only from an endless passion for the poor. Mulu has a dream to see Ethiopia free of poverty; women empowered and free from violence; and all children's poverty alleviated. In her life outside of social work, Mulu is cherished by her family and by society because she is always determined to seek solutions to problems and to teach and motivate people whenever she gets the chance.

Background

Mulu was born in 1951 in Adigrat Town in Tigray, in the northern region of Ethiopia. She is the third child in a family of thirteen children, with nine sisters and three brothers. Her father, Haile Tesema Luelu, during his thirty-five years of service in the Ministry of Health, held different positions, including that of hospital director. Her mother, Hagush Aberha, supported her family by assuming the traditional caregiving role. However, Mulu's family believed in education for all of the children. In particular, her father was determined to give all of them access to modern educational instruction.

Mulu attended Yoannese Secondary High School, which was about seventy-five miles away from her hometown. The distance necessitated her living with relatives. Mulu remembers the time in primary and secondary school as one of the happiest of her life because she had the opportunity not only to learn a lot but also to grow and develop her own unique personality—a dislike for injustice was one of her principal traits. She demonstrated this in the eighth grade by standing up to an instructor whom she felt was behaving unjustly toward her. This challenge earned her the admiration of her peers, specifically the boys in her class, who said, "Let us offer our trousers to her!" Mulu reflected that, in those days, this was the best compliment they could have given her.

The other thing that made Mulu's school days memorable was the support that she and another female student got from the teaching staff. In those days, most of the girls who went to school stopped at the elementary level because they entered into early marriages arranged by parents and the extended family. "But my father," said Mulu, "did not allow even my grandfather and grandmother to get involved. 'All these girls in the house,' my grandparents used to say, 'Why don't you have them married?' And my father replied, 'You have finished your own responsibilities for your children. These are my children, and they have to go to school. The best key for success for my children is to pursue their education.'" Mulu and another girl were the only two girls who finished elementary school and went to high school. "At that time, we did not know what university meant. But our parents and teachers knew and told us that we will go to the university. They were preparing us to enter this [wider world]."

Although Mulu recognizes the role of community and paternal support, she also realizes that hard work and good grades paved the way forward for both her and her female classmate. "I was a good student," said Mulu, "able to participate in class. I remember this particular mathematics teacher—he was Oromo [a native of Oromia, one of nine regional states in Ethiopia]—he used to bring candies to class and the first one who finished without any mistakes used to get those candies and I always got the candies." The fact that she excelled in many subjects meant that she had a lot of choices in education. "I had a chance to go into nursing, which at the time was a vocational training program, but I said no. I think I had realized or sensed that my father was preparing me to go further than that—and for something in the development field."

Entry into the Profession

Opportunity came knocking while Mulu was in the tenth grade. Seyoum GebreSelassie, the director of the Awassa Community Development Training and Demonstration Center, came to Mekele, the capital city of the Tigray region, to select candidates for the newly formed program. Although her teachers and the principal wanted her to study accounting, Mulu was determined to take the chance. She passed the exam and, together with six other students, three boys and three girls, Mulu left high school and enrolled in the two-year program as a member of the first class of only forty students, the majority of whom were boys.

Mulu believes that the best thing about the school was that it taught theory as well as practice, with classes in areas such as agriculture, animal husbandry, and the use of biogas as a fuel, and field placement was a major part of the two-year program. "We had classes on home management and nutrition and recreational programs for the existing cooperatives. We learnt different things, which I think were the basis for my personal growth and work life. We also went on fieldwork in the nearby villages where we had the chance to communicate and interact with the villagers. We talked with them about basic health issues, basic nutrition, child care, community mobilization, and cooperatives with the community." Mulu's placement was in the region formerly known as Elibabour, in the southern part of Ethiopia. At Elibabour, Mulu's love for working with people in poor communities began to grow into what would become her lifelong passion. Her self-confidence also grew. One thing she remembers well is the nickname she earned when the district governor of Elibabour saw her talking about an event and heard her on the radio. He said, "Who is this 'Mitmita' [hot pepper]?" Small and skinny, but also very articulate, she was beginning to attract the attention of government officials.

At the same time, the field placement was a source of conflict between Mulu and her father. He was not happy that his daughter was satisfied with her life in this fairly remote area. This was not his plan for her, and he insisted that she stop and go to the university. He even threatened to take her home if she did not listen. Mulu argued, negotiated, and finally convinced her father to let her stay by promising to enter the only university in the country as soon as she finished her field placement. Mulu's determination and commitment to her training and work were surely tested by her father's wish for her to leave Elibabour, but the pressure extended beyond her family. She was a single woman living away from home, at the prime age when most of the other students chose to marry in accordance with societal expectations, so standing by her convictions was not easy. "It was difficult, very difficult. Even now I tell my two daughters how difficult it was," confides Mulu. "You cannot imagine how strong you would have to be as a single girl in a remote area to come home without any problems. . . . I said no to everybody. There were hospital directors, school directors and doctors, but I said no. I used to say that I had a fiancé back home. And now I realize how strong I was, and how determined. The others—those who were assigned in other regions, and different villages like me—they all got married [during that time] except one, Lemlem Tekuye, my lifetime friend from high school, from the ninth grade up to now." Mulu appreciates the friendship she has built with Lemlem and recognizes the role her friend has played both in her private and public lives. She describes the relationship as one of mutual support: "We complement each other. . . . She is like a gift from God."

Despite the conflict with her father, he remains the most important influence in her life. Strength, commitment, and gender sensitivity are values that she learned from him, and she has taught these to her children. "Maybe what helped me or guided me toward becoming a social worker was also my father's commitment to voluntary work in development activities in the area. He used to go to Addis Ababa and Asmara for fund-raising, in order to construct schools, to construct hospitals, to construct roads and many other things . . . so maybe that's what guided me to be in [community] developmental work." Her father was extremely well regarded in Tigray and deeply patriotic. What amazes Mulu to this day, however, is his gender sensitivity. "He was not like the men of those days. He was a modern man. He encouraged his daughters to continue their studies when others chose to marry. It was important to him that his girls knew how to take care of themselves." For example, when they were children, Mulu's father would take Mulu and her sisters to watch the slaughtering of sheep, which is a man's duty as part of the preparations for a religious or any festive event. "He went to war during the Italian occupation of Ethiopia in World War II, and he needed his girls to know how to take care of themselves, in case of another war or anything that might engage the male members of the family."

After her two years in Elibabour, Mulu joined the School of Social Work at Haile Selassie University I (now Addis Ababa University) in 1971. By that time, her decision to join the School of Social Work was not merely to please her father. Mulu knew that a bachelor's degree in social work would help build her career and be of enormous good for the purposes she had set out to achieve. The good that she wanted to achieve was heavily influenced by her mentor, Professor Seyoum GebreSelassie, the director of the Awassa Center. "He was a role model for me of what a social worker should be. He came out to the villages with us and talked to us about how to work with the people. We discussed what happened, what we learned, and how we could do better. He invited us to his home to celebrate birthdays and held parties for our group of trainees. He influenced us to include recreational programs in our work with communities. He said that social workers needed to learn how to play and how to dance because recreational programs were an entry point for development work." Mulu's coursework and fieldwork through the Awassa Center were stellar, and by arranging to substitute the two-year program for her high school diploma, Seyoum recommended Mulu as his top choice for admission to the university. Mulu regrets that she never had the opportunity to take a social work class from Seyoum, because immediately after her application was accepted, he left Ethiopia to pursue his doctorate at the University of Michigan's School of Social Work. Later, he returned to Ethiopia and became her lifelong friend and social work colleague.

Together with her decision to enroll in the university, Mulu decided to marry. Mulu and her husband, Haile, were neighbors back in Adigrat but met again at the university, strengthened their friendship, and were married. Thus began a period in her life of great challenge and tribulation. In the early 1970s, the country was in the throes of a mass revolutionary movement, organized by students, which had begun a decade earlier. In his book *A History of Modern Ethiopia, 1855–1991*, Berhanu Zewde writes, "The Ethiopian Student Movement went through various phases of evolution starting as a cultural and intellectual forum of an elite, and growing into a mass revolutionary movement in the late 1960s and early 1970s." It was in this context that the (anti–Student Movement) ruling military regime, called Dergue, decided to implement *zemecha*, of which the literal translation is "campaign." In this context, *zemecha* denotes the government's Development through Cooperation Work and Enlightenment Campaign, which required the forced deployment of high school and college students to remote areas to explain the socialist revolution to the peasants and to improve literacy. As a university student, Mulu was a candidate for the assignment, but because she was married, she was exempt. Her husband, who had recently graduated from the university, was employed in Jima, a town about 220 miles away. He asked to be transferred to Addis Ababa, and they started their life as a couple. Soon, Mulu gave birth to their first daughter.

After her daughter was a year old, Mulu returned to complete the fourth year of her undergraduate studies in social work. Shortly thereafter, during the formation of the Ethiopian People's Liberation Front (EPLF), the Dergue regime put Mulu's husband in prison as part of a massive attempt to stamp out the student movement. Haile was in one of the opposition parties and involved in organizing students and fighting for democratic values. "It was really a difficult time . . . [even though] I was not that much involved in politics." She remembers not only the bad times and the difficulties but also the financial support from people she did not know and the moral support from her teachers and classmates and neighbors. When she could not afford to pay her rent because of the loss of her husband's income, the *kebele* (neighborhood-level government) officials wanted to evict her from her rented house, and she was even about to quit school. However, her classmates, adviser, and teachers convinced her that she could complete her education. They promised her moral support, lending her lecture notes, anything that might allow Mulu to continue her education. To complement the fifty birr she received as a student (about US$5 at the current rate of exchange), she started teaching two classes at the Menilik High School. She managed her life with her meager income and the support from friends and family.

The most difficult obstacle was her husband's imprisonment. "Sometimes," she remembers, "I skipped class to go to the place where my husband was in prison, in Arategna Kifle Tor. I was just like a crazy person; I just circled the compound, going round and round. 'Was someone killed today? Was somebody taken from the prison?' It was really difficult, and I had a one-year-old child." But that same year, she graduated with distinction and her husband was released from prison: "This was a black spot in my life. I always feel amazed and I always wonder how God saved me. I've always said, 'God how did you save me from this time?' As Tigrayans (people from the Tigray region), many of my friends went to the bushes [either to evade the Dergue or to join the guerrilla movement], my other relatives were killed, some went to prison, or fled abroad. 'How did you save me?' I ask. Maybe for this work, I think."

Field of Service

During the time of the Dergue regime, workers did not apply for jobs but were assigned to them. Mulu was assigned to the Rehabilitation Agency for the Disabled in the Ministry of Labor and Social Affairs. The agency's mission was to address the needs of elderly people, people with disabilities, and orphaned children. "I think this was the time when I learned how to manage, and how to monitor, programs," explained Mulu. "And that allowed me also to see my country as a nation. At that time we were advocating for a policy for people with disabilities, though they [the government] were not happy to do that. Once the policies were formulated, the hardest thing to do was change people's mentalities. People with a disability can work like anyone if you provide them with appliances, with education and with training. They can do everything like able-bodied people, so this was a hard time for us. It was difficult, very difficult with the [clients] that we were trying to [empower], because they were the product of this society."

Mulu feels that she really learned the profession of social work during those seven years at the ministry. After a short time as a project manager for Pestalozzi International Village Trust (a Swiss NGO), Mulu took a job with the Integrated Holistic Approach–Urban Development Program (IHA-UDP), an organization started by Dr. Jember Tefera, who was one of Mulu's role models. Her initial work was to train grassroots workers in Tekle Haimanot, a slum area of Addis Ababa. "We had thirty young girls who had finished high school and we trained them as para–community development workers. They were a good asset for the area. We called them 'yellow girls' because they usually dress in yellow gowns. All were females, because culturally males were not welcomed in the households to work . . . to teach mothers especially. . . . So my first work was with these thirty young women and I trained them in a way [as what we would now call case managers]—really, they were the best. One evaluator came from Sweden and said, 'How did you train these people? They are even better than the professionals.'"

"They were like a family," continued Mulu. "The 'yellow girls' were supposed to know the situation of about 150 households in their area. They knew the families; they knew their community. They knew which woman gave birth, who died—they had all the information on their area." One day a yellow girl, one of the team leaders, came to Mulu's office. She told Mulu that there was an old man and one of his ears had been eaten by a mouse. Mulu was shocked. This was a bedridden man who did not have any family to take care of him, so, during the night, a mouse would eat bits of his ear. Mulu did not have any resources for these particular problems in the elderly population, but she was quite resourceful. Without any funding, she managed to set up a program in which other abler but underprivileged elderly people would help all bedridden elderly people. Those who could move and were able to take care of themselves were responsible for another elderly person in exchange for the same benefit given to them in the future, should they need it. This assistance program came to be known as Elderly People by Elderly People, and eventually it became a central clearinghouse for the basic human needs of the community's elderly. The program was successful because the caregiver elderly were happy to take care of their peers in exchange for future services. The following year, the program got a sponsor, Help Age International, an NGO whose mission is to improve the lives of older people.

Mulu not only learned from the community she was working with through IHA-UDP but also was sent abroad to conduct training and workshops. After international colleagues observed her as a trainer and participant in a role-play on human rights and women's rights, they urged her to study in Holland. She declined their offer of a graduate education scholarship there because of her family obligations. She did not see why her children, who were nine and thirteen years old at the time, should suffer during what would be a long fifteen-month absence. Nonetheless, Mulu's relationship with international colleagues has continued and she has been invited to be a trainer on human rights and women's rights in many countries in Europe and Africa, as well as Thailand.

Reflecting on her time at IHA-UDP, Mulu concludes:

> IHA-UDP was like a great university for me; I learned so much there. . . . You can see the change, every day you see change. . . . IHA-UDP consisted of many integrated programs with different donors. We constructed houses, we had saving and credit programs, and a clinic. Care for mentally retarded children, kindergarten, and a nutrition feeding program were the areas we were involved in. Thus, in my position as a community development program coordinator, I was coordinating the health programs, the construction program, the income generation program—all these things. You don't have time to think. Sometimes, we even stayed up until twelve (midnight), because we had these community meetings. I don't know—when you have so much attachment with people, when you have the love, it is difficult to stop.

Nonetheless, Mulu decided to leave IHA-UDP. It was an emotionally fraught decision for both her and the community. If Mulu left, they said, the organization would surely close those projects. "And I used to reply, 'If Mulu goes away, another Mulu will come.'" But at the same time, because her involvement with the people was real, she was troubled by this possibility. All great programs must be sustainable and cannot be held hostage to the cult of personality. It is a testament to Mulu that the programs proved self-sustaining.

Mulu next took a position as the country director for Oxfam Australia (in Addis Ababa). "The work was easy, just to appraise and monitor projects, but I was not happy. No, this was not my place. . . . I need to work with people, not in the office. . . . The benefits were so great, the provident fund [pension], the medical [insurance] for my family, all of those things, but I could not stay. Oxfam Australia was a big organization with many resources, but my heart was for the grassroots," Mulu confided, "and I became physically sick also." Mulu realized, "I have to go to the people again because I was so happy when I was working at Tekle Haimanot [with the yellow girls]. It was a slum area; it was so dirty. But whatever you do, the satisfaction you get from that place was so real."

At this turning point in her life, Mulu looked to the impoverished women in other countries who participated in microcredit projects that allowed them to start small businesses. Mulu thought, "I want to establish something like that. . . . I have to begin at the grass root[s]. . . . I don't want to be employed by someone else, because I will not be able to accomplish my own goals, or implement my own ideas. If I establish my own agency, I can use *all* the skills I have."

The Multipurpose Community Development Project (MCDP)

Mulu started by developing a plan on paper, convincing other professionals to serve as board members, and organizing a general assembly. In 1998, the Multipurpose Community Development Project (MCDP) was legally registered as an indigenous or local NGO. With the assistance of local government, she located the agency in an urban slum area with high levels of migration because it was near the bus terminal for transit to and from the rest of the country. The vision of the organization is an empowered and self-reliant society. Its mission is to contribute toward bringing a long-lasting change and improvement in the lives of the community—with an emphasis on children and women through integrated urban and rural development programs with the active participation of the community. The working principles of MCDP are participation, integration, sustainability, nondiscrimination, transparency, accountability, gender sensitivity, compliance with the NGO code of conduct, and networking.

In 1998, MCDP operated on a budget of 260,500 birr; in 2008, the budget was 5.5 million birr. A little more than a decade ago, Mulu began with seven workers. Today, MCDP works in three "subcities" of Addis Ababa and in Chencha and Detta Wereda in Gamo Gofa, a southern region of Ethiopia. The organization employs sixty-four people, operating out of a large new community-based office that includes a community library, meeting rooms, and a large compound for a community-based informal education program for children. Basic Education is a remedial program designed for children who have not been attending school so that they can enter public school in the future.

The MCDP's roster of community development and organizing projects (see http://www.mcdp-ethiopia.org/) provides evidence that Mulu is a lifelong learner. Some of MCDP's programs, such as its biogas project, the construction of sanitary facilities, communal latrines and public showers, and cooperative saving and credit schemes reflect her early experience in rural community development through the Awassa Community Development Training and Demonstration Center. The MCDP's intervention in child labor and the Chencha Child Trafficking Prevention Project brings Mulu's employment at the Ministry of Labour and Social Affairs to mind. The MCDP's comprehensive approach reflects Mulu's more recent experience in participatory community development at IHA-UDP.

But MCDP is not a replication of projects and programs from her previous experiences. A noticeable thread running through the various programs are the concepts of gender sensitivity, empowerment, and self-help. For example, innovative programs at MCDP focus on women's empowerment, including peer-to-peer support for abused women. The women know how to approach the court for legal intervention in an abusive situation. Another gender-sensitivity program intervenes in the situations of young girls who are susceptible to sexual abuse and prostitution when migrating to Addis Ababa. The MCDP also participates in a network of organizations to provide access to a safe house for abused women.

Mulu believes that self-help and empowerment through community organization and community development are the best types of social work methods because they help people assume responsibility for their future, even while living in abject poverty. For example, some of the "yellow girls" followed Mulu to the new agency. "I have, you know, two of them employed here. Strong ladies. One is a loan officer. Her job is to organize and follow up with the members of our eighteen [microcredit] cooperatives. And the other one is a manager in the Basic Education program." Another guidepost of practice at MCDP is to turn over productive and effective programs to be managed by the people themselves through cooperatives, labor unions, or *iddirs*, which are traditional, community-based membership associations in Ethiopia. Mulu believes that the true empowerment of the community occurs when community members become stewards of their own future.

Mulu is particularly pleased with the development of the saving and credit cooperatives that MCDP has organized. The MCDP provided the original seed capital for the revolving loan programs and provided training in leadership, business practices, and literacy education. However, each cooperative of eighty women has its own bylaws, committees, and a separate bank account managed by the women. At first, the loan amount for a member of a cooperative was five hundred birr, which has now increased to five thousand birr, as the strength of the cooperatives has grown. The self-help program is benefiting hundreds of poor households, particularly female-headed households. "Now they become *big-big*! Now the cooperatives—now by themselves—they hired two people from the cooperatives. . . . They have a part-time accountant. . . . Now they are no more MCDP. . . . They become independent because they are efficient!"

The MCDP has developed a baseline survey and strategic plan for the next five years. One area of innovation is broadening the network of stakeholders to include students and policy makers. These new collaborations will help improve the sustainability and growth of MCDP programs, will raise the awareness of those in policy-making positions, and will bring issues of importance to the organization to the national level.

Looking Forward

As this narrative has shown, Mulu experienced significant challenges in her professional and personal lives. Her most difficult moments were when her husband was in prison, but throughout her life, Mulu's achievements continued in the midst of sacrifice. As a professional social worker, she has had the encouragement and support of her husband, who understands the nature of her work. But Mulu confides that he is not a typical Ethiopian husband in the traditional sense. If she is out at meetings until late at night, he never questions her. "He knows I am with my people," she said. As a former member of the Ethiopian Student Movement, her husband also has "respect for the people, a heart for the people." Her commitment to her work has certainly influenced her decisions in relation to her private life. "This is a global problem for women—how to balance personal life and a career." Mulu confides that she limited her family size because of the work that she is doing. She is the mother of two daughters, both very strong and successful young women now. She also wanted them to have the best education they could have. She has certainly succeeded. "They are empowered—so empowered—more than me!" Her eldest has a master's degree from an English university and works at the African Union.

She is married, and soon Mulu will become a grandmother. Her second daughter has a bachelor's degree in management and lives in the United States.

Mulu is the founder and president of the Soroptimist Club of Ethiopia, which is a member club of the International Soroptimist Club, a worldwide organization for women in management and professions working through service projects to advance human rights and the status of women. She also serves voluntarily as a board member in various local NGOs. She has an idea to create an association of women managers who would share experiences and information, as well as their struggles against some of the barriers that women managers come across. Although the idea has not fully materialized, she meets regularly with six other female managers of different local NGOs to discuss the challenges they encounter, to share information about available funds, and sometimes even to design proposals together. "That makes us stronger," concludes Mulu.

Since 2003, Mulu Haile and her friend and colleague Lemlem Tekuye have played an ongoing leadership role in the new School of Social Work at Addis Ababa University (AAU), which, in collaboration with the Jane Addams College of Social Work, now offers a master's degree in social work and a doctorate in social work and social development. This collaboration, known as the Social Work Education in Ethiopia Partnership (SWEEP), has expanded its partnership to include six other organizations that have come together in the design and development of the Community Work and Life Center on the AAU campus, whose mission is to develop employment sites and opportunities for Ethiopians (for more information, see http://www.aboutsweep.org).

As founding members of the new school's Advisory Committee, Mulu and Lemlem have participated in curriculum development and field education, and have served as guest speakers in practice courses. As social work practitioners with more than thirty years of service to their country, these women leaders now play a mentoring role to young MSW graduates in their first years of employment.

Mulu believes that no matter what a person's position is in an organization, men have advantages in terms of promotions, getting funds, and so on. In the traditional society of Ethiopia, men have more opportunities to network at work, receptions, and cafés. "Fortunately this fades away. Once you have proven your leadership skills, it gets easier. Now I don't even have to go look for funding. It comes because of the success of our programs," says Mulu. Success also comes because of the practical methods that Mulu has developed through the influence of her family of origin, her education and training, and her years of experience working for government and for local and international organizations. Regarding others' views of her work, Mulu commented:

"They don't think women will do such kind of things. Or some—like officials—they believe that if you tell her like this, she will shut up. Or, they may think that she will give something of a personal nature that will bribe them. You face a lot of things as a woman, working at the grassroots level."

Mulu believes that part of the reason for her success is her affinity for challenges. "By nature, I like to have challenges. You have to be strong. . . . This is my quality, . . . especially for women managers, for women, you have to be strong and committed. If you are committed and strong, you have everything." This secret of her success as a social worker, program developer, and manager in Ethiopia is encapsulated by the words of a male member of her staff at MCDP: "What I learned from Mulu is, if a door is closed, Mulu will go to another door, and she keeps trying to open every possible door until her goal is accomplished. She never gives up when facing difficult challenges." Mulu Haile will keep working until she accomplishes her goal.

CHAPTER TEN

Sister Patricia Schlosser

From SROs to Women Exiting Prison—A True Pioneer

Patricia O'Brien

Sr. Patricia Schlosser, OSF, has lived by the maxim attributed
to St. Francis of Assisi: "Preach and, if necessary, use words."
Sr. Patricia has dedicated her professional life to work with the
most vulnerable in different settings, including trailblazing
work with women attempting to find their way from prison to
family and community life at a time when social services
simply did not exist to address the needs of that population.
Hers is a long story, spanning more than forty years of dedication. This chapter celebrates her special contributions and
demonstrates some common themes to remind social
workers of the day-by-day good they can do as catalysts for
change. Sr. Patricia's story reminds us to press on, even in the
face of difficulties and challenging circumstances and
systems. I am indebted to Sr. Patricia for the long conversations and years of collegial partnership that inspired this
reflection on her life's work.

Introduction

The United States addresses its most pressing social problems, including violence, poverty, underemployment and changing economies, failing school systems, drugs, discrimination, and inequality through social policies that often heighten invisibility, disconnection, and suffering for those who are most affected. It is at the intersection of these often-failed polices on child welfare, homelessness, and criminal justice where Sister Patricia Schlosser has been anchored. She has spent a professional lifetime advocating for more humane and effective services and responses to these social problems. Although the specific locations of her work have changed over more than forty years of practice, teaching social work, supervision, and advocacy, her focus on social justice and her concern with those who are most in need have remained constant.

Early Influences

Patricia grew up in a small town in North Dakota. Her immediate family had a profound influence on her early values. She recalls that her mother was a very sensitive person who was kind to the children in the neighborhood who had less "without being patronizing." Her father organized his lodge to sponsor what was called Home on the Range, a program for troubled youth. From the beginning, she witnessed both the personal response to everyday private troubles and the organizational or systemic response to larger social issues affecting youths, analogous to the person-in-environment core of social work. She also noticed the social justice–oriented and well-educated nuns in the small Catholic school she attended as a child. As she said, "I had these well-educated teachers who had us reading the *Catholic Worker* (a newspaper produced by the Catholic Worker movement), so we knew about Dorothy Day and pacifism and war." When she went to college (at a small women's Catholic college in Winona, Minnesota, that is no longer in operation), she said she had "no idea" about social work. But "my friends helped me to realize what I cared about, and other mentors at the College began steering me in the direction" of social work, which, in the 1950s, was not well known as a career path for women. She recalls that when she took a class in her sophomore year, she thought, "My god, this is it! Where had I been? It just opened up everything—it was exactly the way I could do what I thought was important."

A Merging of Personal and Professional

After completing her BA in sociology in 1955, she worked in foster care for Catholic Charities in Minneapolis. An important aspect of this first job was the diversity that a larger city offered as well as "excellent" social work supervision. "I had a particularly marvelous supervisor—she really helped me through my first year of social work and we are still in contact."

A new path opened up when she decided to join the Catholic community of Franciscans. This particular order "didn't have social work; we only had teachers and nurses." So, Sr. Patricia taught high school social studies for seven years. It was a "great experience," she recalls, because she felt like she could use some of her social work experience with the students. In 1968, the community supported her enrollment at Catholic University in Washington, D.C., where she would earn her master's degree. It was a time of great social upheaval and change. She characterizes the period as a very important stepping-stone in her development as a social worker. She recalls that it was "a frightening time" but also a marvelous time that "opened up another part of life to me" and inspired action. "We were in every welfare rights march in Washington—we were part of the poor people's campaign." Sr. Patricia remembers the tragedy and aftermath of Reverend Martin Luther King's assassination when "the whole city was on fire." She tells the story of when, during the riots following the assassination, she and other social work students borrowed veils and collars and went down to the inner city dressed as nuns and priests and helped in food pantries: "We were a peaceful presence and [we] told them that they had a right to be angry. We were sort of fearless and young. It sort of encapsulated what I thought about where social workers should be. And my vision has never changed."

She describes what she calls the two principles that would govern her social work life. The first was that she would do social work with the most vulnerable and oppressed—that is where, she said, "I am going to choose to be." The second was to never be controlled or governed by the need for salary. This was particularly advantageous to her later when continuing her work with women in correctional settings.

Ironically (she says), after completing her MSW, the community asked Sr. Patricia to teach social work at the college from which she had graduated. She said she decided, "I could contribute [at least] this much" to the community that had fostered her growth and supported her graduate education. She said she enjoyed teaching college students, but "my heart is really to be with the people," and in 1970, after two years, she left for Chicago, where she has lived and worked ever since.

In addition to working with the most oppressed, Sr. Patricia indicated that where she lived was also important to her professional life. "I decided that if I'm going to work with who I see as a vulnerable population, I really want to know them well. I wanted to be in solidarity on lots of different levels. I think that was very helpful to me in under-standing city folks—especially since I came from small town stuff." She lived in Uptown, a neighborhood in Chicago characterized by mixed income levels and a high proportion of homeless and mentally ill per-sons, for thirty-four years. She currently lives in the Rogers Park neigh-borhood, one of the most racially and ethnically diverse neighborhoods in the country, in large part because of its incredible array of immigrant groups.

As a sister, her reliance on the Franciscan community for both financial and emotional support enabled her to make her own choices about where she worked and, to a certain extent, where she lived. "I always worked for not-for-profits—I didn't have to take a job because of what it paid or I didn't have to not take a job because it didn't pay very much." As an agency-paid and then later as an unaffiliated "volun-teer" in correctional settings, she has been bound by the rules for secure access to correctional facilities but has a freedom in what she does that is not based on correctional system objectives. And she was able to live with other members of the Franciscan community who had similar commitments to solidarity with their neighbors.

It was in Chicago where Sr. Patricia launched her social work career in earnest, first showing up to do the work of attending to individuals in need and then by cultivating her ability to create new social pro-grams across multiple settings. She reflects, "I think in my whole social work career, I've had great opportunities to be at the right place at the right time or be invited to be on the cutting edge for creating something new."

Professional Social Work Development

In about 1970, Sr. Patricia began her post-teaching career with the Juve-nile Protection Association (JPA), a "magnificent agency" where she worked as a family caseworker for ten years. The JPA, one of the oldest and most respected child welfare agencies in Chicago, was founded in 1909 by some of the women associated with Jane Addams's Hull House. Initially, its mission was to "stem the tide of 10,000 young offenders who passed annually through the city's court system" (Addams, 1909). The agency has evolved over the decades since to become notable for its concern with child protection and advocacy on behalf of children and families. At the time that Sr. Patricia worked for the JPA, the focus was on addressing the needs of abused and neglected children in their homes. The goal was to prevent the removal of children by providing direct services with families. As a consequence of these efforts, social workers rarely had to do so. Sr. Patricia believes that she contributed to the efforts by helping her coworkers to look beyond the daily turmoil that many of the families were experiencing and to explore and exploit both internal and external resources that would shore up their capacity to be effective parents.

After about five years at the JPA, Sr. Patricia recognized that the child-care center in the middle of a public housing development where she provided some staff consultation could also serve as an extension for the agency, "so I started the outpost there at the daycare/nursery school [Mary Crane Nursery]. We could be right there—working with preschoolers and the after-school program: it was in the middle of the Julia Lathrop housing projects. We could attempt to interrupt cycles [of neglect and abuse]." As a caseworker at the child-care center, she worked with center staff to understand the families and "know what could be done, which in turn, made a tremendous impact with the families."

After ten years of working with abuse and neglect issues in poor families, Sr. Patricia was ready for greater variety. The outpost, though, continued at the public housing project after she left. For a short while, she worked with an alternative school for dropouts, specifically for adults with low literacy skills. "We had literacy classes and GED and computers—it was a marvelous experience."

Shortly thereafter, in the early 1980s, she was contacted about a new project in an organization that was establishing what was described as a new response to homeless people: single-room occupancy (SRO) programs. The term *SRO* commonly refers to a building that houses people in single rooms with shared bathrooms and kitchens. These types of temporary housing have existed in the United States since the 1930s, often located close to the rail yards of major cities and characterized by a very transient population. Lakefront SRO staff wanted to provide a social work model for their residents so that the individuals who used the SRO (mostly people with addiction problems and mental illness) could have greater stability in their lives: "They needed a lot of support and help to do that and that was the essence of what I did in developing their approach." Sr. Patricia recounts, "We were able to create support services—I was able to hire an activity director so there could be some point to their lives other than just living in their little room." She reflects, "We actually formed phenomenal communities."

As she thinks about the development of her social work life, she concludes that "this was a very important experience because I believed that if there was sufficient support, really social services in the sense of having people reflect on their lives and look at their addictions and then use referrals to places that could help them, they could be stabilized in housing and have a stable life. . . . Lakefront went on to become the leader in SRO housing [in Chicago] and I was happy to be a part of that.

That had fallen to me as an opportunity because I was living in Uptown and there were so many homeless people; we had to have some creative way of working with them."

After Sr. Patricia had worked at Lakefront SRO for five years, she realized that it was again time to look for new opportunities. After taking a sabbatical provided by her community, she went to work at the Salvation Army as a supervisor of casework services. It was there that she began to first recognize the effects of incarceration on women and their families. As she explains, she observed the effects in two different client systems: caregivers who looked after children while their mothers were incarcerated and released mothers. She explains:

> We had grandmother after grandmother coming into Salvation Army, toting these little children—for the food pantry, for clothing, to get rent and utility help. They just economically couldn't make it. And every story was that these tots' mother was in jail or prison. And the caregivers loved their grandchildren but they had already raised their children. This is not what they expected to do so they had a lot of feelings about it. They also felt they had seen it coming and had warned their daughters and nevertheless it still happened. And then the daughters would come home—and they would be coming in for food stamps or transportation and they were beside themselves—there weren't resources for them, they were so discouraged, and they weren't well received at home. . . .
>
> People were angry; their kids were angry—their mothers wanted them to hurry faster [to resume parenting their children] than was possible—it was chaotic and crisis-ridden.
>
> I thought, "Where are the social workers?" I was appalled and it was such a huge overwhelming issue and problem. I thought, well, I'm part of the social work community so I have to do something. So I called around to everybody I could think of to ask who was doing something about women in prison?

Social Work with Women in and out of Prison

A current reality in the United States is the enormous number of men and women, more than in any other country in the world, whom we hold in our nation's prisons and jails—more than 2 million at this point, and a total of 7 million are under some form of correctional supervision (probation, jail, prison, and parole). These individuals—with their assigned numbers and complicated backgrounds created out of the nexus of poverty, trauma, victimization, violence, and addiction—reflect every imagined individual and social ill, and cross all social work settings. Women, especially poor women of color, represent the fastest-growing group of prisoners; today there are more than 115,000 women in state and federal correctional facilities (West & Sabol, 2009). The majority of these women are also mothers or primary caregivers to family members outside the system. Thus, when women are incarcerated, children's lives are also severely affected. The increasing rate of women's imprisonment, then, is also a crisis in our society's ability to create a viable future.

Sr. Patricia's question, "Where are the social workers?" is an important one. Although corrections and social work have seemingly different purposes, it has not historically been so. Rehabilitation of "fallen women," in particular, was central to the women engaged during the progressive era in some of the early institutions where girls and women were held—often, it was believed, for their own protection while they could be reformed and shaped into morally good housewives or, at the very least, domestic help (Rafter, 1990). Kann (2005) notes that the prevailing attitude about female criminality in early U.S. history had everything to do with the idea that women who defied their ascribed gender roles were more disgraceful and disturbed than even men who committed the most serious crimes.

Although women still constitute less than 10 percent of all incarcerated adults, the rapid increase in their rate of incarceration and more severe sentencing for mostly nonviolent convictions is intricately related to policy changes stemming from the war on drugs initiated during the Nixon administration. These changes led to mandatory-minimum sentencing (an automatic sentence length based on the classification of the crime and the person's legal history that does not consider any mitigating factors) and truth-in-sentencing laws (policies and legislation that aim to abolish or curb parole so that convicted felons serve a greater percentage of or the entire sentence). These federal and state laws often applied to the most vulnerable members of our society—those without the resources to secure decent legal representation.

Parallel to the rampant increase in the use of incarceration in every state and federal jurisdiction is the shift to fewer services or program offerings to inmates to facilitate rehabilitation. The belief in the mantra "Nothing works" with respect to reforming criminals (based on data from Martinson's 1979 meta-analysis of criminal rehabilitation programs between 1945 and 1967—after years of critiques of his findings, Martinson noted that they were derived from limited data) contributed to a correctional philosophy that, for years, opposed rehabilitation and influenced the move away from liberal interventions. It has also resulted in a greater reliance on retribution or deterrence as the major justification for punishment.

Some have argued that this overreliance on deterrence, even when not supported by evidence of its effectiveness, has led to the mass incarceration and warehousing of inmates without any effort toward rehabilitation or addressing the issues that contributed to their involvement in criminal behavior (Mauer & King, 2007). These major shifts in "tough on crime" sentencing policies, which have resulted in still-increasing numbers of U.S. citizens being held for longer periods of time, have been a costly enterprise. A recent Pew Report that determined that one in one hundred men and women are "behind bars" today argues that the great investment of billions of dollars in state and federal monies in punitive measures has not resulted in an appreciable impact on public safety because so many inmates are low-level offenders or people who have violated the terms of their probation or parole (Pew Center on the States, 2008). In addition, to support this dramatic increase in punishment of recent decades, our society has had to transfer financial and social resources from education and social services into criminal justice.

It is in this context that social workers have recognized the necessity to be involved in working with those who are entangled with the criminal justice system, many with a particular focus on reentry services to prevent recidivism, or return to prison. They have also grown in their awareness of the concrete and emotional harms experienced by the almost 2 million children and other family members who are left behind when an adult member is sentenced to prison.

Providing Services to Incarcerated Women: Fulfilling "Two Dreams"

Sr. Patricia discovered that a major family counseling and support agency, Lutheran Social Services of Illinois (LSSI), was providing transportation for children to prison facilities to visit their mothers. "They received me gracefully and said yes, we need social workers to do something, but no one was hiring anybody to do it. After I talked with them, they were able to hire me under the AmeriCorps program to develop a resources guide for women returning to the community in Chicago." During this two-year period of developing the resource guide and educating prison staff about what was available, Sr. Patricia realized that the women exiting prison were often reluctant to go to resources that they didn't know and came up with the idea of a one-stop center. She remembers, "There were two dreams with that: the women would have a place to go when they came out that would be supportive and also be of immediate help in making use of community resources, and . . . we would hire formerly incarcerated women to work there. I thought that would build credibility for the agency but could be most helpful for the women coming out so that they could see women working there who had had the same experiences and understood how difficult it was to make it outside of prison."

Her dreams bore fruit when, about a year after the completion of her AmeriCorps term and her hire by LSSI on a full-time basis in the Family Services division, the agency acquired foundation funding to establish the ReConnections program, for which she was able to hire several formerly incarcerated women to work with her in assisting women in transition from prison to the community. During the two years she worked with ReConnections, Sr. Patricia coordinated efforts with the Illinois Department of Corrections in their preparation of women exiting prison, continued to build the network of resources available to women reestablishing themselves in various neighborhoods throughout Chicago, and provided crisis intervention and counseling regarding the making of efficacious choices for themselves.

ReConnections was one of the nation's first, if not the first, freestanding agency program dedicated to working holistically with women exiting prison. It was a community-based, safe place where women could begin learning about what they needed to do and gaining support while they took small steps toward reintegration. In addition to help with immediate and concrete needs, Sr. Patricia and the other staff provided nonjudgmental support and understanding of the reentry process. An evaluation of the ReConnections program found that it was the nonjudgmental support and caring that the women identified as crucial to their commitment to making use of community resources and staying in touch with the staff (O'Brien, 2006). Many of the women participants talked about how Sr. Patricia's ability to really listen to them helped them believe in themselves and take the next steps toward recovery, moving forward in their lives, and success.

Serendipity, Skills, and Compassion

In reflecting on her social work career, Sr. Patricia tells me she has had "great opportunities to be at the right place at the right time or be invited to be on the cutting edge." She also refers to the casework skills that she learned in her graduate education and the relational skills involved in interviewing techniques that she believes have been fundamental to her work. She observes a difference in how social workers intervene with others: "We might all be in the same work but there [is] a different perspective that I really appreciated: when social workers do it, they are trying to lead the person to take a look at what they can do and how they can develop their own selves."

When asked what she believed were her greatest accomplishments in her career, Sr. Patricia talked about the pleasure she has found in "creating something new." For example, "to see the problem of the effects of incarceration on the family system and then find a way in to address it." She recalls, "It was a lot of hard work, from doing a little guide for the counselors to making all these contacts, to being able to start something where women could come to get both immediate assistance and long-term support." Since Sr. Patricia left LSSI several years ago, the ReConnections program continues to provide information and referral services to formerly incarcerated women but in a more abbreviated fashion. Jane Otte, executive director of LSSI's Prisoner and Family Ministry commented that Sr. Patricia's "passion and social work experience helped us to develop the first reentry nonresidential program in the city of Chicago" at a time when the Department of Corrections was not doing very much to prepare women who were exiting prison (J. Otte, personal communication, June 17, 2009). ReConnections was not only innovative for Chicago and unique in the state of Illinois; there were very few programs of its type anywhere in the country.

Currently, in the phase she calls semiretirement, Sr. Patricia is still active as a volunteer with Grace House, a community-based residential center for women exiting prison, and she continues to visit area state and federal prison facilities to provide reentry groups and work one-on-one with women in transition to home and community. In the reentry groups with women, she focuses on building self-esteem, dealing with feelings (particularly anger), discussing healthy and unhealthy relationships, and setting goals. She is still interested in developing the network of resources for people coming out of prison: "All that we need to do is not finished."

Lessons Learned

The inspiration that Sr. Patricia gained from the *Catholic Worker* and her early introduction to Dorothy Day (whom she once met) continued in all the jobs where she "stood with the poorest," doing her work in the community and living as a neighbor and friend with people affected by oppressive social welfare and criminal justice policies. When asked how she believes that her work has contributed to social change, she laughs and says, "I have been changed!" She goes on to reflect, "It's been reciprocal and mutual. I've learned a lot from the people I've worked with and I believe that people are changed by having something reflected back about their possibilities for self-transformation." While the voice of this pioneering social worker reflects what many social workers in the everyday trenches in hundreds of agencies might humbly believe, showing up, being creative, and persevering in solidarity with those who so often are made invisible is testimony to the central focus of social work and its contributions in the real world, regardless of what it is called, and to the specific roles and functions of the individuals who take up this work.

Sr. Patricia's narrative describing her journey in social work demonstrates some noteworthy characteristics, including her flexibility and willingness to learn from new situations. For example, she was able to accept the position with Lakefront SRO, which taught her about program development even though her interest had not been initially focused on homeless men. She was also able to be flexible and recognize the serendipitous opportunities she's had to develop innovative services when the problems often loomed larger than the solutions.

Although it is very common for social workers to experience burnout in the emotional and sometimes traumatizing work they do with people who experience major and repeated life problems, she has not appeared to do so. She has learned how to draw on her community for support, continued to believe in what she is doing, and known when to seek new opportunities. As noted earlier, she continues to travel to federal and state prison facilities to help women see their potential and possibilities for change. What makes that possible for her at the age of seventy-five when many others have retired? Her persistence is intertwined with flexibility—Sr. Patricia said she knew when it was time to move on, to try something different or more challenging than what she was already doing. In moving on, she also moved up in responsibility, which created other possibilities and new avenues. She also mentioned the importance of taking care of herself, physically, emotionally, and spiritually.

Sr. Patricia's religious roots have also sustained her social work practice over time. These roots are very intertwined with her thirst for social justice. The community of Franciscans has been crucial in providing support for the struggle to live out or "preach" the gospel. Finally, in the context of mentoring others, Sr. Patricia hopes that future social workers will continue working to make a difference. As she puts it, "I would reinvite them to look at how important it is to bring their energy, new technology and skills" to the oppressed and the vulnerable.

In addition to individual helping and social reform efforts, Sr. Patricia has been involved in teaching, in writing articles, and in creating curricula for use by other social workers and helping professionals. She has also been involved in evaluations of her work with formerly incarcerated women. Constructing knowledge about what works with whom at different junctures of involvement with the criminal justice system enables social workers to inform the field and expand the possibilities for change.

Social workers should and can make a difference in hard-to-access settings such as prisons. To make a difference, social workers have to be actively engaged in using what they have already learned about effective practice. Moreover, social workers must contribute to the systematic observations that are integral to developing new interventions and progressive social policies to advance the rehabilitative ideal that joins corrections and the practice of social work, a task that Sr. Patricia has executed with creativity, clarity, and faith in people's strengths and possibilities for change.

References

Addams, J. (1909). *The spirit of youth and the city streets.* New York: Macmillan.

Kann, M. E. (2005). *Punishment, prisons, and patriarchy: Liberty and power in the early American republic.* New York: New York University Press.

Martinson, R. (1979). New findings, new views: A note of caution regarding sentencing reform. *Hofstra Law Review, 7,* 243–258.

Mauer, M., & King, R. S. (2007). *A 25-year quagmire: The "War on Drugs" and its impact on American society.* Washington, DC: The Sentencing Project.

O'Brien, P. (2006). *Evaluation of ReConnections.* Chicago: Lutheran Social Services of Illinois.

Pew Center on the States (2008). *One in 100: Behind bars in America 2008.* Washington, DC: Author.

Rafter, N. H. (1990). *Partial justice: Women, prison and social control* (2nd ed.). New Brunswick, N.J.: Transaction.

West, H. C., & Sabol, W. J. (2009). *Prison inmates at midyear 2008—Statistical tables* (NCJ No. 225619). Washington, DC: Bureau of Justice Statistics.

CHAPTER ELEVEN

Reverend Debra Trakel

Fighting for Milwaukee's Hungry, Homeless, and Displaced

Deborah Padgett

Recently, Rev. Debra Trakel's office was awarded the Hole in the Wall Award by staff at the neighborhood meal program. Large, comfortable, and packed with books, couches, and other accoutrements of her work, Rev. Debra's office may be a bit out of the way by downtown standards, but it is central to the church and the people she serves. Rev. Debra is an ordained pastor and the rector of St. James Episcopal Church, in the center of the city of Milwaukee. As pastor, Rev. Debra serves her parishioners and the local community in one of the poorest zip codes in the state. She is also an MSW.

Her daily work involves the details of being a parish priest: responsibilities to her parishioners, oversight of programs and services that the church supports, and attention to the physical structure of the church. But Rev. Debra is also responsive to whoever may appear at her door in need, and she works to encourage the community's response to the

Quotes and information about Rev. Debra Trakel's life and career are from an interview conducted on March 3, 2008, and a written autobiographical statement that she provided.

needs that she sees. She blends her spiritual and social work training in her roles as pastor, administrator, community practitioner, and clinician. Rev. Debra credits her understanding of systems as an essential benefit of her social work education. Sometimes "encouraging" a community response means facilitating a partnership and bridging competing interests; other times, a confrontational strategy is required. Her commitment to the needs of Milwaukee's poor is fierce and clearly reflects both her social work and her spiritual values.

Although I have lived and worked in Milwaukee for some time, I had never met Rev. Trakel. I am grateful for the opportunity to have met with her, because it allowed me to meet someone who has done so much to change the world of the dispossessed in this city.

Personal History

The story of Debra's adoption is that her birth mother met a man in a bar who was sympathetic to the tears of an overwhelmed and unmarried new mother. The man's wife could not have children and they had been considering adoption. He offered to take the infant Debra home. With the approval of Lutheran Social Services, six-week-old Debra was suddenly part of a new family in West Bend, Wisconsin—sudden enough that the new baby slept in a dresser drawer until there was time to buy a crib.

Debra's new father had sons from an earlier marriage but these stepbrothers were old enough to be independent and out of the home when Debra was growing up. Both her new parents were alcoholics and, she says, "I loved them both fiercely." They divorced when she was six. She and her mother moved to Milwaukee so her mother could find work. Debra's mother located a job at a local department store, and they lived downtown near Debra's maternal grandfather, not far from where Debra works now. Debra's grandfather and her mother could often be found together at the neighborhood bars when they were not at their jobs. Debra describes her ability as a young girl to evade all babysitters to try and locate her mother, at work or at a bar: "All of the local bartenders knew me as I padded up and down Lincoln Avenue, going in and out of all the bars looking for my mother, in my pajamas with the feet in them. God was surely with me on those lonely and frightening sojourns because I was never hurt and, eventually, I always found my mother. I used to be proud of that ability. Now, of course, I see that little girl as very sad and troubled."

When Debra was in the third grade her mother broke a leg. Because her mother was unable to work, mother and daughter had their furniture repossessed and went on welfare. When Debra was in the fifth grade, her mother remarried and their lives became financially stable. However, this stepfather was also an alcoholic—one who was mean when drunk and abusive to Debra's mother. Debra describes her efforts to protect her mother, diverting his anger, avoiding fists, and calling the police after her mother had been beaten again. Debra's childhood of alcoholism, abuse, and poverty not only required elements of self-reliance but also allowed for an understanding of life on the margins: "My mother taught me about tenacity and grit and the dangers of alcohol abuse. She taught me about strength and about having compassion for the most vulnerable in our society. . . . Parental alcoholism, child abuse, domestic violence, and abandonment became the grist for my own compassion."

Along with resilience, she inherited a love of reading, finding escape in books and ultimately the familiarity and comfort with words that lends itself to success in school and into a professional life. She thrived in school, working hard and finding nurturing adults.

A teacher introduced Debra to the Catholic Church. There, she found a community of loving and healthy peers and adults and, in the ninth grade, she converted to Roman Catholicism. After high school, Debra entered the convent, which she describes as a way to give back for the blessings of what life had provided—a loving and protective God and friends. While in the convent, she attended Mount Mary College. She credits Mary Ann Suppes for awakening her to the profession of social work during those years. It was in social work that she found her interest in helping others to be a profession. After seven years, Debra left the convent with a BA in social work to continue to give back but now as a social worker.

Rev. Debra's employment experiences have alternated between traditional faith-based work and social work jobs for much of her adult life. Both her faith and her belief in helping people have been central to Debra's professional life. She started out as a sister, had various jobs as a social worker, and now serves as a parish priest. She says, "I remember thinking when I turned eighteen that I had been so blessed because many horrible things that could have happened to me had *not* happened. I was well loved by many friends and felt very loved and protected by God. I wanted to give back what I had received."

Her career transitions have reflected this commitment to serve with changes that reflect choices about how she could best serve others. In her midthirties, Debra made the decision to leave Roman Catholicism for another religious tradition. She left Catholicism, she says, because

she experienced the oppression of so many of her peers by the hierarchy of the church. Eventually, she found her way to the Episcopal
Church. Although she was happy with her social work career, she felt
that not being able to discuss religion and her deep faith left a gap for
her. Her pastor convinced her to consider seminary. Debra says, "God
spoke to my heart"—being a priest did not mean she would have to
renounce social work and instead would allow her to combine both
passions. She ultimately entered seminary and became ordained in the
Episcopal Church.

Career Trajectory

Debra earned her undergraduate degree in social work from Mount
Mary (1975), her MSW from the University of Wisconsin, Milwaukee
(1981), and her master's degree in divinity from Seabury-Western Theo-
logical Seminary (1995). Early in her social work career, Debra worked
in nursing homes as a medical social worker. She found herself, as a
young social worker, working in an agency with some unethical policies, which were harmful to the clients. The decision to report her
employer, especially as a new social worker, was stressful but also
reflective of her commitment to remedy structural injustices. She soon
"fled" medical social work and started her career in corrections.

Initially, her work was with probation and parole, which led to her
becoming the supervisor of the Sex Offender Unit for the Department
of Corrections in Milwaukee County. In that role, she was responsible
for supervising agents who worked with sex offenders. In addition,
Debra worked at the Corrections Academy to train new agents to
address domestic violence situations. She also helped to create the
Domestic Violence Coalition, now known as the Task Force on Domestic Violence. Her own childhood experiences added to the meaningful-
ness of the work. She also says that work in corrections can be
rewarding because you know that you are doing important work that
most people don't know how to do and likely don't want to know how
to do. However, it is also work that "takes a toll" personally.

Later, for two years, Debra worked as the chief of training and
employee development with the Department of Natural Resources.
When her mother and stepfather became ill, Debra returned to Milwaukee until their circumstances stabilized. She was then promoted to
chief of human resource development in the Department of Transportation. Both positions provided experience in macro social work with
employee assistance and training, organizational development, and
quality improvement.

These jobs in medical social work, corrections, and occupational social work taught her to use her skills in understanding systems to advocate and locate resources for her clients. She reports that, throughout her career, she has been able to see the relevance of policies and institutional structures for the individuals they served. She is adamant that social work is about understanding systems—that doing so is what makes the social work profession unique from other types of helping professions. Being able to assess the organizational and community contexts within which people function allows social workers insights into negotiable pathways for making change—or at least, initiating a connection, she says. Evident throughout Rev. Debra's work is her understanding of the role of larger systems in the lives of the people she sees.

Interestingly, her experience with sex offenders as a social worker led to a call from the bishop after she completed her time in seminary to work on the bishop's staff as his assistant for pastoral care. In this capacity, she worked with troubled clergy and in the area of clergy sexual misconduct. For four years, Rev. Debra ran investigations and provided recommendations to the bishop and parishes. As a "case manager" for the bishop, she was responsible for the investigations. In retrospect, she says, she is proud of having helped both women and children who had been victimized and to know that she had helped prevent continued victimization. However, the case manager also often faces the anger of parishioners who need to blame someone for the departure of their beloved priest. Much like corrections, the job requires a willingness to work with unwelcome issues of the church and of people. Although there were often positive outcomes that created opportunities for healing, the process was personally difficult. And the job was part-time. She now provides education and training about the issues surrounding clergy sexual abuse and serves as an expert witness around the country in legal proceedings.

St. James Episcopal Church

For the past nine years, Rev. Debra has served as rector of St. James Episcopal Church with what appears to be a natural blend of her previous career experiences, professional trainings, and personal passions. Several programs that are a part of her life at St. James reflect values and beliefs that will resonate with social workers.

MEAL PROGRAM AND DOOR MINISTRY

St. James is located in the poorest area of Milwaukee. The church feeds more than three hundred people each day, in a meal program known as the Gathering, a program available to anyone who needs a meal. When she arrives at the church in the morning, Rev. Debra says there is a line of people extending down the sidewalk, all waiting for a meal. These guests of the Gathering are typically people who are desperately overwhelmed by the challenges of a life with few resources. Over the course of one year, the church distributes ninety thousand meals through this program.

Door Ministry is a program in the church that attempts to respond to the needs of people who show up at the door of the church. Many people who are referred have been referred by guests of the Gathering. Others have been referred by area churches, homeless shelters, and the community resource hotline, 211. Some individuals have been evicted from area facilities where they had sought warm shelter. Requests include clothing, money, food, bus tickets, medicine, rent assistance, and a multitude of other needs for survival. St. James dedicates a monthly offering for a discretionary fund, and community agencies know that St. James has some unrestricted resources that might help a client's situation. But obviously, the funds are limited and the needs are great.

Many guests of the Gathering and those in need of the Door Ministry are not members of the congregation, officially, but may still need to talk with Rev. Debra. The director of the Gathering, as he meets with guests, may refer people to her who have concerns or needs beyond food. Rev. Debra says, "I also work with the poor who come every day to the door, even though they are not members of the parish. I try to assess their situation to see what systems can best be helpful to them, to help them to make good life decisions, and to refer them to places where they can receive the help that they need that I can't provide. Often, I simply listen to people who are beaten down by poverty and just need for someone to take them seriously. It is the hardest and most rewarding work that I do."

Conversations may involve discussions about strategies to negotiate community agencies, health-care options, and state welfare systems. Rev. Debra often becomes aware of problematic community policies and systems through these conversations.

As Rev. Debra says, sometimes people just need someone to listen. As a licensed clinical social worker in the state of Wisconsin, Rev. Debra can function as a clinician. She notes, however, that as an Episcopal priest, the church limits her to six sessions with people who come in to talk with her. She says she is comfortable with the time limitation for counseling people because most priests lack clinical training.

INDIGENT BURIALS

As a unique effort on behalf of the very poor, Rev. Debra created a program in which St. James offers a burial service for the indigent in

Milwaukee County. Although it is not a widely described aspect of social work, providing a respectful burial for people who have no resources or family is consistent with other tasks of social workers (Castex, 2007). However, the effort to initiate the burial services was quite cumbersome, as it required that the Office of Indigent Burials be convinced to give permission to the funeral home to contact St. James when there was an upcoming burial, then appealing to the funeral home to make the contact with St. James, and organizing the service.

Ultimately, the church has developed a relationship with the funeral home in town that buries those who are indigent, unclaimed by another person, or would otherwise not be noticed in their death. Rev. Debra and members of the church who can attend offer a prayer at the grave site. Because there is no grave marker, a plaque exists in the church with the names of those buried so that those who were not otherwise noted are remembered somewhere. St. James has provided services for fifty-three indigent individuals in the two and a half years of this commitment (St. James Episcopal Church, 2008).

RADICAL HOSPITALITY

The Benedictine concept of inclusion called radical hospitality is a commitment to welcome all people. Brought to contemporary life by Catholic Worker Movement cofounder Dorothy Day, the concept of radical hospitality requires an acceptance that extends beyond passivity to activities that demonstrate inclusion and welcome. The expectation is one of activism, not merely of awareness and quiet agreement. Social workers will recognize the commitments to diversity and social action in this concept. Rev. Debra introduced the concept of radical hospitality to the congregation of St. James, which has incorporated it into the mission of the church.

As with most efforts at inclusion, radical hospitality can create unique experiences for parishioners who may come from conservative, privileged backgrounds; those challenged by the urban streets of poverty; or others who have chosen a lifestyle that others consider different. For any congregation—including the members of St. James—truly embracing a mission of radical hospitality is transformative, requiring a welcome of others who are unlike themselves. Church members from affluent areas of the city may find themselves needing to understand what it means to welcome the lines of homeless people in the front yard of the church. Others from conservative backgrounds may need to figure out how to welcome members of the congregation whose sexual orientation or lifestyle is different from their own. As a social justice mission, radical hospitality requires a commitment to understand how one genuinely enacts welcome and inclusion.

Urban Poverty and Community Systems

There are several aspects to life as the rector of St. James that illustrate community-level challenges. St. James is in the center of the city and next to Marquette University, a private Jesuit college. The three hundred people on the front lawn of St. James every day for a meal are not generally the constituents of the university or downtown businesses and are often targeted as "the problem" of the neighborhood.

Problems created by institutions and agencies working at cross-purposes are often identified through conversations with parishioners and community members, Rev. Debra notes. For example, downtown businesses have entrepreneurial goals, Marquette University has an educational mission, and the city police department is concerned with safety. Parents of students sometimes call St. James to complain that their child has to pass a homeless person on the way to class. Rev. Debra says she has learned to recognize the complaint as reflecting fear, not genuine risk. And she is happy to talk with them about how to help their young-adult child cope with the reality of student life in an urban school. However, if parents just want that "reality" to go away, Rev. Debra is less patient. She notes that it is important to have relationships with Marquette University and other institutions already in place when shared issues arise. So, she develops and maintains those relationships both to keep track of potential challenges and to nurture the kind of partnership necessary for community change.

For local businesses, the response has often been to refuse to let homeless people access to restroom facilities. Rev. Debra meets with the business association to maintain a relationship, framing the issue as a shared problem of no public restrooms. The police department often responds by ticketing homeless people for exhibitionism (public urination), loitering, or jaywalking. With people without the resources to pay such tickets, Rev. Debra functions as an advocate, writing letters on behalf of individuals, talking to area police, or lobbying the district attorney.

"Don't mess with my lambs"

But these challenges reflect ongoing battles. Rev. Debra indicates that people are welcome to confront her but should not "mess with [her] lambs." Her protectiveness of those least able to defend themselves against community systems is fierce and apparently legendary, as evidenced by the quantity of stuffed lambs in her office that people have given her: "I also fight systems for them. The police. Welfare. Food stamps. Food pantries. Health care." As an advocate for the poor, Rev.

Debra uses her skills in understanding a systems perspective and in her familiarity with these systems specifically. She reports having no tolerance for unjust authority and for people who abuse the authority they have, a posture clearly reflected throughout her career.

At one time, there was an effort to stop the church's ministry that allowed homeless people to sleep on the property. The police threatened to fine St. James into bankruptcy. Rev. Debra organized area ministers, priests, and parishes, garnering a sufficient display of support to end the threat of fines and to allow the ministry to continue.

She has battled the city attorney in an effort to protect people from unnecessary tickets, noting that Marquette students do not receive tickets for jaywalking. A ticket for loitering can cost $120, and with enough outstanding tickets, individuals spend three days in the house of corrections. Obviously, these are not fines that people who are homeless can pay, resulting in costs to the court system, jails, and ultimately taxpayers.

Common Ground

A relatively new community organization in Milwaukee is Common Ground, where Rev. Debra is a founding member and serves on the board. Common Ground is an affiliate of the Industrial Areas Foundation, an organization created by Saul Alinsky and reflective of his perspectives on power and social change. The group focuses on the need for social change and the issues specific to southeastern Wisconsin. The membership represents a broad spectrum of the four county area with a defining phrase of "on this common ground, we will build" (Common Ground, 2008). The vision of the organization speaks of inclusiveness, personal dignity, and strategic change (Common Ground, 2008) without, as Rev. Debra says, Alinsky's "in your face" style. "There is an excitement in a group of people willing to come together with a vision of a different Milwaukee," Rev. Debra says. The challenges that Milwaukee faces are extensive; they cross gender, race, and income groups. Common Ground offers opportunities for community participation to address shared problems. Capacity development, as a model of community change, encourages participation from a broad spectrum of members (Cnaan & Rothman, 2008; Rothman, 2007).

Recently, the group successfully challenged a ban against storefront churches in Wauwatosa, a mostly white, relatively affluent suburb of Milwaukee. When a faith-based community group unknowingly set up in a storefront, they were confronted by the city ordinance. Common Ground gathered a very large group of Wauwatosa pastors to speak to the city board about the implicit racism in their ban. Subsequently, the

Wauwatosa mayor worked with Common Ground to facilitate the needed changes.

Professional Issues

Finally, as professionals, there are challenges to this commitment to social work practice principles. Reflecting on the personal characteristics helpful to sustaining oneself in social work, Rev. Debra had several observations. Surviving the rigors of the profession of social work, she says, requires a heart, a sense of humor, a curiosity tinged with wonder, and never-ending personal growth. One needs an essential curiosity about people, to be able to be outside of him- or herself, in the work that is done as a social worker. There is, Rev. Debra says, a "grittiness" to what social workers do in their profession; and, if they are doing it well, "there is no way not to get messy." Your heart will help you lead with compassion, but, unguarded, it will create problems for you and the people you serve. Rev. Debra commented, "I am blessed with an essential curiosity about people and what makes them who they are. I find people endlessly fascinating. And I am relentless about my own growth and development. . . . I also find amusement in almost everything—and I do think that a sense of humor is essential to remain healthy in our profession."

A sense of humor helps sustain us in distinguishing the trivial from the tragic, but this also needs to be guided by compassion, she notes. Being able to always feel challenged and to find new directions for growth will help one stay invigorated. Although Rev. Debra seems tolerant of multiple degrees of competence among new social workers, she views a lack of compassion as fatal to the effectiveness of a social worker and potentially the profession. "In the midst of the mess of human life," Rev. Debra says, "our job is to find wholeness."

Also critical is knowledge of systems, but unlike some of the earlier personal qualities necessary for effective social work, Rev. Debra says, this is a skill that can be learned. Social workers need to know how to manage both systems and roles. Although other professions may do battle over lines of responsibility, she argues that social workers need to understand and be willing to navigate those lines and create competence in institutions and systems. It is also necessary to understand power, a skill that Rev. Debra identifies as particularly important to facilitating change on behalf of those who have none.

Bridges versus Battles

Social workers frequently need to decide whether a collaborative or a combative approach is warranted, by drawing on their assessment of the situation, circumstances, and personal resources (Netting, Kett-ner, & McMurtry, 2008). They need to know whether to mount a battle or to build bridges to address social issues. Rev. Debra reflects that she has had to learn to be "smarter" about these decisions, strategic about choices. Sometimes, she says, the process has merely reflected matur-ity, presumably representing a thoughtful choice rather than a reaction-ary one. She also asserts that available personal resources are critical in selecting a strategy, because confrontations take time and energy, which may not always be available in the face of competing priorities.

She does sometimes select a quixotic battle, she acknowledges, refer-encing the posturing of Don Quixote. However, she notes that doing so also needs to be strategic and offer either energy from the loss or a critical symbolic gain. An awareness of the power and politics around community issues is critical to facilitating community change. Rev. Debra notes the importance of "being at the table" when community decisions are being made and resources—whether money, people, or time—are being allocated. She says it is also critical to know how to leverage power, to mobilize allies, and to draw on established and nur-tured relationships.

Social Work Practice Principles

A commitment to justice and human dignity requires several types of skills and energies that Rev. Debra has demonstrated. Social workers need to be willing to persist in the face of complicated community sys-tems, in addition to knowing how to navigate those systems. Initiating a burial service for those who would not otherwise have one involves time and resourcefulness in working within community systems. Being able to resolve challenges and identify achievable goals is also critical. When people who cannot afford a home are being excessively ticketed, it is important to be able to think about the people in the community who might make a difference and to identify strategies for working with those individuals and institutions. Listening skills help social workers in community work become aware, through individual conversations with people, of the injustices and challenges that are implicated in a life of poverty; social workers in contact with individuals frequently identify macro issues (Netting et al., 2008). An additional micro-level skill is building relationships with those who are interested in resolving issues, others who may have the resources to be helpful, and those who may be working toward competing goals. Finally, social workers need to know how to sustain themselves, to be able to be responsive throughout a lifelong career: "I don't honestly imagine myself ever completely retir-ing. Too many people, too much need, too little time. I begin more and more to turn to where I began: systems. If we can help change our systems—education, welfare, health care—we can make an even greater contribution to the lives of people in great need."

Rev. Debra works within a neighborhood and a community. The problems are not new: poverty, injustice, health care, homelessness, and social service systems continue to create challenges for communities; and these issues continue to resonate with the goals of social work.

References

Castex, G. M. (2007). Social workers' final act of service: Respectful burial arrangements for indigent, unclaimed and unidentified people. *Social Work, 52*(4), 331–339.

Cnaan, R. A., & Rothman, J. (2008). Capacity development and the building of community. In J. Rothman, J. L. Erlich, and J. E. Tropman (Eds.), *Strategies of community intervention* (7th ed., pp. 243–262). Peosta, IA: Eddie Bowers.

Common Ground. (2008). Who is Common Ground? Retrieved June 9, 2008, from http://www.commongroundwi.org/who-is-common-ground/.

Netting, F. E., Kettner, P. M., & McMurtry, S. L. (2008). *Social work macro practice* (4th ed.). Boston: Pearson.

Rothman, J. (2007). Multi modes of intervention at the macro level. *Journal of Community Practice, 15*(4), 11–40.

St. James Episcopal Church (2008, January 27). *Annual report of St. James Episcopal Church.* Milwaukee, WI: Author.

CHAPTER TWELVE

Sister Jean Abbott

Bringing Healing to Victims of Trauma Worldwide

Jami Curley and Susan S. Tebb

All the world is full of suffering. It is also full of overcoming it.

—Helen Keller

The effects of war and civil conflicts on a survivor's mind and body can be devastating, particularly when abuse and torture are involved. According to the World Health Organization (2002), depression and anxiety, suicidal tendencies, alcohol abuse, and posttraumatic stress disorder (PTSD) are among the psychological and behavioral problems resulting from the collective violence that ensues from the chaos and disorder of civil unrest. Many victims flee their homeland out of fear for their lives or are forcibly displaced to other countries in search of asylum. Known as refugees, these people often seek safety and protection from their home countries. At the end of 2006, approximately 14 million refugees and asylum seekers were in need of protection worldwide (U.S. Committee for Refugees and Immigrants, 2007). Of the 69,400 refugees that were resettled in other countries, more than 41,000 were resettled in the United States (U.S. Committee for Refugees and Immigrants, 2007).

It is these people to whom Sister Jean Abbott has devoted more than a quarter century of service. As the founder and clinical director of the Center for the Survivors of Torture and War Trauma, she has assumed responsibility for the emotional well-being of more than nine thousand such clients living in the St. Louis area, from places as diverse as Afghanistan, Bosnia, Ethiopia, Iran, Somalia, Liberia, Iraq, and the Democratic Republic of the Congo. We interviewed Sr. Jean at the center, in person, and by phone during the summer of 2008.

The Early Years

Jean Abbott is the fourth child of eleven, born in a working-class neighborhood of St. Louis. In our interview, she noted that "everybody there was working class, good families and all of them big families. They didn't serve wine at the parties, they served beer. A lot of them were factory workers, salesmen, milkman drivers—we had a milkman in those days, and it was a good old neighborhood."

Her father was a millwright at General Electric and a proud union member—so proud, in fact, that he refused a promotion to management because it would have meant a move out of the union. Sr. Jean's father saw the union as the protection he needed to support nine kids. Her mother, busy raising the nine children, often worked outside the home when financial difficulties struck. After the death of her father, her mother moved permanently into the workforce, taking a job at McDonnell-Douglas (now Boeing), a major aerospace manufacturer and defense contractor. Sr. Jean remembers her mother really struggling with her values and beliefs because, at the time, McDonnell-Douglas was very much involved in making weaponry for the United States, which was involved in the Vietnam War, a war that her mother did not support; yet she had to have a job to support the children who were still at home. Sr. Jean recalls people telling her mother that she was not actually fighting the war, but her mother always had the sense of participating and assisting in it, which caused her great pain. Sr. Jean was always proud of her mother for her consciousness of the struggle. Sr. Jean's mother knew what McDonnell-Douglas was participating in and believed that made whoever benefited from its work somewhat responsible. Sr. Jean attributes her sense of justice, a belief that all people are a part of the system and need to acknowledge and take responsibility for their actions, from both her mother and her father. However, neither one of her parents would have risked their children's well-being to fight the system and protest. Because of their experiences growing up in extreme poverty, stability and family were the highest priority for both. They did not want their children to experience poverty, and together they built a decent life for their family. Sr. Jean does not believe that she was born or raised in childhood with a mission to serve, but her desire to give to others slowly evolved as she grew up watching the kindheartedness of her parents.

Clearly, Sr. Jean's deeply religious upbringing had the greatest impact on the direction of her life goals: "I can remember being in the kitchen with my mom and dad listening to the radio when the troops rolled into Hungary and my father saying, 'If anybody comes to you hungry, and asks you for something to eat, you treat them as if they were a king. You treat them like they were doing you a favor.'" Sr. Jean stated that this desire came out of his own memories of being so hungry that it affected his vision: things changed colors. Thus, as she and her siblings were growing up, they were always waiting for somebody to ask them for food. "My sister was watering the lawn one day when somebody came by and asked if he could have a drink of water. She made him come in the house and she fixed him breakfast and embarrassed the heck out of him because she thought this is it, this is my chance to do what Dad said I should. And we all are living our lives that way. Our parents gave us sensitivity and helped us to realize that everyone is a human being with feelings. And I hate it when we say 'the poor,' because that is us in a different circumstance."

On the Path to a Life's Work

Growing up, Sr. Jean thought that Catholic sisters were the most beautiful things in the world. They walked on water—at least in her mind, anyway—and their feet did not touch the ground. Both her parents wanted her to go to college, so when she finished high school, she went to a local women's college, Fontbonne, which happened to be run by the Sisters of St. Joseph. Because of her admiration of Catholic sisters, it was natural for Sr. Jean to take what she considers the easy path and become a sister by beginning the training to take her vows. As Sr. Jean looks back on her life and the decision to become a nun, she believes that her parents unconsciously made it for her. She recalls, "As a baby, I got very high fevers and the doctor told my mom that she had to let me go because I might die. So my mom promised me to the Blessed Mary. When I made my final vows I realized that this was a setup: I was set up to be a Sister of St. Joseph from the get-go. Mother was a converted Catholic. She made that promise that I would be a sister so I would survive. I entered the order at seventeen, and she just thought that was too young. I agree now that I was too young. I had been sheltered. I went to a Catholic girls' high school and spent most of my young life sitting on a bus getting back and forth between home and school. She was not happy with the fact that I entered the convent, but she never tried to stop me. She always made sure that I knew I could leave the order anytime and I would be welcomed at home."

Sr. Jean remembers that her dad almost ran down to the convent with her as soon as she graduated from high school. None of her other sisters or brothers went into religious life. Sr. Jean shared, "I am not sure why I joined except that I had very high ideals and had grown up with the Sisters of St. Joseph. They inspired me as I was growing up, but I didn't know when I made the application that the Sisters of St. Joseph had taken my father in as an orphan and raised him."

Sr. Jean's father died when she was twenty-four years old. By then, she had graduated from Fontbonne College and had taken her vows to be a Sister of St. Joseph. "I was in Denver working as a grade school teacher and right before he died, he sent me a poem. Dad didn't write to me ever, but he sent this poem and it said, 'When all the cats begin to crawl, and from yard to yard they roam, this little kitten will not howl because she has found a home.' And I thought, 'This doesn't feel like home to me, being a Sister of St. Joseph,' but it was to him. He grew up in the St. Joseph Orphanage for Boys, from the age of about five on, because his mother was too sick to take care of him. I was going back to his home and it never registered with me that he was talking about himself."

As Sr. Jean reflects back on her life now she knows that for her, joining the order was not a personal mission choice but more something to do at that time as a young woman. She notes that had the Catholic Church not changed because of Vatican II she probably would have left the order because she found it very confining, and it did not allow for independence or respect of personal ideals. She continues to live as a Sister of St. Joseph today because she sees it as a community that encourages sisters to be involved intimately in people's lives.

A Growing Awareness

Armed with the values of her parents, particularly her father, who had been raised not only in but also by the church, Sr. Jean maintained her teaching position in Denver for three years. At that point, the order called her back to work in St. Louis. One of her first positions on her return was to direct St. Henry's Community Center, on the city's south side. Under the auspices of St. Henry's Parish, she also became a community organizer. The area was quite poor, and she worked with others to form the St. Louis Association of Community Organizations, known as SLACO, whose mission was to advocate for increased quality of services to low-income residents. Trained by a disciple of Saul Alinsky, Sr.

Jean found aspects of the advocacy work a poor fit with her own personal style: "I am not the best community organizer in the world, mainly because you have to confront and I'm not a good confronter. I'm a good organizer in the sense of pulling people together, but other people would have to do some of the serious confrontations." But it was through this group that she became more aware of international events, particularly in Central America, where civil wars were raging. As her awareness continued to grow, she returned to school and received her MSW from Saint Louis University in 1982: "During that time, I saw what was happening in Nicaragua and Guatemala. I didn't know a lot about Guatemala at the time, just that the United States had participated in the overthrow of their government."

It was also at about that time that Sr. Jean became aware of another church in the North City area of St. Louis that was involved in providing sanctuary to people fleeing Central America, El Salvador, and Guatemala. As she was learning about the efforts of this church, she discovered the group Witness for Peace, which was sending people interested in working for peace to Nicaragua. Sr. Jean believes that the opportunity to work for Witness for Peace came along at a time in her life when she felt she needed to be more proactive.

She recalls that as she interviewed with Witness for Peace, she didn't even think, "Am I prepared?" she just signed up. Because she did not speak Spanish, she was told she would have to study it while in Nicaragua. So for the first six weeks in Central America, Sr. Jean was tutored each morning in Spanish. A woman with a rifle in one hand and a baby in the other was her teacher, and her sessions were without a book. The experience of being taught by this woman made such an emotional impact on her that she will always be able to remember the words for struggle and women. She learned Spanish, as Sr. Jean says, "on a gut and need basis." Sr. Jean found language to be more of an emotional activity, as opposed to a scholastic activity, and thus, she can never remember the words for ceiling or floor, but she can remember the words for hurt, work, and weep. Sr. Jean acknowledges that her preparation for the work she was to do while there seemed to just emerge. She notes that before the opportunity arose, she did not have the maturity or the ability to be other centered, but being in a war zone and being overly centered on one's self just does not work.

Sr. Jean spent a year in Nicaragua, where the work of Witness for Peace was to help bridge communications between different parties. She originally was to be there for three months, but she renewed her contract and stayed for a year. During her year's stay, however, her passport expired, and to renew it, she had to leave Nicaragua for three days, so she traveled to Guatemala. While she was there, she could not believe the difference in the unrest between the two countries. In Guatemala, she was enchanted and horrified at the same time. Guatemala was the country that the United States publically noted as being democratic, but Sr. Jean found the tension and the fear palpable. On her return to the war zones of Nicaragua after her three-day absence, she realized Nicaraguans had much more freedom to discuss and talk among themselves than Guatemalans did, and Nicaragua felt much safer than Guatemala. Sr. Jean did not believe that the Nicaraguans were safe from the effects of the war but that they were safe from political persecution from their own city and national governments, and they could critically talk openly about the war, which Guatemalans could not.

Moved by what she saw in Guatemala during her short stay, Sr. Jean visited a Guatemalan refugee camp on her return to Nicaragua. There she found that everyone in the camp either had lost a family member or had been threatened by the government in Guatemala. Their plight inspired her to return to Guatemala once her term with Witness for Peace was finished, this time with a group called Peace Brigades.

It was her experience in Guatemala specifically that led her to the desire to heal and work with torture survivors: "As I was flying to Guatemala, three people whom I had met earlier and who were associated with Peace Brigades were kidnapped, killed, and found by the sides of the road and in ditches, all tortured to death. I thought, 'This is the Guatemala I am going to.'"

Sr. Jean's responsibilities with Peace Brigades involved coordinating a project in which persons from the international community, mostly from North America, would be placed with Guatemalan people who were organizing and speaking out. The hope was that if there was a North American at the side of the brave Guatemalans, then the government would not hurt them, because if they did, there would more than likely be a great deal of publicity and media coverage.

Asked about the impact of these activities, with their attendant danger, on families, Sr. Jean explained that just undertaking the activities was a terrible risk. But, she said, "the effect of a disappearance on families is incredible. It caused families to break up, members would lose their courage. . . . [I]t would make people crazy because the person would just disappear. There is no end to that kind of suffering; your imagination plays out the torture. I have seen brothers and sisters start to go into a dissociative state and sound like the disappeared sister. And guilt! There [are] the 'if you would have,' 'did you speak out?' 'it's your fault' thoughts that continue to play with your mind. It is absolutely destructive."

When the time came for elections in Guatemala, all of those working for Peace Brigades were deported. Because Sr. Jean was technically working for the Catholic Church, the group made a decision to leave her behind; her job would be to pull together some Guatemalan students to look after the citizens who were at high risk. "They left and suddenly I felt so alone," she said. "I went back to the Peace Brigade house and there was a knock on the door. At that time every knock was menacing to me because I thought, 'Girl, you are alone!'" But instead of trouble, there stood a small woman who had been protected by our group when she went to the mutual support group. "She said to me, 'You walked with me; I am going to walk with you.' So this tiny, vulnerable woman, whose daughter had already disappeared, went with me everywhere. It was one of the most moving things. When I left Guatemala, she also applied to leave."

Finally, the church could protect her no longer, and Sr. Jean's letter came saying that she was to be deported. Her name, along with the others, was seen on Guatemalan television. The U.S. embassy could not help protect her because she had not left the first time when all Peace Brigade members were supposed to leave. As soon as she was satisfied that those she had been protecting were in good hands, she left. It was 1985—she had been in Guatemala for one year.

On her return to the United States, she was told that she had been deported from Guatemala for political reasons, but the Guatemalans coming into the United States at the same time as her arrival were seen as fleeing for economic reasons. One's designation as a refugee is important because if a nonresident comes to the United States for economic reasons, they are treated very differently from those who are seeking asylum in the United States for political reasons. As an economic refugee, one is given no resettlement assistance. So, drawing on her earlier exposure to sanctuary, Sr. Jean, in collaboration with a friend, organized an effort to raise money to purchase a house that would serve as a sanctuary for Guatemalans and Salvadorans who made it to St. Louis but who had escaped for political reasons, not economic hardship in their own country. From 1987 until 1994, many Central Americans, politically persecuted in their homeland, found shelter in St. Louis because of Sr. Jean and her friend's efforts. They also obtained legal representation for the refugees and helped them begin the asylum application process. Sometimes they even found jobs for them. Sr. Jean and her colleague also organized the community so that if she or her colleague were arrested, there would be a cadre of people who could be relied on to continue their work. They put together a phone tree so that neighbors would come and surround the safe haven and accompany those inside. Ultimately, the sanctuary consisted of the entire community around the refugee house. The sanctuary house sheltered five individuals and four families, each with five members. For Sr. Jean and her community, keeping the sanctuary was a long-term endeavor because no one left the home until he or she was granted asylum, often not in the United States, but in Canada. In those cases, the refugees were provided assistance to help them get to Canada. Sr. Jean said, "One woman arrived here without her five-year-old daughter. We then learned that an attempt had been made on the little girl's life. So I went to Guatemala, without papers, to try and find the daughter and bring her to the U.S. I found the daughter, but then we had to get her out of there. We traveled by bus because traveling by plane required identification. One day, we were stopped by the military. They got on our bus to conduct a search. Before I left the United States, people who ran the underground helped me get ready and told me to not get separated from the little girl, no matter what, because little kids get sold. Well, I thought, 'If I get arrested on this bus what is going to happen to her?' I was scared. We were sitting in the bus, and the military started at the front and moved towards us in the back. There were some nuns in front of us and they even made them stand up and take off their veils. I am sitting next to this child and I thought, 'It's over; what am I going to do?' But just as they got to us, she broke out in one of those huge nosebleeds and it spurted. I mean it didn't just bleed, it spurted and she threw her hands into the air and she collapsed on to the people behind us. The military took one look at all the blood and the collapsed child and they turned and left the bus never checking the rest of us on the bus for proper identification papers. Her dress was a bloody mess but I saved that dress for years. It was my proof that the child was an angel. As soon as the military left, she was fine. I was so relieved I was almost sick. We brought her to the sanctuary and reunited her with her mom."

She went on, "As I worked with these people I realized that those who had been tortured or seen torture were not resettling. They couldn't sleep at night or hold down a job. One time I came into the house and found a man beating his wife. I said to him, 'This is a house of nonviolence, we don't settle our differences this way.' He turned to me and screamed, 'Violence, you don't know anything about violence; you don't know anything about it.' He pulled up his shirt and his chest was filled with burn marks. He had been taken as a teenager, tortured until he gave them names. The names were just of people he knew. Shortly thereafter, some of these people were found dead at the edge of the road. This was a technique used to control innocent people and this experience completely changed him. He had guilt; he had hatred; he didn't trust anybody. He was an embodiment of the effects of torture. I did not know how to help him. He was raging and we had to ask him to leave the sanctuary house. We got him on the underground to Canada. I felt sorry for Canada! We gave his wife the option to not go with him and she chose to stay and we helped her find another avenue to remain in the United States. She had not been tortured and could not apply for exile as he could."

Of all of Sr. Jean's experiences thus far, it was this experience, with one violent man, that ushered in the realization that the community needed to help these people heal from the severe trauma of torture and repression and to give hope. The political situation in Guatemala had changed, and there was no longer the need to provide sanctuary for those coming into the United States from Central America. However, Sr. Jean saw that many others were coming to St. Louis from other war-torn countries and did not have the help they needed to heal. In 1994, Sr. Jean and her colleagues stopped offering sanctuary but continued to take in refugees from the African countries of Rwanda, Botswana, Nigeria, and the Congo. "Most of these people really suffered terrible times," she said. "One woman saw her children slaughtered. When she was living with us sometimes I thought the foundation of the house would crack with her grief. It was so awful, but we prayed, we talked; we took care of her and did as much healing intervention as we could and knew how to offer. And I began to see that if a person had enough internal resources and was surrounded with active, intentional compassion that she was going to be able to touch that inner strength and begin to heal. One never gets over the loss, but one can start to get their life back."

Sr. Jean began to seek out ways to help those who suffered from torture and trauma. She could find no classes on the subject at the time, nor could she find many articles or books in the professional literature. So Sr. Jean began to use her organizing skills and she listened and talked to people about how people suffering from war could be helped. "Someone told me that if you want to study torture, [you should] study human or childhood abuse, because it is a similar situation, in which an authority or a power causes untenable suffering to a vulnerable person who has no way out. This is how I started studying torture. Now there is a whole lot about post-torture trauma and posttraumatic stress, but not when I started." Sr. Jean even accepted a position at an agency that served child abuse clients so that she could gain more knowledge and experience. She sought out other agencies that were beginning to notice the need for services to the survivors of torture and war trauma. It was at that time that Sr. Jean made a promise to herself that for the rest of her working life she would serve only those who suffered from war torture. She traveled the nation, taking every workshop possible on the topic, and then began to talk about the issue. In talking and sharing her experiences with others, she began to find resources, and the more she talked, the more her dream began to fall into place, to have a center to help those suffering from war to begin to heal.

In 1997, articles of incorporation were filed and the Center for Survivors of War Torture and War Trauma was in business. A nonprofit organization, the center provides mental health services to refugees who suffer from PTSD as a result of torture, war, and/or forced relocation from their homeland. The center offers a wide range of services for adults and children, including individual and group therapy and programs to help refugees both cope with the effects of the violence they encountered in their home countries and help them transition into their new lives in the United States. The center also has an outreach program and training for professionals who serve survivors.

The staff has increased from its original two employees to a current staff of eight in the main office, as well as drivers for those who need them and staff that help with children's programs. The center is presently one of only twenty-one U.S. member agencies of the International Rehabilitation Council for Torture Victims, a Denmark-based worldwide advocacy organization whose mission is to prevent torture worldwide and to promote the rehabilitation of those who have been its victims. Through the center's participation in this organization, as well as by reputation, the center has become a critical resource for those lucky enough to survive torture and terror in their home countries and make their way to the United States.

Recently, the center hired a new administrator, allowing Sr. Jean to return to being a therapist, therapist supervisor, and program developer. She hopes that she will now be able to delve in and look at how specific interventions work with different populations. For each culture, she tries to develop something appropriate for its unique needs. It is remarkable to think that there are so many nationalities represented in her current caseload of fifty-five to sixty (mostly young) adults, whose assessment and treatment may differ markedly. Sr. Jean's decision to offer treatment differently has come from her daily experience in working with the people and in her search for knowledge. She found an article by Wylie (2004), "The Limits of Talk Psychotherapy," which cites a variety of notable scholars who argue that it is not helpful for people who have experienced trauma to sit and talk; rather, they need to be involved in some type of action or movement, because people learn only when they can move and act. So Sr. Jean began to experiment with what type of action or movement might work best, and she found that tai chi and yoga work well for the Bosnian clients. The Afghan clients think that yoga is crazy, so with Afghans, she found art and stories more helpful. Sr. Jean's experience has shown that different cultures store trauma differently; often, the result of torture is to align it with a body part or physical ailment. The survivors cannot find the expressions or put their experience into words, but they do know that a part of them is hurting. Sr. Jean has found that with movement therapies, she can get clients to work on a specific body part, and as that gets better, they begin to talk about it. All survivors need to eventually articulate their experience, but often it is so horrific that one needs to find another way to express it, and movement allows for this outlet. Movement is often the inroad to the healing process.

When war survivors become physically involved in their treatment, they begin to realize that they can take control of themselves again. Talk therapy is relevant for those who have been traumatized, but Sr. Jean agrees with Wylie (2004), who notes that it is more successful when combined with some type of action or physical exercise. Much of the healing occurs when one begins to develop a relationship with one's body, bringing the mind and body together.

Sr. Jean found that one approach to treatment that brings the mind and body together is known as body-oriented therapy. This type of therapy can take several forms, including dance or movement therapy, yoga, and healing-touch therapy. All have been shown to have positive outcomes for individuals suffering from PTSD. The idea is to allow the person to get back in touch with his or her inner self and to begin to heal from the inside out. Dance or movement therapy relies on the flow of dance and movement to relax the muscles and connect a person's spirit and body together as one entity. Sr. Jean draws from an article by Gray (2001) that suggests that movement therapy can help torture survivors rebuild their self-trust and increase relationship capacities. Sr. Jean recommends that any student serious about studying social work practice with traumatized clients should, of course, avail him- or herself of this literature.

Asked to elaborate on how clients are referred to the center and to talk about some of the tasks that require the center's assistance, Sr. Jean said, "People hear about us by word of mouth, or are referred by outreach workers or the legal or health care system." By way of example, she discussed one person with whom she is working right now: "One young man was referred to us by the legal system to help him get ready to present his trauma situation in court. We have been working with him for eight months, but the closer we get to the court date the more anxious and afraid he becomes. His first torture by his government was at [the age of] seventeen. One day here in St. Louis, he was picked up by the police, not because he did anything wrong, but because he didn't have his papers. While in jail, he had such a serious flashback that he could no longer understand English. I will be there for him when he goes to court. He will do all right, if he has a judge with any sense of humanity. This is the work that we are supposed to be doing. It's restorative. They were treated so cruelly, and if we treat them with grace and love we can replace some of that with them. Constant cruelty and torture takes away your strength. It makes you sick, and destroys your ability to remember and think. It leaves you with a sense of mistrust and fear and this blocks one's adjustment. It is our job working with these people to be present, give respect, go that extra mile, care, and not be afraid of their suffering or a flashback. I can't be afraid of their pain."

Sr. Jean says that the best knowledge for social workers in her line of work is to realize that "therapy doesn't just happen in an office. It is learning to use a person's whole sense of well-being and connectedness, which is when healing happens. If a person is upset you can't say, 'Leave that anxiety outside, I'm only going to help you with this.' You need to be considerate of where that person is and have a whole sense of their context so healing can occur. Have a respect for that context." She believes that a social worker needs to be able to sit next to the client rather than just sit as an expert. It is important for the social worker to be able to "help normalize daily life for that person." Social workers need to be strong advocates for people in different aspects of their lives, such as going with them to immigration, to their lawyers, and to their psychiatrist. "Networking is huge; you need many people to help you help them. . . . I would also add that most of the social workers in this line of work are kicking, screaming, and banging on doors for their clients. Sometimes we bend the rules. But we are advocates!"

A particularly universal aspect of the conversation with Sr. Jean turned to the subject of gifts from clients. Many social workers work in agencies in which there are rules against clients giving gifts. The question, then, often arises about what to do when politely declining a gift from a client is culturally inappropriate. Although the center has no such rule, Sr. Jean's handling of such a situation is very appropriate. She said, "Clients are often grateful, and because we do not charge for these services, they want to give us something for the work we have done together. We let that happen but only after we have achieved a goal. We will say, 'Let's see if we can get this far, and then we will celebrate.' I have had some great meals and some weird ones. We talk about this at our staff meetings: if giving a gift is a way for a person to feel that they have equalized the relationship, then we take the gift. We do not embarrass them and turn them down, because, as you have noted, giving gifts is very important in many cultures. You don't start amassing gifts from your clients and you help control it, but you certainly let them have that dignity." Sr. Jean tells the story about a young man she is helping get ready for court. After he finally received his green card, he got a job in a pizza place. One day he called her and was very excited and told her he had a surprise for her. He brought in a pizza and when Sr. Jean opened it up it wasn't just a pizza, it was a *pizza*! He had put everything he could on the pizza, so that it was a mound. She got plates and they shared it together. It was so big they couldn't finish it, but the young man was beaming. When the next client came in, a very thin person, she smelled the leftover pizza. So Sr. Jean got it out again and shared it with her. "It is so good to watch people get better and it is so sweet when you have a client who once said, 'I will never have a life again,' start to have a life again."

Social workers must be vigilant about the impact of secondary trauma, a phenomenon in which caring individuals absorb the trauma through the eyes and ears of the people they are trying to help. It can also be thought of as secondary posttraumatic stress. And given the nature of her work, Sr. Jean has to be especially vigilant: "I have learned that Providence often walks in front of you. But there are some times when I get tired of Providence or I do not see it. When I came back from Nicaragua I had a very poor reentry. I threw myself into my work; there were a lot of talks and presentations to give. I arrived home right after a massacre occurred where a U.S. plane shot into a children's military school. There were children with bullet holes in their head and we were working so hard in our talks to try and bridge communication. I never slowed down and took care of myself. I guess I was depressed, but I felt so separate, so alone. I was looking for a job but could not find one; I just didn't care about anything. I look back now and know I was in a serious depression."

Secondary trauma victims need to care for themselves and acknowledge that they are at risk (Herman, 1997). Weinstein-Moser (2008) found in speaking with social workers that they must practice self-care to work with people who are in seemingly impossible circumstances. Self-care tools that are used include meditation, yoga, daily exercise, walking, music, massage, prayer, retreat attendance, dancing, drumming, laughter, spending time with kindred souls, chanting, and eating healthfully with friends. Sr. Jean encourages all who work with her to practice self-care: "I now care for myself by enjoying dear friends. I think all social workers should exercise this concept. I believe networking with caring human beings and caring for each other is the key. We can either be hostile, catty or destroy each other, or we can really love each other and care for each other."

A Moral Obligation to Hold the Mirror to Ourselves

In the recent debate about the practice of "water boarding" so-called enemy combatants in Guantánamo Bay, the question of what constitutes torture, and who is doing it, took center stage. Although the Bush administration argued in favor of its use to coerce prisoners into revealing future attacks, a majority of Americans believe that it constitutes torture, marking a disturbing breach in the moral and legal framework on which this country was built. This, too, is a central concern of Sr. Jean's: "One of the things we aren't tackling but [that] we need to tackle is the torture that goes on in our own prisons. Isolation for five years, except for an hour a day—that is torture. It destroys the human being. . . . We become so tolerant of things that really are so destructive. . . . The fact is the outrage and the horror at what we are making commonplace and acceptable—it is so great that if I couldn't be working with [victims of torture], I would go nuts." Sr. Jean notes that there are 189 books on torture in prisons and 89 percent of the prisons in question are U.S. prisons. She says that she asks herself and others daily, if the United States defines torture in other countries, is it willing to apply that definition to its own prisons? She strongly believes that the United States needs be accountable for the torture procedures that it uses. Sr. Jean freely depicts the horror of torture and the lasting effects it has on the people she works with, and she speaks out on it. Ultimately, though, she believes her work continues to be with the survivors at the center. She still calls for the United States to use the *U.S. Military Training Manual*, which says that torture is not an effective means of getting the truth. She would like to see this manual used in all states and to have people be able to define what harsh treatment is and what torture is.

Conclusion

Sr. Jean measures the center's achievement qualitatively by the stories and the small personal successes she sees each and every day, such as someone being able to live through a July 4 fireworks display without having flashbacks, or having them, but of a shorter duration, and the client knows they are coming on and how to handle them. Or when people can articulate the torture that happened to them and then use their experience to help another person who has been through something similar. She believes that evil cannot win and that there is no greater act of protest to violence than to work with and for the survivor. Sr. Jean wants to get people to the point at which they are not ruled by the experience of torture but can live with it; she sees that as strength.

Asked about her future, Sr. Jean shared that she would love to see the center with all kinds of services, housed in a lovely, safe building, but she stops and says, "That is not really my dream, for here we are with a house and a tavern and both these buildings house the center's offices, my home and a community of people who are offering all kinds of services." Since hiring the center's executive director, Sr. Jean is not making the daily decisions, and the center has a working board and a board of community advisers (who are clients or former clients). With these additions, Sr. Jean is moving away from the decision-making apparatus for the center. This, she says, is her dream for the future of the center and those it serves. Sr. Jean believes the greatest thing a social worker can do is to work him- or herself out of a job; she has surrounded herself and the center with talented, creative people and she wants the center to continue and to be able to "keep its soul."

Sr. Jean has learned important skills and knowledge as she has practiced social work throughout her variety of experiences, but it is her ability to live the symmetry between her strong faith and the profession's highly articulated code of ethics that placed her on this life path of service. In the end, we think she would just call it Providence.

References

Gray, E. (2001, March). The body remembers: Dance/movement therapy with an adult survivor of torture. *American Journal of Dance Therapy, 23*(1), 29–43.

Herman, J. L. (1997). *Trauma and recovery* (rev. ed.). New York: Basic Books.

U.S. Committee for Refugees and Immigrants. (2007). *World Refugee Survey 2007.* Washington, DC: Author.

Weinstein-Moser, E. (2008, March–April). Spirituality in social work: The journey from fringe to mainstream. *Social Work Today, 8*(2), 32.

World Health Organization. (2002). Collective violence: Fact sheet. Retrieved March 30, 2008, from http://www.who.int/violence_injury_prevention/violence/world_report/fact sheets/en/collectiveviolfacts.pdf.

Wylie, M. S. (2004, January–February). The limits of talk psychotherapy. *Psychotherapy Networker, 28,* 130–141.

PART III

Bringing Social Work to the Rest of the World

The women profiled in this section laid the foundation for social work and social work education worldwide. At nearly one hundred years old, Katherine Kendall, it could be said, has occupied a front-row seat in the development of our profession. But that would imply that she has been a passive observer, which, to anyone who knows her, is laughable. In fact, social work education worldwide exists today as a viable profession largely because of her efforts, a fact to which both Dr. Armaity Desai (chapter 14) and Sattareh Farman Farmaian (chapter 15) would attest.

These women are rather unique in that they are all professionally related: both Sattareh Farman Farmaian and Dr. Armaity Desai credit Katherine A. Kendall for support and assistance when they were developing their programs.

About Katherine Kendall much has been written. But the Council on Social Work Education's executive director, Julia Watkins, has written a warm and affectionate portrait of her predecessor that has taken her remarkable history and made it fresh.

The same could be said for Mahasweta Banerjee's profile of her mentor, Armaity Desai. Although Dr. Desai was modest about her accomplishments as a social work education pioneer in India, Banerjee asked the important questions, whose answers enable us to see how different social work can look to those of us in the West and yet still be social work.

Sattareh Farman Farmaian lives a quiet life today on a tree-lined street in Los Angeles. If you saw her on the street, on the way to the classes she still takes, you would never guess that she has lived one of the most remarkable lives, a life that includes birth into a royal family (and all the privileges implied therein), an incredible voyage halfway around the world as a young girl all alone, and after a lifetime devoted to the establishment of the Tehran School of Social Work, an appointment with death (obviously thwarted!). Her story perhaps best exemplifies the difficulties of truly carrying out the mandate of social work—empowerment, self-determination, and freedom—in non-Western countries.

As you read about these women, think about your own social work education. We think you will come to a greater appreciation of what it means to be a social worker.

CHAPTER THIRTEEN

Katherine A. Kendall

The Founder of International Social Work

Julia Watkins

It is fair to say that international social work would not be what it is, or where it is today, without Katherine Kendall's tireless efforts to expand its reach. Born in Scotland during the Progressive Era (and the halcyon days of Hull House!) and undoubtedly influenced by limitations society placed on her as a woman, Katherine fit well in a profession whose core principles include self-determination and the according of respect and dignity to all. An example of Katherine's worldwide influence on social work is found in the fact that two other women in this book—Armaity Desai and Sattareh Farman Farmaian—cite her as a most valuable source of consultation and support in attaining their professional goals in their respective countries.

I had the pleasure of interviewing Katherine over two visits to her apartment in the Washington, D.C., area. Her memory is sharp, and the stories were fascinating.

Introduction

The year was 1950. The accomplishment was the passage of a resolution by the United Nations Social Commission that declared social work a professional function requiring professional preparation in universities or equally qualified educational institutions (United Nations, 1950b). The same commission then asked for continuing study of social work training. During the subsequent decade, five reports were produced addressing the matter.

The prominent placement of social work on the agenda of the United Nations—an organization devoted to worldwide peace, social justice, human rights, and economic development—reflects great internal logic. After all, what profession, other than social work, is better positioned in our global configuration to address and further such noble aims and purposes and to do so from an action-oriented and value-based agenda?

This focused attention on the profession of social work had a political dimension as well, one that continues to this day: challenges to the legitimacy of the profession in many parts of the world are ongoing and rise to the top of the agendas of government and nongovernmental organizations (NGOs) across the globe. But behind these agendas, actions, and aspirations are individual social workers. And whether or not they know it, these social workers are the professional descendents of one in particular—a social worker whose heart, mind, and soul have inspired, challenged, and honored those with whom she comes in contact. She is the focus of this chapter, because it was she who laid the important groundwork for the passage of that UN resolution in 1950 that contributed to the subsequent growth of the profession worldwide. Katherine A. Kendall is to be treasured as an individual and esteemed as a social worker whose life and actions mirror the very best of our profession, our aspirations, our pride in the past, and our hope for the future. The depth and breadth of her influence and her life, spanning almost a century, is nothing short of breathtaking.

Significant lifetime experiences and accomplishments have rendered Katherine Kendall an iconic figure in contemporary and worldwide developments in the profession of social work. Only a few social workers have been accorded more public written and visual space in the past two decades than she has. This chapter, then, brings to readers the thoughts, life themes, and aspirations of a woman of significant contribution and influence, with more than sixty years of professional life and ninety-nine years of profound engagement in life.

In our two structured interviews, and during numerous informal moments as Katherine and I traveled and attended meetings and social events together over the past five years, I have been constantly struck by her intelligence, energized by her creativity, humbled by her modesty, and always impressed by her attribution of credit to others for professional successes when it was she who clearly contributed the fundamental keys for success and change. It is the discovery of these characteristics—and the intellectual and personal pleasure of seeing them develop as life themes marking Katherine as an intellectual, an internationalist, and an activist for change in the contemporary world—that elicits idealism and reinforces aspirations.

The Beginnings

Katherine Anne Tuach Kendall was born September 8, 1910, in Muir of Ord, Ross-Shire, Scotland. She was the third child and only girl in a family of four children. Katherine describes her childhood as happy and memorable. Of the home in which she grew up, she says, "The cottage in which I was born is one of those that you see in fairy tales—a stone cottage, covered with roses, no indoor plumbing, no interior heating except for one huge fireplace in the kitchen, where we spent most of our time." Katherine goes on to describe warming the bed with stone hot-water bottles, water that was pumped into the kitchen, and baths on Saturday nights with water that had been heated in the large kitchen fireplace.

Her memories of her childhood are as vivid today as they have ever been. But as Katherine reflects on those early beginnings and considers her longevity, she notes the luck of good genes: her grandparents lived into their late nineties, her mother lived to be ninety-five. Her father died at a younger age, suffering for many years from a gunshot wound to his leg that he sustained in World War I. Of her own ninety-nine years, Katherine says, "I came by this old age, as a Scot, because actually, life there is hard. And you have to be hardy in order to survive it. And if you're hardy enough to survive it, you'll probably live a long time. I have good, strong, hardy genes."

Katherine Kendall's biography was presented in detail in *Global Leaders for Social Work Education: The IASSW Presidents, 1928–2008* (Healy, 2008). In that book, a great deal is written about the events shaping Katherine's early life—the immigration of her father first to Canada in 1913 and then to Chicago after World War I, where he was joined by the family in 1920, and the later return of her parents to Scotland during the Great Depression of the 1930s. Healy (2008) also captures Katherine's sense of humor about who she was as a child: she remembers "having her head in a book" and was "something of a nerd" (p. 214)—to hear a ninety-nine-year-old woman use contemporary slang the way Katherine does attests to her continuous, deep engagement in the modern world! Always important, however, was Katherine's sense that she was going to do something important in her life, and that her own intelligent mother's thwarted ambitions were to play out in her children, especially her "little girl." The *Anne* in Katherine's name is her mother's name.

Katherine knew it was expected that she would excel in school. She expected to be president of the class in high school, and she was; she expected to be editor of the school paper, and she was. She recalls that once she did not get an editorship because she was a woman. Instead, she was offered the "consolation prize"—editor of the women's section of the paper—which she declined. Katherine says of herself that she never really felt like a feminist but that she has always acted as one. Seldom did she experience overt discrimination because she was a woman. The pattern of her life, as she describes it, played out in this way: opportunities presented themselves, challenges were enticements to action, and an absolute commitment to social justice and a prevailing self-confidence to make a difference were essential elements of her life accomplishments.

Although Katherine describes herself as an outstanding student, she understood very well that she needed to have a formal university education. After working in a factory for a year and saving some money, she entered the University of Illinois. Her field of study was humanities. She was elected to Phi Beta Kappa in her junior year, and she received her bachelor's degree in liberal arts in 1933. Her aspiration was to become a foreign correspondent.

During her undergraduate years, Katherine met the man who would become her husband, Willmoore Kendall. She describes him as a child prodigy, and though only one year older than she was, he was already working on his doctorate. In Katherine's words, he was "extremely intelligent, brilliant." He was also her Spanish teacher. Katherine and Willmoore, known as Ken, became engaged following her graduation. She left for London, where she lived for a short time with an uncle, found a job, and married Ken Kendall, who was already at Oxford as a Rhodes Scholar.

Katherine describes this time as one "of the awakening of a strong social conscience and a time of searching for a professional role" (Healy, 2008, p. 216). In another interview (Billups, 2002), Katherine describes the contact with social movements in Oxford as coloring her "pink" (p. 146) (in this context, the color pink is a reference to the term *pinko*, another word for *communist* that is often used derogatorily). More important, perhaps, than this descriptor was the growing intensity of Katherine's commitment to do something important. In her own view, that translated into addressing the ills of society—the social injustices that she had become aware of through her reading and her developing circle of friends at Oxford.

It was not just the contact with Oxford leftists, however, that galvanized her intense emotional commitment to social justice. It was also a result of experiences she had that first year in London as a waitress and management trainee in a restaurant. The lack of respect shown to employees and the pitifully low salaries prompted Katherine to take on the cause of unionizing the kitchen staff. This brought a quick end to her management career—at least the management of restaurants.

In 1935, Katherine and Ken moved to Madrid, Spain, where he served as a foreign correspondent with United Press. This sojourn in Madrid before the Spanish Civil War was, as Katherine describes, "a very exciting period there. We were involved in the Popular Front Movement that, in our view, was moving the country in the right direction. We were quite ideological, except that I was less so than my husband. I was in the middle, left of center, sometimes more left than other times, but never, never over the edge of communism." When it appeared that elections in Spain were a victory for democracy, Ken made the decision to leave, return to a teaching assistantship, and complete his doctoral studies. But their time in Spain was very eventful.

In what seemed a very traditional way, Katherine followed her husband, or as she says, tagged along, first to England and then Spain. Yet she always found interests and made achievements of her own accord, and it was always understood in her marriage that she, too, would have a career. This aspiration was to develop more fully after the Kendalls returned from Spain to the United States. In Madrid, Katherine's plans to attend university courses were derailed because of problems in scheduling. In looking around for something to do beyond tourism and wifely responsibilities, she found that fashionable women in Spain went to millinery and dressmaking establishments to get exact copies of the latest hats and fashions, as seen in *Vogue*. Being very fond of hats, she persuaded the management of a millinery shop to take her on as an apprentice. At first, because of her rudimentary sewing skills, she was the laughingstock of her fellow apprentices, most of whom were young girls with little education and no prospects for more. However, her command of Spanish saved the day as she talked with the girls, elicited the stories of how they lived, and visited several in their homes. From them, she learned not only how to sew but also valuable lessons about poverty and the constricted lives of women there. Soon, her interest in hat making waned and she took up cooking, which became a lifelong hobby.

The multiple layers of strength and achievement kept emerging as Katherine shared her life story. She and her husband belonged to a swimming club, and the story unfolds that Katherine was very good on the diving board. Spanish women were not divers, and Katherine was persuaded to enter a national championship swim meet. Reluctantly, she agreed, and with her swan dive she brought victory to her team. For that brief moment, she was high-diving female champion of Spain. And with typical self-effacing modesty, Katherine says, "It was not a record I should brag about because I didn't earn it. It was a fluke, but it was fun." It also reinforced Katherine's view that women could compete in this larger world, even though in Spain, as in most other domains in the 1930s, that was not the case.

During her rather brief sojourn in Spain, Katherine recalls that her commitment to a professional career continued. Knowing, however, that she and her husband would be in Spain for a limited time, she was motivated to simply experience life, and not to pursue her career aspirations.

The Professional Self

Leaving Spain to return with her husband to the University of Illinois in 1938 seemed the right thing to do. Katherine once again followed Ken, who had accepted a graduate assistantship as he worked on his Ph.D. in political science. Katherine, in turn, still wanted to do something in the sphere of social justice. But to supplement Ken's assistantship, she worked for a local newspaper and tutored female students in a sorority. Mostly, she recalls, "I made them study. One of the problems was they never studied." Here again, Katherine's career aspirations were more or less put on hold, but she did influence younger women by exhorting them to study more!

Katherine and Ken left Illinois to follow one of his professors to Louisiana State University at a time of institutional growth for that institution, including recruitment of high-profile faculty from other institutions. Rather serendipitously, Katherine discovered a direction that would build on her intellect, her creativity, and give shape to her motivation to make a difference.

On the suggestion of her husband after his first day at the office, she looked into what he had described in the following way: "You know they have something here called social work. It sounds like what you're interested in. Why don't you look into it?"

She did and decided, "Yes, this is what I'm looking for because its main focus is on public welfare." She was admitted to the new social work program at Louisiana State and was its first graduate. As she describes, "Later, when I was responsible for accreditation and curriculum consultation, I teased them about letting me in, with no questions about my personality and no psychiatric evaluation of my motivation.

Nothing. They just admitted me on the spot and I learned later that I was the only student without a scholarship from the newly established Department of Social Welfare, staffed largely by experienced social workers from the North."

"In the beginning, my insistence on the need for social reform was something of a pain to the faculty. In fact, they even had a faculty meeting wondering what to do about me. Fieldwork changed my one-sided view. I soon recognized that help with personal problems was just as important as changing social conditions and ended up convinced that social work must be involved with both."

After one year of class and fieldwork and a second year of highly individualized tutorials and fieldwork, Katherine received a master of arts degree and then began working as the first trained social worker in the Baton Rouge welfare office. The Louisiana Department of Social Welfare wanted to demonstrate that individuals could become productive and independent if they received the services of a qualified social worker—in this case, Katherine. Again, from fieldwork, her first job, and others that followed, Katherine recalls successful cases in which personal help combined with resources led to independence. Those experiences solidified in Katherine's mind the importance of both individual and social change and the strength of the interaction between them.

Katherine knew that social work qualifications mattered. She methodically reviewed her caseload and applied her classroom and field learning to help her clients (about twenty-five) to success in their own life aspirations.

As her husband prepared to return to Illinois to complete his doctorate, and at the urging of one of her supervisors in Baton Rouge who was a graduate of the School of Social Service Administration at the University of Chicago, Katherine returned to Chicago and entered the doctoral program. The supervisor had emphasized the importance of Katherine studying with luminaries such as Edith Abbott, Sophonisba Breckinridge, and Charlotte Towle. At the same time, her husband completed his doctorate and became a professor at Hobart College in upstate New York.

Katherine says, "It took me years to get my Ph.D. Of course, I was always in and out of the program to follow interesting employment opportunities. I had completed a great deal of the class work, but there was still the dissertation to complete." But during this time of separation and sporadic trips between Chicago and upstate New York, Katherine's marriage began to unravel. Ultimately, it ended in divorce in 1950, but Katherine's friendship with Ken remained. Katherine received her Ph.D. from the University of Chicago in 1950.

Her career gained momentum as Katherine assumed increasingly complex and important work. Interspersed between semesters of Ph.D.

studies, Katherine became the assistant director of the international unit at the U.S. Children's Bureau (1945), social affairs officer at the United Nations (1947), executive secretary of the American Association of Schools of Social Work (1950) and, following the launch of the Council on Social Work Education [CSWE] in 1952, she served in the capacities of educational secretary, associate director, executive director, and director of international education. Katherine authored a definitive history of the Council on Social Work Education (Kendall, 2002). Who better for the task than one who has lived our professional history the way she has? And finally, she served in several roles with the International Association of Schools of Social Work (IASSW). Most notable were seventeen years as volunteer honorary secretary followed by seven years as full-time secretary-general of IASSW, which is based in New York City. She officially retired in 1978 (Billups, 2002).

The Personal Self

The early childhood years and adolescence, the high educational expectations, and the interpersonal relationships with a spouse and friends from a global network all have shaped Katherine Kendall. And no doubt, there is reciprocity in that influence. Those most significant have been described. There is one set of relationships, however, that may not usually emerge in a chapter that seeks to understand the essence of a life and career. In the case of Katherine Kendall, these are sustaining to this day—her extended family of nieces and nephews and her godchildren.

Her nieces and nephews and now her grandnieces and grandnephews are part of Katherine's extended family—as are her godchildren. A tragic accident took the lives of her very dearest friends from the days at Hobart College and later Chicago. Although the clear intent was that Katherine would be the guardian of their children, the absence of a written will to that effect resulted in the children being raised by their maternal aunt. Katherine, however, has maintained strong and wonderfully warm and enduring relationships with these children, now adults and grandparents themselves; they remain active participants in her life.

Also, Katherine and her mother, Anne, were incredibly close for all the years of her mother's life. In fact, Katherine persuaded Anne to return to the United States and live with her in New York City, which Anne did for a decade until her death at the age of ninety-five. Katherine describes the influence of her mother in part as one model of the immigrant experience: "Well, actually what happened is something that I've often wondered about myself. When she came to this country, it was disconcerting, I suppose. Everything was so different. She didn't seem to feel any real control of her being in this new environment. I mean the kind of control one develops by studying a new setting and understanding how one should operate in it. And the same was true for me. I was very much on my own in many ways [when I came to this country]."

"She was a wonderful seamstress," Katherine says of her mother. "She made all of my clothes. I was one of the best-dressed people at the university, although we had no money. Beautiful clothes. See, that's what she did. She dressed me; sent me off into the world as best she could, and that was it. But what I did in the world, I don't think she ever understood."

Professional Contributions and Impact

Assessing the professional contributions of social workers is a task of great importance and one with which we often struggle, because clarity often does not emerge until a significant period has elapsed. However, Katherine's impact on the social work profession is both clear and profound. In particular, Katherine notes four projects as her greatest accomplishments in a life of many.

The UN SURVEY AND RESOLUTION

According to Katherine, "It was my work with the United Nations that made it possible for me to have all those wonderful experiences later. It immersed me in social work education around the world and put me on the track for the rest of my professional life" (Billups, 2002, p. 153). Katherine had pioneered the groundbreaking UN survey of training for social work that was published in 1950 under the title *Training for Social Work: An International Survey* (United Nations, 1950a). This led to the internationalization of social work and to a decade of seminars, expert work groups, scholarships, and faculty exchange programs funded by the United Nations and UNICEF, as well as by other international organizations and national governments. The involvement of the UN Social Commission in the survey—receiving and reviewing comments from governments after the survey had circulated—was instrumental in the passage of the resolution cited earlier. In Katherine's words, "It was a tremendous relief and honor to have the commission pass the resolution declaring that social work was a professional function requiring professional preparation." Recounting later her involvement in the UN survey, Katherine describes herself as the author, developer, and implementer of the project—she did everything from conceptualize the ideas to type up the report. She knew the members of the commission and understood their interest in the report and their positive disposition toward its findings.

Today there are international associations and nations that struggle with attacks on the legitimacy of social work as a profession. This is particularly true in many developing nations. But the UN resolution stands as the watershed in the profession's ability to engage around the world. And it is the work of Katherine Kendall that is referenced and acknowledged as the definitive recognition of the profession, superseding contemporary assertions of various regulatory and educational bodies (United Nations, 1950b).

THE PARAGUAY MISSION

A second significant project in Katherine's view was a short-term consultation on social work education performed at the invitation of the U.S. government for the government of Paraguay. Only later did Katherine learn that her assignment was meant to prevent Eva Perón (the popular and powerful first lady of Argentina from 1946 until her death in 1952) from carrying out her offer to arrange for Argentine assistance and oversight of the Paraguayan efforts to establish social welfare services and training.

Whatever was defined and available as social welfare in Paraguay was located at that time in the Ministry of Public Health. Social workers and midwives shared training facilities. Katherine described the experience as one of the most challenging of her expertise, as the advanced education given in American schools of social work was obviously somewhat removed from the Paraguayan reality, which lacked anything resembling good, progressive social legislation.

Katherine explained how she organized the consultation as an interactive seminar attended by a leadership group from the school and all existing agency programs: "First, we identified the major fields of service for social workers and then, from papers prepared by the Paraguayans and myself, we discussed, in fluent Spanish, their programs and problems and looked at what from American experience might be useful for them. A major problem that emerged early in the seminar was the lack of any guidance or financial support from the Ministry of Health. Fortunately, the minister had similar questions and became involved in the consultation with happy results."

It was the minister's enthusiasm that convinced the Paraguayan legislative body to authorize an expansion of the work of the Ministry of Health and a change of name to the Ministry of Public Health and Social Welfare, signaling a move toward progressive social welfare policy at the national level.

In a letter dated December 1954, the minister of public health and social welfare wrote to Katherine, "You and I have obtained a triumph on December 2 just past on Pan American Health Day. The Ministry of Public Health has changed its name to the Ministry of Public Health and Social Welfare. This should be a cause of satisfaction for you and for me, especially for you since it marks one more achievement in your work as a social worker." He went on to describe the significant internal organizational changes within the ministry and requested Katherine's assistance in further defining its functions. The letter closed, "You can understand that at this moment we need your valuable advice more than ever" (Zacaroas Arza, 1954, p. 1). Katherine not only was made an honorary midwife and social worker but also recalls dancing the polka with the minister.

Katherine's work was social action at its very best—effecting dramatic change in government structures. And it only intensified her interest in the international arena.

THE FAMILY PLANNING PROJECT

The Family Planning Project was a five-year project with a one-year extension (1971–1977) carried out with funding to IASSW from the U.S. Agency for International Development. Katherine describes it as an initiative designed to demonstrate the value of social work in the promotion and acceptance of family planning, or more directly, "to develop qualified personnel for population and family planning work in developing countries" (Healy 2008, p. 226). The project promoted an approach that connected family planning with social development and respected indigenous, culturally specific curriculum development and more effective work with other disciplines, including medicine. More than thirty schools participated with pilot programs, but the real impact was demonstrated through the more than one hundred seminars and other project activities that involved most schools of social work in Asia and some in eastern and western Africa and the Middle East. The disappointment was in Latin America, where the project was ideologically interpreted as an attack on indigenous populations.

Describing herself as the "mother of the project," Katherine secured the funding, developed and implemented the project, and participated in many of the seminars around the world. The significance of this project is not to be underestimated; it was pioneering in its integration of social work and social development and in the manner in which it accounted for the culturally specific needs of populations. More important, particularly in today's globalized world, social work educators respect the cultural specifics of a context and use their skills to help their colleagues and students determine and use interventions that promote the culture, values, and strengths of differing contextual settings. Katherine understood this imperative very well and speaks eloquently to its inclusion in social workers' thinking about international social work education and practice. This understanding forms the basis of the Katherine A. Kendall Institute for International Social Work Education, which the Council on Social Work Education created in 2005 from an endowment fund whose primary contributor was Katherine A. Kendall (see http://www.cswe.org/CSWE/centers/kendall/).

THE INTERNATIONAL ASSOCIATION OF SCHOOLS OF SOCIAL WORK (IASSW)

Without doubt, the signature and most important professional accomplishment in the life of Katherine Kendall has been her leadership in reestablishing the strength, vitality, and global prominence of the IASSW.

Following the publication of the UN Survey of Social Work Education in 1950, Katherine was invited to give the keynote address at the 1950 congress of the then International Committee of Schools of Social Work (ICSSW) held in Paris. This congress signaled the rebirth of the organization after World War II. Hopes were high for the future of the organization and for the world. As Katherine would later note, the pioneers were old and exhausted by the suffering and dislocations of the war. Following her presentation and in recognition of her leadership potential, Katherine was asked to become a member of the board of directors. In 1954, she was elected secretary of this all-volunteer organization and served in that position until 1966, when she was named secretary-general—a part-time position held simultaneously with her major responsibilities at CSWE.

Katherine recalls that the executive director of CSWE, Ernest Witte, was also an internationalist. He made it very clear that Katherine could do her work with IASSW but that it had to be on her money and her time. That meant that she spent weekends and all of her summer vacation working for IASSW—a great pleasure for her.

Her leadership in CSWE provided a strong base for her work with IASSW, and in 1966, she left the position of executive director of CSWE and became its director of international education so that she could be more active in IASSW. She became IASSW's full-time secretary-general in 1971, serving until her retirement in 1978.

Working globally and in concert with her many friends and colleagues, Katherine brought a diverse group of nations to participate in IASSW. She also established a scholarly journal, carried out the Family Planning Project, and in short, extended the global recognition, reach, and impact of the social work profession.

Of her service to CSWE, it has been written:

> During those years she worked throughout the United
> States with schools of social work, social agencies, public
> authorities, and foundations; no one then had more standing
> or knew more about social work education. All who worked
> with her attest to her executive ability, her sense of key
> issues, her professional acumen, and her unfailing verve and
> spirit during those years of ferment and of change in national
> curriculum policy. She worked fast and furiously, writing
> speeches, memoranda, and letters in the office, on planes, or
> at any time and place when she had an odd moment to
> spare. She never lost sight of the goal of excellence in social
> work education and the importance of opening up curricula
> to new intellectual and practice currents. She could keep
> many different balls in the air at once, yet in all these admin-
> istrative preoccupations she was always available to col-
> leagues and friends, always ready for a good time. (Kendall,
> 1978, p. iv)

Throughout these projects, the identification of Katherine
A. Kendall as a true internationalist was solidified.

Vision of the Future

Does an icon ever lose her hope and enthusiasm, even her idealism,
about social work's ability to change the human condition and secure
a world future that embraces difference and stimulates the advancement of human rights globally? Katherine notes often that she was
always an idealist, but today she sees the future of social work as very
difficult. The growing encroachment of other helping professions, the
complexity of social and economic issues, the bureaucratization of systems of change, and the scarcity of resources—including the growing
scarcity of food and energy—place societies worldwide in peril. In contrast, advances in science and technology and the resilience of the
human spirit may prevail, as social workers continue on their journey
to create a just and equitable world order.

Katherine Kendall has not lost her optimism, but she does recognize
with some dismay the difficulties posed by differences in time and
space and the continuing daily struggles to maintain global peace and
the social development of nations and peoples. Continued vigilance
and engagement by social work is a prerequisite to ensuring global
human rights and human progress. For Katherine, the key ingredient is
one of education; from an understanding of her biography, this is not

surprising. She has always promoted education as the cornerstone to a more humane and just society. And the one transcending element in education is a global perspective—one in which geopolitical boundaries are permeable rather than obstructive to our desires to be part of something larger than ourselves and in which myopic vision and rigidity of intellect have no place.

The Advantages of Longevity

Most individuals reflect at one time or another on how long they may live, what contributions they may be recognized for, what differences they may have made in the lives of others—spouse, children, friends, colleagues, neighbors. They also ask those searching questions about what allowed them to do what they have done or, at times, failed at what they have attempted to do. The response configuration is probably as unique as is each individual, even in the same cultural or geographic context.

For Katherine Kendall, the themes that have evolved, strengthened, and persisted over more than ten decades of life are wonderfully strong, clear, and consistent, suggesting a life of fullness and satisfaction. The fundamentals of success as she describes her lifetime of accomplishments are hard work, a bit of luck, motivation and aspiration, self-expectation, and the connections and ability to work with others—and she adds that a sense of humor also helps. A conclusion that a biographer suggested is that here is a woman who absolutely and persistently discovered opportunity in any situation, exploited it for the ultimate good of society and a cause to which she dedicated her life's work, and enjoyed to the limit the intellectual and personal challenges inherent in making a difference.

The Future

There has been no retirement for Katherine Kendall. With vision and hearing difficulties, she maintains an active life of engagement in CSWE, her retirement community, and connections with lifelong and new friends and colleagues around the world. It was only three years ago, at the age of ninety-five, that she stopped riding the Washington, D.C., Metrorail (with a transfer) to come to the CSWE office. She logs on to her computer on a daily basis to write and follow her e-mail. When Katherine talks about age, it is with a sense of the inevitable, but she is now planning how she will celebrate one hundred years!

References

Billups, J. O. (Ed.). (2002). *Faithful angels: Portraits of international social work notables*. Washington, DC: National Association of Social Workers Press.

Healy, L. (2008). Katherine A. Kendall, since 1978. In F. W. Seibel (Ed.), *Global leaders for social work education: The IASSW presidents, 1928–2008* (pp. 211–238). Boskovice, Czech Republic: Verlag Albert.

Kendall, K. A. (1978). *Reflections on social work education, 1950–1978: Collection of articles by Katherine A. Kendall*. New York: International Association of Schools of Social Work.

Kendall, K. A. (2002). *Council on Social Work Education: Its antecedents and first twenty years*. Alexandria, VA: Council on Social Work Education.

United Nations. (1950a). *Training for social work: An international survey*. Lake Success, NY: Author.

United Nations. (1950b) Social commission report. (ECOSOC Official Records, 13th sess., suppl. 12, 3). Lake Success, NY: Author.

Zacaroas Arza, E. (1954). Letter to Dr. Katherine Kendall. *Social Work Education*, 2(6), 1.

CHAPTER FOURTEEN

Professor Armaity Desai

Interpreting Social Work in a Developing Country

Mahasweta Banerjee

I am honored to be able to write about a person I loved and admired in the initial years of my professional life. Dr. Armaity Desai has been a role model, mentor, and someone I have known since 1984. At that time, I was catapulted, through a set of unforeseen circumstances, into the positions of acting principal of the Calcutta School of Social Work and deputy director of the Jaya Prakash Institute of Social Change. I had yet to go back to school for my doctorate, and it was Dr. Desai who helped me to see the necessity of this move.

Initially, Dr. Desai was hesitant to be interviewed, although there is professional literature about her contributions in both the United States and in India (Billups, 2002; Desai, Pimple & Jaswal, 2000; Wadia, 2007). I was able to persuade her—happily. Because I was in India as a Fulbright Scholar during the 2007–2008 academic year, I was able to speak with Dr. Desai by phone; I was based in Kolkata (formerly Calcutta); she lives in Mumbai (formerly Bombay). The conversation was a full-circle experience in many ways. It was also stimulating and (for me) very joyous.

Dr. Desai's considerable contributions to social work education and practice span more than fifty years. She started her career in 1957, as lecturer at the College of Social Work, affiliated with the then University of Bombay, and later became vice principal and then principal there. From 1982 to 1995, she functioned as the director (equivalent to the chancellor of a U.S. university) of the Tata Institute of Social Sciences—the first and most prestigious social work educational institution in India. Although she worked primarily as an educator and an administrator, she was simultaneously involved with initiating numerous innovative field activities to address Indian social problems.

Growing Up in Bombay

Armaity Desai was born in Bombay, India, on April 28, 1934. She and a younger brother are the children of Sapur F. Desai and Tehmina S. Desai, a Parsi couple. The Parsis arrived in India 1,300 years ago from Persia (Iran) to overcome religious persecution. The Parsis are Zoroastrians by religion. In the ancient Avesta, the Zoroastrian religious text, Armaity is one of the feminine aspects of God, symbolizing purity and representing the earth. Dr. Desai says, "That is why I am so earthy—pragmatic!" Dr. Desai is very cosmopolitan. She says, "I don't look like a Parsi, as I don't dress typically like one in Western clothes or the types of saris generally preferred by them! I am an Indian. Wherever I go, people mistake me for some state or the other. They don't equate me with any one place."

Her father was the joint secretary of an organization called the Parsi Punchayet Funds and Properties. This three-hundred-year-old trust, with headquarters in Mumbai, provides welfare services "from womb to tomb" for disadvantaged members of the Parsi community. He directed the activities of the organization, adapted its programs to suit the times, and professionalized its methods of service delivery. Her mother also grew up in Bombay and, after earning a bachelor's degree, worked as a schoolteacher and subsequently as the principal of a girls' school in her father's hometown, Navsari, in Gujarat, where she was known for her innovative style. Her parents met in Navsari and lived in Bombay following their marriage. When Armaity's mother left full-time teaching, she volunteered as a social worker. She developed a day-care center for the organization Armaity's father worked for when nothing comparable existed in the city. Later, she was involved in many other activities, such as establishing a child guidance clinic and participating in several committees tied to children's welfare for the Maharashtra State Women's Council. She was also an active member of the Women Graduates' Union. Thus, Armaity Desai's exposure to social work, and to the unrelenting problems associated with poverty, began early in her life.

Her parents were involved in India's freedom movement, much to the distaste of some Parsis who were supporting British rule in India. When Mohandas K. (Mahatma) Gandhi undertook his famous salt march, Armaity's mother was one of those who welcomed him to Navsari en route to Dandi—the final destination (for more information about the salt march, see http://www.dadalos.org/int/Vorbilder/vorbilder/gandhi/salzmarsch.htm). With pride in her mother's varied accomplishments, Dr. Desai recalls that her mother sat next to Gandhi on a stage in a public meeting. Following Gandhi's recommendations, she also spun the *charkha* (spinning wheel) to make thread for handloom material that she wore. Many years later, as a volunteer in the children's organization Balkanji Bari, she mounted an exhibition of that work that the first prime minister of India, Jawaharlal Nehru, inaugurated, and she met him personally. Without hesitation, Dr. Desai says, "As a woman what I am today is because of my mother. It was easy for me. My mother went through a lot of struggles in a patriarchal culture to be able to do what she did in her time. It was her struggle and not my struggle that made me who I am today."

Dr. Desai has one brother, who has had an outstanding academic career, a graduate of Oxford University in politics, philosophy, and economics. He worked for the well-known Tata company and pioneered for it the manufacture of quality Indian watches—Titan—that captured the Indian market and for Tanishq, which manufactures quality jewelry. Now retired, he is developing a model school for the employees of Tata factories and working to provide them with housing ownership. Also he is interested in urban planning; he is on the governing board of the National Institute of Advanced Studies, funded by the Tatas; and he is the chair of the city's Oxford and Cambridge Society. He lives in Bangalore, the information technology capital of India.

Studying in India

Dr. Desai's parents chose a private Protestant missionary school for her in Bombay. Her schooling brought forth two major advantages: she learned to speak and write in English, and she developed an orientation toward service, as the school's motto was "Others." Growing up in a social service–oriented family and school, it is no surprise that, after completing high school, she confidently declared, "I know what I want.

I want to be a social worker." Dr. Desai says that it is her home upbringing that taught her to communicate openly, to think for herself, and to
argue her own point of view. She acknowledges that her home was different from other Indian homes, where children were expected to be
seen but not heard. In addition to parents and school, her paternal aunt
Aloo, one of the first graduates of the Tata Institute of Social Sciences
(TISS), strongly influenced her decision to become a social worker.

Although Dr. Desai was too young to be involved in India's freedom
movement, it also influenced her career choice to be a social worker.
She was thirteen when India became independent in 1947. She remembers her parents instilling in her the belief that India had to be independent and that the struggle was important. She remembers the painful
Hindu-Muslim riots of 1946 before the partition of India, and her aunt,
who was by then a hospital social worker, walking to her work about
three or four miles from her home until the hospital's dean found out
and sent an ambulance to pick her up. Before independence, Dr. Desai
recalls making badges by hand with the motto "Do or die" and wearing
them to school. She never met Gandhi, who was assassinated in 1948,
but she saw him from a building when he came to attend the famous
Quit India meeting with other leaders at the August Kranti Maidan (an
open public space so named after the event) when they were picked up
and imprisoned. Those were difficult times, she recalls, but nurtured in
such an environment, the resolve to do something for her country
became stronger.

As were her parents, Dr. Desai was influenced by Gandhian philosophy, but she did not feel it necessary to follow some of his ideas (e.g.,
living an ashram, or hermitage, life and wearing *khadi*, or handloom
clothes, all the time). But to this day, she believes in the Gandhian
notion of *swaraj* (self-rule) that promotes local self-governance at the
grassroots level and of privileging Indian goods (including handloom
saris, equipment, and medicines) over foreign products.

With her strong resolve, she wanted to enroll in a social work program right after graduating from school. But there was no bachelor-
level social work program in India at that time, so, somewhat begrudg-
ingly, she enrolled in a liberal arts bachelor's degree program at St.
Xavier's College in Bombay. She majored in sociology and with minors
in anthropology and political science. She believed that this combination would be ideal as a base for her future study in social work. During
college, she was active in the Social Service League and participated in
various activities, such as working in poor neighborhoods to improve
their physical infrastructure and offering recreational programs for children and spending a summer in a rural area working with a women's
group and helping to make bricks to build a school. She recalls that the
stray grazing cattle would squash the bricks at night because straw,

which had been strewn on the bricks for drying, lured the cows. These experiences taught her lessons about poverty, culture, and relationship building. Thus, her college education, through its classroom and field exposures, prepared her well for her entry into social work training and her future work in the profession.

After completing a bachelor's degree with honors in 1955, Dr. Desai enrolled at the TISS for graduate education in social work. It was a two-year program, but at that time, TISS offered a diploma in social service administration, not a degree in social work, as the institute was then outside the university system. Because of her prior experiences, she wanted to specialize in community organization in her second year, but it was not offered that year, so she accepted her second preference and specialized in family and child welfare. However, not willing to give up her first love completely, she negotiated a dual field placement. She worked part of the day in a children's setting and spent the other half working with a potters' community in Dharavi, which is one of the largest slums, with extremely poor-quality housing and living conditions, in Asia today.

By the end of her first year of social work education at TISS, a French nun, Sr. Maria Piva Couceiro, who headed the Daughters of the Heart of Mary in India, was just starting two programs: the College of Social Work (CSW) and the College of Home Science. She contacted Dr. Desai and asked her to teach there after graduation. The women had known each other through Dr. Desai's undergraduate social work field exposures. At their meeting, Sr. Maria also wondered whether Dr. Desai could help her by supervising three first-year students from the CSW. At a very young age, she was mature enough to understand the reason for such a request: there was a lack of trained personnel to teach social work in India. Confident and fearless, a second-year student with a high propensity for risk taking, Dr. Desai started a community project in a slum so she could develop a practice setting and supervise three students from the CSW.

By the time she graduated from TISS, Dr. Desai had gained experience in casework (direct practice with individuals and families and clinical practice), group work, community work, and supervision through varied field placements. Dr. Desai says that her TISS years laid the foundation for all she did later. Right from the start, she disliked following only one practice method. Her field placements provided her with the opportunity to develop an integrated approach, using all methods. In terms of social work courses, she learned most about human behavior in the social environment and practice courses, both individual and group practice. She uses knowledge and skills gained from these courses in her everyday functioning, finding them most applicable in her work as an administrator in the institutions she has served as well as in the field-based activities she has initiated.

Studying and Working in the United States and in India

After graduating from TISS in 1957, Dr. Desai joined the CSW, which was in its second year of establishment, and she was the only full-time faculty member, as all others were part-time in that initial phase. She taught there for a year and then came to the United States to extend and deepen her social work knowledge and skills. At that time, formal social work education was new to India, and as such, it was shaped and influenced by two U.S. social work schools: the University of Chicago and Columbia University. She obtained an AM degree in 1959 from the School of Social Service Administration at the University of Chicago. She was thoroughly happy in America: "I came from a nice home, but I was never homesick." She had a good social life with friends and was fully engrossed in whatever she was doing. But she knew what she wanted to learn and bring back to India. Although she felt that the coursework was heavily biased toward casework, she was able to enroll in a community organization class as well. She took two classes from Charlotte Towle, whose influence on the profession continues to this day. Because her interests straddled all methods, she did her field practicum at two places: the Jewish Family and Community Services for casework and the Urban Renewal Project of Hyde Park–Kenwood for community organization, and she fell back on all the skills she learned there while practicing in India. She says that at that time it took much persuasion for the school to agree to two types of field placements.

After completing her degree, Dr. Desai worked in Chicago for twenty months to gain practical experience that would help with teaching at the CSW on her return to India. She wanted to work in an area that was sufficiently developed in the United States but nonexistent in India so she could transfer her learning. Consequently, she chose to work in child welfare (at the Chicago Child Care Society), where she learned about adoption and foster care services along with legislation for adoption and how to work with single mothers.

She returned to India in 1961 and rejoined the CSW, teaching courses, providing field education, and guiding the research of MSW students. At that time, another faculty member was managing the project in the slum community that she had initiated before leaving. So the principal of the CSW, Dr. Dorothy Baker, an American, requested that she take over the Family Service Center, which had been newly established by a volunteer group that wanted the college to manage it professionally. She felt that this was a serendipitous opportunity for her to use her newly acquired knowledge and practice in family casework, child adoption, and foster care.

At that time, the adoption of children unrelated to a family was a foreign concept in India, which made her work very challenging. A great believer in teamwork, she identified a network of existing institutions that could provide adoption services. But at that time, some of the institutions were unwilling to place their children in unknown families. So her job was to educate the institutions about such adoptions of unrelated children and the advantages in contrast to institutional placement for life. Further, the government of India was promoting foster care at that time as a noninstitutional option and was seeking a person with experience in the field. She took up the challenge and did some preliminary work before returning to the United States to earn her doctorate.

She returned to the School of Social Service Administration at the University of Chicago for her Ph.D. in 1965 and completed it in 1969. Long before social workers had raised issues about cultural competence in the United States, Dr. Desai's doctoral dissertation focused on social work education for international students. It examined the content of social work education with its cultural parameters in relation to its applicability and transferability for practice in other countries. She asked, how should social work education be restructured for international students in relation to the socioeconomic and cultural contexts of the practice realities in their own country? What should a U.S. institution that receives students from other countries understand about those students? She did a survey of all 166 social work international students enrolled in the United States in 1967 and a more in-depth study of 25 students to answer her questions. Dr. Desai says: "It uncovered many misconceptions . . . about the requirements for foreign students and their learning needs, especially with respect to fieldwork. It made me sensitive to how, in my own situation [in India], I would need to work with my students in a culturally sensitive way" (Billups, 2002, p. 64).

As a doctoral student, she again sought work opportunities related to her future work aspirations. During this time, she had three consecutive part-time jobs: as a medical social worker (supervising social workers at the University of Chicago hospitals), and as a field instructor and then a casework instructor at Loyola University. She also drew on her prior experiences in India to initiate a school social work program in a Chicago neighborhood with a large number of Cuban refugees. There had been, at the time, a huge exodus of Cuban families to the area. Through this work experience, she learned a great deal about what displacement meant to these families. Much later in life, as the director of TISS, she accepted on behalf of the institute the task of monitoring the people who had been displaced by the controversial Narmada Dam project in India. Her colleagues carried out the work, but she shared with them responsibility for arguing their case with the state government and the World Bank, which funded the project, and suggested appropriate policy initiatives.

Working in India

Dr. Desai's professional career is strewn with several innovations in the field of social work education and practice. Her pathbreaking contributions to the field of social work continued after she returned to India in 1969 with a doctoral degree and work experiences from the United States. First at the CSW and then at TISS, she contributed significantly to the social work profession by emphasizing an integrated methods approach to teaching social work. Her work experiences in India and the United States demonstrated that effective social work practice required the simultaneous use of a variety of methods to address social problems and issues. Thus, she believes that students ought to learn the unique contributions of each of the methods of practice: casework, group work, and community work. Simultaneously, they ought to be able to conceptualize a method for practice from an integrated theoretical framework so they can analyze and address the problem holistically and decide on the focus of interventions in a particular problem situation. As there were no available courses for teaching integrated social work at that time to promote her vision of holistic practice, Dr. Desai developed the first integrated practice syllabus in India and taught it both at the CSW from the early 1970s and subsequently from 1983 at TISS.

Furthermore, given the Indian reality of poverty and marginalization of a vast majority of its people, she also recognized and emphasized the need for a developmental focus to social work. She believes that a developmental focus with an integrated social work approach is appropriate for India because it allows social workers to identify and address socioeconomic and sociopolitical factors that impede various groups of disadvantaged people from fully participating in Indian society.

In addition, as the vice principal in charge of the academic program at the CSW, she provided leadership to her faculty colleagues to develop a unique BSW program suitable for the Indian context. There were very few existing models of undergraduate social work education at that time. Given her own desire and interest to move quickly into social work after high school as well as her later professional experiences, she believes that, in a country like India with scarce resources, it is more cost-effective for junior-level social workers and paraprofessionals to perform tasks requiring beginner-level skills than for MSW graduates to do so. Thus, with help from colleagues, she designed the BSW program at the CSW and the University of Bombay awarded the first degrees in 1971. The first year of the course was designed in such a way that it provided adequate skills to work as a paraprofessional; should students have decided to stop at that level, they would have earned a university certificate. However, most students finished the full degree. Consequently, she formed a group of colleagues to design and teach a one-year certificate course for paraprofessionals. This course was offered mostly to those who had completed high school. (In India, high school education is for ten years, higher secondary is for two years, which is also known as junior college, and undergraduate education is for three years). This strategy was conceptually and philosophically different from that at TISS, located on the other end of the same city, as at that time, their programs moved upward to the M.Phil. and Ph.D. degrees. The objective was to make the master's degree a model for advanced practice and management, focusing on policy, planning, and administrative capability. However, in addition to BSWs, the intake of students from other disciplines at the MSW level continued at the CSW.

A precursor to the paraprofessional course was the redesigning of students' fieldwork for community work. Dr. Desai was distressed at the state government's policy for slum dwellers. She believed that, instead of adopting and working in one slum, the CSW needed to develop a federation of slum dwellers that would have greater capacity to negotiate with the government. Thus, a new strategy was promoted with MSW students: instead of placing them in one slum or a low-income neighborhood to bring about change, the faculty members at the CSW organized groups of students to work in various slums of Bombay with the aim of creating a federation so that together they could push for the desired policy changes.

Parallel to this strategy, Dr. Desai also pursued her interest in school social work by starting a project with the Municipal Corporation of Greater Mumbai, Department of Education. Starting with two schools in slum locations, in time the project covered seventeen slum-located schools with an enrollment of eighty thousand students. The focus was on arresting the large dropout rate, even at the elementary school level, and the large number of grade-promotion failures. The strategy was to make the school attractive for children to attend through curriculum changes and new teaching methodologies at the point of entry. When children and families needed special attention, school social worker teams intervened, using the integrated method of social work practice. The teams employed at the schools were a mix of MSWs, BSWs, and paraprofessionals who were recruited from the local community. Each team member learned and was allocated responsibilities on the basis of his or her expected level of knowledge and skills.

Unlike most social work education institutions at that time in India or in the United States, Dr. Desai and her colleagues promoted an activist orientation in the program at the CSW. At the University of Chicago, she had written a paper on Edith Abbott for one of her courses by researching in the university archives. She was very impressed by Abbott's activism with which she took on the government of the day. Dr. Desai was convinced that such a dimension of social work practice had become lost in its subsequent therapeutic orientation. After creating a hospitable environment for social work as an instrument of social change, in addition to working for slum dwellers, Dr. Desai and her faculty colleagues at the CSW worked on the right to housing and rights of construction workers, women, and street children. They initiated and worked on these projects and brought their live field experiences into classroom teaching. Dr. Desai believes that, as they were young and inexperienced themselves, this enriched the capacities of the faculty as well.

After serving the CSW for a quarter century, she was invited by the governing board of TISS to become its director. She eventually accepted the prestigious position, remaining for thirteen years (from 1982 to 1995). On the board, Dr. Desai again pursued her ideas about making social work relate to the needs of the country through course work, fieldwork, research, and practice. The Ph.D. program was modified to add an optional module of producing a monograph based on an actual field project implemented by the scholar and then analyzing it in relation to the existing theoretical framework, or a monograph on substantial work experience with a similar analysis. The objective was to create indigenous literature for social work based on the field realities, and especially to give students with less work experience an opportunity to carry out a project with an academic underpinning.

She encouraged the faculty to develop new professional degree programs at TISS, such as the part-time evening diploma in hospital administration to become a full-time degree. Degree requirements were offered in a modular pattern so that working doctors could come in at various points as time permitted them to access the courses. A part-time certificate course in social work for volunteers and an advanced course in social welfare administration for trained social workers also were started. Faculty members were also encouraged to develop field action projects, which demonstrated new areas of practice, new strategies, or new models of work. When Dr. Desai left TISS, there were sixteen such innovative projects in the field that various faculty members had started, thus releasing in them their own creativity. Examples of such projects include working with the victims of domestic violence through police stations; accessing justice for poor people by helping them through the labyrinth of the legal system of courts, jails, and after-care; demonstrating telephone emergency service for children; working with indigenous people living in villages about three hours from the city; and working with people using drugs and other chemical substances. Some of the projects were later handed over to the Indian government. For example, the project that demonstrated the effectiveness of marital counseling in divorce cases in the city's civil court led to the introduction of social workers in family courts when they were established, and the child telephone help line project was adopted by the government of India for replication in various locations in the country. Thus, Dr. Desai states that the belief that schools of social work have a role in demonstrating new services to people or a new method of work has been vindicated. Not only through research but also through live demonstration, it is possible to impact policy. Dr. Desai also took the lead in social workers' disaster-response work in various parts of India, as she believed that social work had a major interventive role to play in both natural and man-made disasters.

Last but very important, under Dr. Desai's leadership and guidance, TISS started a rural campus to help poor and marginalized villagers reconstruct their lives. Wadia (2007) reports that, in 1985 and 1986, when TISS was celebrating its golden jubilee, Dr. Desai decided that it was time for the school to have a rural presence: "I felt we needed to have social work in the rural environment but we didn't have any good role models. There were some attempts at rural work in some schools of social work but there was no adequate focus, or they used urban models of social work which were inappropriate." The TISS rural campus at Tuljapur (an eight-hour journey from Bombay) was the direct result of her efforts and those of her colleagues, endorsed by TISS's governing board. The campus was set up on a hundred-acre property, gifted by the government of Maharashtra (the state in which Mumbai is located), in a region of high poverty and low rainfall, as requested by the institute. Over a period of years, many programs were developed in the villages. The programs began with first developing a relationship of trust in the community, even before the campus was established. As a result, "women have learnt, through livelihood and education initiatives, to fight for their rights. Local labor has been supported in its battle against low wages and corrupt practices. Water management and other developmental work have helped farmers in the area" (Wadia, 2007).

The first objective of setting up the TISS rural campus was to establish courses for paraprofessionals at eleventh- and twelfth-grade higher secondary school educational levels so they could qualify for the educational mainstream and a BSW in rural development with recruitment of largely rural students who would eventually work with the government and the volunteer sector. The BSW program has been established recently and the first two classes have graduated. Dr. Desai is very appreciative of TISS furthering her dream project and making it a reality.

To summarize, at the CSW and TISS, Dr. Desai's emphasis on practice-oriented projects not only provided valuable service to people and learning for students but also kept the teachers actively involved in practice in one way or another—supervising students, managing programs, coordinating overall practice strategies and methodologies, and documenting their work. Through these projects, faculty members not only were able to demonstrate to the community how social work could and should be done but also helped further the learning and research of the students. The curricula were designed in such a way that they could innovate in teaching courses, guide students' research, participate in community projects, and intervene in crises.

Sharing Practice Wisdom for Practitioners and Students

Armaity Desai, an Indian woman, must have had to bypass and overcome Indian patriarchy to have made such pathbreaking contributions to the field of social work. Surely there are lessons for social workers to learn from her experiences in this arena. It took some probing to get to the crux of the matter. At first she said patriarchy did not bother her at all. However, as she relaxed a bit more, she acknowledged some difficult situations with men that she was "able to handle professionally." For example, as chair of the University Grants Commission, she worked primarily with men, who at first referred to her as "sir" and then would correct themselves and say "madam." Suppressing laughter, she says, "They themselves were possibly a little uncomfortable in the beginning because they had not dealt with a woman heading the organization in the recent past." Consequently, it took some time for her colleagues at the commission to call her "Ms. Desai" or "Dr. Desai," which were preferable to "madam." Another incident had to do with white men from the developed world when she worked on a committee to develop education for postapartheid South Africa (for details, see Billups, 2002). In her work on the Committee on Human Resource Development for Post-Apartheid South Africa, Dr. Desai was challenged repeatedly in convincing other committee members that programs should focus on professionals but also community-level and grassroots workers. Eventually, her point of view prevailed.

When asked what she would tell students about to enter a social work education, Dr. Desai said that she would encourage students to think independently, to critically analyze situations for themselves, to question what they read in their books and what their teachers say. She shared that she used to tell her pedagogy classes that Ralph Waldo

Emerson said, "Don't make your students like you. One of you is enough." Also it is important for students to have a strong commitment to social work issues. Consequently, it is OK to be angry about things that they see or experience as unjust, because such anger or ability to feel and recognize something as wrong motivates them to address the injustices.

Dr. Desai says, as a social worker, the first and the most important thing for her is to understand people. She tries to understand who they are, what they want, why they think as they do or their frame of reference, what games they may be playing with her. Irrespective of where people come from, she always tries to establish comfortable relationships, making sure others are not put on the defensive. She respects people and expects respect from them, even when men treat her differently because she is a woman. When faced with a conflict, she tries to understand the issues, thinks through possible ways to deal with them, clarifies her own stand, and conveys her position clearly and firmly. She believes it is important to let people know that she is not threatened in any way even when she is the only woman in a group of men, as has frequently been the case. She relates comfortably with them and makes it known that she has a clear mind and can substantiate her position with logic and facts. She never attacks people but clearly addresses the issues and articulates her difference of opinion. She states that with these strategies it is possible to address and overcome dominating persons and groups.

Identifying Significant Accomplishments and Current Involvements

On being asked which achievement she treasured the most, Dr. Desai said that three things bring her satisfaction. The first is the nurturing of the College of Social Work from its initial years to its twenty-fifth anniversary, laying down the perspectives and processes that guided their further development, including the establishment of the BSW degree. Second, she is "most satisfied and proud" that she could start a rural campus of TISS and acquire additional land at no cost for extension of the campus, which has made its further development possible and increased its endowment. Third, she is very happy that she could demonstrate the need for an integrated approach to the family through her work at the Family Service Centre at the CSW, where she added family casework, adoption, foster care, and sponsorship (financial assistance to children) as noninstitutional services back in the 1960s, when institutional care of children was the only approach. However, she could see its full impact only recently, when the government of

India adopted the integrated service delivery model for children as national policy. It has taken the Indian government more than forty years to understand its value, and as such, it feels like "a whole life's journey" that has come to fruition.

The key to Dr. Desai's accomplishments is her simultaneous interest in poor communities and the plight of women and children. These interests are tied to the overriding issue of injustice and exploitation that keeps the poor as poor. Right now, she says, "I have more dishes in the air than my two hands can keep them from falling!" Yet it seems that the one thread that runs throughout her career is her interest in children's well-being. She agrees, saying, "I have always enjoyed working with children right from the beginning."

Since formally retiring from work, she has been attending to her long-abiding love for children through her involvement with several NGOs, such as the Pratham Mumbai Education Initiative and the Childline India Foundation, a partnership with the government of India's Ministry of Women and Child Development. As a trustee of the Childline India Foundation, she has been guiding its staff on planning, administrative, and program matters. Currently, the organization is dealing with international pedophilia tourism by fighting a case involving two foreigners. Beginning with the sessions court and up to the Supreme Court of India, the case has received attention and support from activist-oriented lawyers, a well-known legal luminary, and the media.

Because of her involvement with the Pratham Mumbai Education Initiative and the Childline India Foundation, she worked as a bridge between the two organizations to help start a program for rescued children of the state of Bihar, from where many are sent to work in Mumbai. Childline is currently developing grassroots groups to keep vigil on the families to ensure that the children are returned to their families and that new children are not recruited for work. They also provide staff training and monitoring, and Pratham operates a district call center in its Shelter Project, forwarding calls to the workers in the field and ensuring that the children receive their legal due. Both Pratham and Childline are national organizations, ensuring that the problem is monitored broadly throughout the country. Very proudly, Dr. Desai says, "They are both run by my [former] star students!"

In addition to working with these two NGOs, Dr. Desai is working with the University Grants Commission (UGC) to enhance women educators' status in academia (referring to our discussion related to patriarchy, she says that generally women are not in decision-making positions in academia). She also chairs the National Consultative Committee for the Capacity Building of Women Managers in Higher Education. As a result of her extensive work in this area, female faculty members have learned to advocate for themselves when positions become open. Some women have now become department heads when they were likely to be bypassed by men, two have become registrars at their universities, and there are many other positive outcomes.

The fascinating story of Dr. Desai's professional career does not end here. Dr. Desai is also a member of the UGC Women's Studies Committee. Recently, the UGC invited her to head a small subcommittee of women for the 11th Plan, which drafted the required programs for women in universities and colleges. These programs that target women include professional courses, technology courses, special hostels, and benefits during pregnancy and childbirth. Much will depend on how much the UGC can implement given competing budgetary demands, although the attempt has been to make an impact on a gender-sensitive budget allocation.

Conclusion

Armaity Desai has received many awards and honors, including two *honoris causa* degrees from Indian universities and the Professional Achievement Citation of the University of Chicago Alumni Association. But the honor she prizes the most is the Katherine A. Kendall Award for a lifetime of distinguished international service to social work education, which she received in 1992. She takes so much pride in this honor because Kendall is her role model. Dr. Desai admires Kendall's contribution to social work education worldwide, her keenness of mind, and her friendly and warm disposition. Dr. Desai feels that she has always enjoyed a special relationship with her, which she deeply values as significant in her professional growth and development.

Dr. Desai has contributed her expertise to many national and international committees, associations, and commissions. She was a member of the Commission on Self-Employed Women and Women in the Informal Sector, appointed by the late prime minister of India, Rajiv Gandhi. Through her work on this commission, at times it became necessary to demonstrate to government officials that a large percentage of women in India are sole earners or major providers for their families, instead of the traditional belief that men earn and take care of their mothers, wives, sisters, daughters, or daughters-in-law—the traditional view of women in India. In the 1980s, she was appointed by the chief justice of India to inquire into mistreatment of women under trial (or women who had been jailed but had not been given a trial). With support from her CSW colleagues, she completed the study and presented her written report to the chief justice in two weeks, as directed by the supreme court. The chief justice was so impressed with the report that he still remembers it and talks about it whenever he sees her (Billups, 2002).

Dr. Desai currently lives in her childhood home in Mumbai, where she lived when she was five years old. Sure-footed and with clarity about how things ought to be, she is leaving behind strong and colorful strands of change in the world without giving up her treasured roots. As she moves closer to full retirement from her many activities, she can take tremendous satisfaction in the knowledge that thousands of lives, particularly those of women and children, have been improved because she was here in India.

References

Billups, J. O. (Ed.). (2002). *Faithful angels: Portraits of international social work notables.* Washington, DC: National Association of Social Workers Press.

Desai, M., Pimple, M., & Jaswal, S. (2000). Social work education and its application to general university education: An interview with Prof. Armaity S. Desai. *Indian Journal of Social Work, 61*(2), 316–339.

Wadia, J. (2007). A rural revolution. Retrieved May 7, 2008, from http://www.tata.com/index.htm.

CHAPTER FIFTEEN

Sattareh Farman Farmaian

Bringing Social Work Education to Iran

Alice Lieberman

Born into the ruling Qajar dynasty in Iran, Sattareh Farman Farmaian brought social work to her country when she founded the Tehran School of Social Work. At the time, the concept of professional social work was so foreign to this tribal culture that there was no equivalent in the Persian language for "social worker," so she made one up: *madadkar*, which means "one who helps." But that, she says, is not the most important professional contribution she made in her life. I visited her in October 2006, at her home in Los Angeles. It is filled with photos, books, and art that reflect her devotion to family, and her love for this rich culture.

Sattareh herself is a small woman, with classic Persian features. Of course, I had a sense of what she looked like, because her autobiography, *Daughter of Persia: A Woman's Journey from Her Father's Harem Through the Islamic Revolution* (1992), contains photographs of her and her family. And because I read her book, I knew a great deal about her as well. I thought that it might be disconcerting for her to know so little about me, a visitor to her home, when I obviously knew so

much about her. But she is used to that: her book was
remarkably successful, often required reading in social work
and women's studies classes. Thus, it was that yet another
stranger came calling to talk about her life, this time at her
breakfast table over a cup of hot tea.

Growing Up in Iran

In her excellent autobiography, Sattareh Farman Farmaian (called
"Satti" by her family and friends, and hereinafter) provides a richly
detailed description of her life in Iran. She was the fifteenth child of the
thirty-six born to a prince and military commander and governor during the Qajar dynasty and a deeply religious mother, the third of his
eight wives, who had married him at the age of twelve. Shortly after her
birth, the Qajars were defeated, and the British-backed Pahlavi dynasty
took control of the country. It was a powerful blow to Satti's family. Her
father (called Shazdeh, which means "prince" in the Persian language)
never regained his standing, and slowly the family lost its land and a
significant portion of its wealth.

Despite this misfortune, the family—including all the wives, children, and servants—lived a comfortable life in Tehran, although all
lived with the knowledge that the secret police were watching them.
There was always a palpable fear among the adults that her father could
be arrested, or killed, yet Satti spent her youth relatively protected from
such concerns. Everyone seemed to look out for one another—wives,
children, servants, and servants' children—and all lived under the protection of Shazdeh.

Some of Satti's earliest memories are of her parents taking care of the
villagers outside the compound. Because there were no governmental
institutions to rely on, the villagers—poor, uneducated, and vulnerable
to exploitation—had to rely on the landowners. Satti describes the
efforts her parents made to sustain the villagers. But this perpetual
dependence on others fed a deep insecurity that, Satti notes, "everybody felt, and it went so deep [that Iranians] didn't even think about it.
It was just there, like the sky or the desert. In Iran, everybody depended
on somebody higher for survival, some benefactor who was richer or
more powerful than they were and who could take care of them" (Farman Farmaian, 1992, p. 24). And this insecurity drove counterproductive
behavior: "Just as we and my mother depended on Shazdeh, Mashti
[their servant] depended on [my mother]. He feared that if he lost my
mother's favor by admitting ignorance or fault, she might fire him, and
then he and his family would have to beg or starve. . . . [H]e would come

up with the most ridiculous lies and excuses to avoid taking responsibility for his actions" (Farman Farmaian, 1992, pp. 24–25). This observation of dependence on others, and its consequences, would stay with Satti and have far-reaching implications in her professional and personal lives.

Satti attended Tarbiat, an elementary school run by adherents of the Bahai faith. A cornerstone of the faith is its emphasis on tolerance and kindness to others, and it is likely that her early education, coupled with her sharp observations of the lives of villagers outside the compound, planted seeds that led her to her eventual career path.

But seeds require nurturing, and the American School for Girls, where Satti went to high school, provided this fertile ground. Presbyterian missionaries from the United States ran the school, at a time when U.S. foreign aid was contributing significantly to the well-being of the poor and illiterate in Iran. It was at the school that Satti was exposed to diverse cultures, lifestyles, religions, and social classes. She learned English there and took every advantage of the liberalized atmosphere.

Throughout Satti's childhood, the shadow of Reza Shah grew inexorably darker and more malevolent. In his quest to modernize the country, he outlawed the wearing of the veil, a humiliation for religious women like her mother. He had Satti's beloved older brother killed because he had European connections that the shah did not trust. For Satti's family, it was the beginning of the end of life as they knew it. Their home was destroyed.

To take her mind off her family's difficulties, Satti threw herself into service work, sponsored by the missionaries who ran her high school. She worked in the medical dispensary and, for the first time, ventured into South Tehran, where the poverty was unimaginable but where Presbyterian missionaries, with few resources, tried to help improve lives with food and medicine. For the first time, she learned about poverty, poor housing, and the plight of having too many mouths to feed.

Strongly influenced by her independent female teachers, Satti resolved to continue her education in the United States. She knew that she wanted her life's work to be helping her people, but social work as a profession did not exist in her country. And yet, through the missionaries, she had learned about an educational path that she could take in the United States that would help her learn how to help her people. And the time was right: her father had died, and Reza Shah had been deposed, making way for her cousin, Dr. Mohammed Mossadeq, to lead the country (after years of house arrest, he was freed and elected to the parliament).

Satti's travels through Iran and to the port of Bombay (from which she would depart for the United States) were an adventure, to say the least. And the adventure continued once she boarded the ship bound for the United States. Because it was wartime (1944), the ship's route was kept secret, but this did not stop them from being torpedoed, and ultimately rescued and escorted back to Bombay. When she finally left the port of Bombay for good, it was on a U.S. Navy troopship, bypassing the European ports to avoid dangers.

Coming to the United States

The journey to the United States has to be viewed with considerable awe, as it was undertaken by a twenty-two-year-old woman, from a culture in which one did not go many places unescorted and for whom English was a second—and baffling—language. In fact, Satti was not even aware of where in the United States the ship was headed, because the route had to be kept secret for security purposes. She had been waiting throughout the journey to see the Statue of Liberty and the port of New York, and only when she arrived did she find out exactly where she was—southern California!

With the help of the American Red Cross, she found the former educational director of her Iranian alma mater, the American School for Girls, Dr. Samuel Jordan, who happened to live nearby. He helped her enroll at the University of Southern California, where she earned her bachelor's degree in sociology and then enrolled in the school's MSW program.

One of the things that most impressed Satti when she first came to the United States was that Americans were able to speak freely, something denied to her people under the regime of the shah. And it was this openness, she believed, that allowed Americans to be so decisive. If you can talk about problems, she reasoned, you can do something about them. The term "taking the initiative" had no Persian translation, but it was the key, she felt, to her country's hopes of becoming a great nation.

Crystallizing Life Goals

The graduate program in social work was a perfect fit for Satti, both professionally and temperamentally. In her book, she says, "By my second week there, I knew that I had found the weapon I needed to fight Iran's human miseries" (Farman Farmaian, 1992, p. 167). She resolved to learn everything she could about the U.S. systems of social welfare, from child welfare to health care and mental health. During our conversation in her apartment, while she was searching for photos, I reflected on my own, rather modest goals as a graduate student not much younger than she was at the time she was in school. The very idea of wholly transplanting my new profession to even a small locale in the United States would have been immobilizing! But here was Satti, determined to bring a profession that did not exist back to not only her entire country but also into a tribal culture, where getting assistance from outside one's own family was unheard of.

During her graduate school years, Satti married briefly and had a daughter, Mitra. Mitra was, and is, a beloved child who now has grown children of her own. Their photos adorn the tables of Satti's home, and she speaks of them with obvious pride. But it has to be noted that Mitra was raised by a single mother and, like so many single mothers, economic insecurity and concern for her child's general well-being were ever present. In this way, Satti was no different than so many single mothers who balance the primacy of their children's needs with their own work and pleasure.

After graduation, through a series of serendipitous events, Satti obtained a job in New York with an independent oil company sympathetic to Premier Mossadeq. Her job was to serve as a cultural liaison to U.S. citizens doing business in Iran and to monitor what the U.S. and foreign presses were saying about Iranian oil policy. She immersed herself in the international community and made many important contacts.

When Satti returned to Iran in 1954, it was a different country. Mossadeq had been overthrown and imprisoned, and the Pahlavi dynasty was back in power. However, her new position, as a social welfare consultant with UNESCO to the government of Iraq, allowed her the opportunity to practice her profession among people whose culture and lifestyle she profoundly understood. After a short visit with her family in Iran, she went to work with the social welfare ministry of Iraq to develop a social welfare system. She worked with nomadic tribes, participated in ongoing social welfare projects, and taught all over the Middle East. This experience served her well: in those years with UNESCO, she worked in Baghdad's slums, with Nile farmers who lived in mud huts, and in Palestinian refugee camps in Lebanon. The experience prepared her for the primary work of her life, bringing social work to her own people, through the establishment of the Tehran School of Social Work in the fall of 1958.

Bringing Social Work to Iran

All of Satti's life experiences—her early years in Iran as a Qajar daughter, her primary school education at Tarbiat, her years at the American school, her life in this country as an outsider to American culture, and her role as a mother—coupled with the social work skills she was subsequently able to put into practice following her American professional education served her well when she founded the school. Independent of both the university system and the government, it functioned more as a private not-for-profit enterprise. I think that Satti would underscore the nonprofit aspect—"I certainly did not get rich!" she told me.

Of course, the first order of business was to make precise the mission and goals of the school. As noted earlier, there was no word for "social worker" in Persian. So she made one up: the word was *madadkar*, or "one who helps."

The curriculum was structured as a two-year program with a six-week orientation. The education was free (Satti had obtained funding from the government), and a guaranteed work position was available for all who graduated. During the academic year, students attended classes and worked in the field six days a week, including summers. I asked Satti about the course work offered at the school. She smiled and said, "If my dean of the School of Social Work [at the University of Southern California] would come to Iran, she would shoot me if she saw what was taught in my school!" Course work in family planning, diet, sanitation, agriculture, and first aid was taken alongside courses in social and individual psychology.

Here in the United States, the idea that professional social work education is built on a liberal arts base is so widely accepted that no one even questions it. This is because the liberal arts foster the analytical skills necessary for good practice. But as Satti notes in her book, Iranian public schools were established to produce not critical thinkers but loyal, unquestioning subjects. "Young Persians," she writes, "learned that unthinking authority was a virtue, that critical discussion was both rude and dangerous, and that to prosper they must not show initiative but, on the contrary, must attach themselves to an influential mentor" (Farman Farmaian, 1992, p. 212). Thus, to reverse this process and to prepare the students with the analytical skills necessary to observe and ameliorate the country's intractable social problems, the school also required students to take logic, statistics, political science, philosophy, and law.

Sustaining a school such as this one requires money, and Satti said she was always looking for funding. Teachers were needed. A library had to be built. Field instructors were needed. Through a combination of luck (several Americans in Iran who had MSWs volunteered their time as field supervisors) and strong moral and financial support from her family, the school slowly took shape. Ultimately, Satti was able to build a freestanding building just for the school.

It was clear from our discussion that one of the most difficult things to accomplish at the school was to move beyond the cultural barriers that could prevent students from becoming the best *madadkars* they could be. For example, although both males and females were admitted to the school, many were shocked and not a little dismayed to realize that they not only would be taking classes together but also were expected to discuss ideas with one another and to look one another in the eye! Furthermore, Satti insisted that a *madadkar* was never to refuse to help because he or she did not agree with the political views of the client. It was quite a while, and required a great deal of trust among the students and with Satti, before their professional socialization took hold, but eventually it did.

Satti also noted that it was very important to her that the students never betray a trust with clients, always dress professionally, and always—always—arrive on time for appointments. "Persians are notorious for not being on time," she told me. But her students were required to be punctual. "You have to be a [role] model," she said.

One of the first major projects undertaken by the school and its students was the rehabilitation of an orphanage and an asylum in the nearby town of Aminabad. Through a combination of sheer will and persistent coaxing, Satti was able to get the mayor to visit the institution and to see for himself the deplorable conditions in which babies and children were living under the city's authority. What he witnessed brought him to tears (as one example of how bad things were, the children had no real identities or names—to that point, the orphanage workers called them only "Rabbit," "Dog," or "Rat"). Afterward, he agreed to provide the funding needed to clean the place up and to give Satti and the students the authority to find and train orphanage workers and doctors to attend to their medical needs. These projects, and others like it, allowed the students to practice their skills and gave them confidence in their ability to solve problems.

In all of her work, I think that there were two problems that Satti faced that never really went away. The first was the cultural propensity, which she first noted as a child, of Persians waiting until someone bigger, wealthier, or of higher status came along to solve one's problem. Social workers can do many things, but reversing a fatalistic worldview that is deep in the bones of a people is pretty close to impossible. The second problem, also cultural, has to do with the limitations imposed on Satti because she was a woman in a patriarchal culture. For example, shortly after she went with the mayor to inspect the orphanage in Aminabad, her brother chastised her for setting herself up as a potential object of gossip because she and the mayor had been in the car together, without familial supervision.

And yet the Tehran School of Social Work became an indispensable element in the effort to build a social service infrastructure in a country where the government was trying to modernize, and Satti, as the director, was the go-to person. Students found themselves doing everything from teaching the rural poor more efficient farming methods to delivering what we would call employee assistance services (on-site counseling and referral) in factories.

One of the most important contributions of the school was its collaboration with other private entities to establish the Community Welfare Centers of Iran. These centers, located in the country's metropolitan areas, provided much-needed services to families who had moved there from rural areas. The families often had no resources to survive in their new environment. Many were illiterate, and the skills they had honed in their formerly agrarian lifestyle did not transfer. Furthermore, the communities to which the families had relocated were not immune from problems found in deeply impoverished communities everywhere: drug trafficking, crime, and child neglect.

The centers worked to combat these problems by offering services designed to meet the specific needs of the communities: day care for children, so their mothers could work or learn a trade; vocational, homemaking, and literacy classes for young women; recreational and educational programs for teens; cultural activities for adults; and individual and family counseling (directors for the agencies were graduates of the school, as were many of the professional staff). Over the years, Satti developed a warm relationship with the wife of the shah, Queen Farah Diba, who appreciated what the school was doing for the country and whose ability to bring positive publicity to this and other endeavors undertaken by the school was undeniably helpful.

Family Planning Comes to Iran

When I asked Satti what she believed to be her most important professional contribution, she did not hesitate: "The most important thing that I did, and the [most important] contribution of my life, is to [help women] stop having babies, so they could space their children in order to have the needed time to get their education." And indeed, the school was clearly instrumental in bringing family planning to Iran.

Muslim beliefs and tradition hold that children are a gift from God. In addition, the number of children a woman had determined her social status. There was also the reality that, for poor families, sons were needed to help farm the land and to support their parents in old age. But even with these strictures, self-induced abortions were not uncommon and were undertaken using dangerously unsanitary methods. Severe infections and death were common outcomes. Clearly, family-planning education was desperately needed. In consultation with the International Pathfinder Fund (an organization devoted to funding population control programs worldwide), Satti set about to change this.

Trying to institute family planning in a Muslim country is risky business. It was important not to offend traditionalists in the country, who could prevent their wives from coming to the clinic. Compounding this difficulty was the fact that there were literally no words in the Persian language that were suitable for a sexuality education class. There was not even a word for "intercourse," because discussing sex was culturally taboo. For this reason, a physician from the United States had to be brought in to train social workers, nurses, and other health professionals in comprehensive family planning. Then, from what they were taught by the doctor, Satti says, "we invented our classes!"

Eventually, family-planning services became part of the network of services offered to Iranian women through the community welfare centers. By locating family-planning services in a larger social service context, the social workers were able to reach a wider population. Women coming to the center to take advantage of its other services would find that they were also able to receive education in and devices for birth control (the pill was introduced to the United States in 1960 and available worldwide shortly thereafter). Eventually, classes for men were designed as well.

Satti told me that her success in bringing such services to Iran hinged on the fact that the government had a strong interest in curbing population growth. It had even instituted laws that were supportive of population control, such as raising the legal age of marriage and liberalizing the institution of divorce. But just as important was the approach that Satti and her students took when introducing the clinics to the local populations, to overcome the resistance of traditionalists. She noted, for example, that the Koran devotes an entire chapter to the health of women. And while it is largely silent on the topic of abortion, an abortion to save the health of the mother is interpreted as permissible by most in the religious community.

One of the most innovative endeavors that she told me about was the creation of family-planning services for prostitutes who lived in an area called the Fortress. Prostitution was not legal in Iran, but many young girls were kidnapped and taken to the madams and then forced into prostitution. These madams were no better informed about contraception than anyone else. So, in addition to teaching family planning methods to the adult women in the Fortress, Satti and her students went to the Ministry of Justice and secured the release of the little girls there who, since their kidnapping, had become sexual slaves, financially dependent on the madam. Satti and her students also paid the debt owed to the madams to secure the release of many children. As a result, quite a few of them were able to pursue normal lives and were even able to marry, something that had not been possible before.

Now Satti was wearing several hats: in addition to her work as the founder and director of the Tehran School of Social Work, she also carried the title of founder and director of the Community Welfare Centers and the Family Planning Association of Iran. Building on these experiences, she also consulted with the International Planned Parenthood Federation and the South Korean government on the media's role in population control and social development, and she was a member of the board of directors of the International Planned Parenthood Federation, on whose behalf she traveled extensively.

Portents of Tragedy Amid Success

The 1970s was a productive decade for both Satti and the school. The graduates were finding excellent jobs, and the admissions process was highly competitive. In addition to practice with individuals, families, and communities that the school prepared them for, *madadkars* were also publishing scholarly work on the effectiveness of their interventions, expanding what today would be called best-practices literature. The school was truly in its heyday.

But portents of trouble were appearing with ever-increasing frequency. The Pahlavi regime had built a powerful secret police force, the SAVAK, which terrified the people into silence. Eventually, in 1975, the shah announced that the two-party system in Iran had been abolished, and from then on, there would be only one party. Everyone was expected to join, and those who did not wish to do so were invited to leave the country. Spectacular corruption, starting at the very top, proliferated.

As Satti says in her book, "Disappointment, envy, repression, and the government's lies, corruption, and injustice were building an explosive, poisonous resentment that had no outlet" (Farman Farmaian, 1992, p. 283). The only thing keeping a lid on the simmering cauldron was the shah's half-million-man army. In other words, the ground was being laid for revolution, and a voice from exile, a holy man, exhorting the people to rise up and to overthrow the shah and the trappings of Western society was becoming louder and louder.

The people rose up, and the revolution came, in 1978. By the time the shah had figured out the trouble he was in, it was too late. He left Iran in January 1979, putatively to receive medical treatment but really because staying was no longer a tenable option. In April, that holy man, who had been the nominal leader of the revolution, came into power. His name was Ayatollah Ruholla Khomeini, and his first order of business was to establish theocratic rule, in which society was to be governed according to Islamic law, as he interpreted it.

Facing a Firing Squad

Satti made it very clear to me that she saw both the ruthless corruption of the government of the shah and the appeal of the promises made by the ayatollah. Her politics were and are moderate, however, and as with most of the highly educated in her country, she did not favor turning the clock back on modernization. She nevertheless had, up to that point, assiduously avoided getting herself, or the students, embroiled in politics.

In February 1979, as she was preparing to enter the school, one of the staff came out to talk to her. His words were chilling: "There are students inside with guns, waiting to kill you" (Farman Farmaian, 1992, p. 330).

She faced her accusers. Her "crimes" were that she had received her education in the United States (an imperialist country), that she had had positive relationships with the previous government, and that the school was a front for the CIA. "We are going to ask Ayatollah Khomeini to execute you. He is going to kill you" (Farman Farmaian, 1992, p. 331). With that, she was taken to police headquarters, along with several other hapless faculty members who had shown up for work. From there, she was taken to the ayatollah's residence, where she stood against the wall of his compound for about twenty-four hours.

When she was finally allowed to speak with someone who had the power to dispose of her case (one way or the other), it became clear that her arrest had not been instigated by the ayatollah but by her students, who had accused her of eleven specific crimes that implicated her as an enemy of the revolution. Among the accusations were those that she had worked for SAVAK, the shah's hated secret police force, as well as for the CIA and Israel; that she had committed theft (from the school and the community welfare centers); and that her membership in the Imperial Sports Club (a local athletic club) was evidence of collusion with imperialists. And while those were quickly discounted, the last one was most serious: "The students testify here that, as part of their education, they were required to attend courses on how to prevent the birth of children and to work for a semester in clinics you started for this purpose. In these clinics, they say, doctors gave women medicine that prevented the births of at least five thousand children in the last year alone. You were responsible for bringing these activities to Iran, and if you had not started these clinics, millions of Iranians would have been alive to fight for the Ayatollah Khomeini and support the revolution" (Farman Farmaian, 1992, p. 360).

At this point, one might wonder how her students could turn on Satti so quickly. Although she never addressed this, it is important to note that the assumption of a group identity (Khomeini loyalists, in this case) can be a powerful behavior changer. Ordinary people can fall victim to a "mob mentality" and participate in extraordinary acts of cruelty that, in more peaceful times, they would never take part in. (The Rwandan genocide is an extreme example of this: members of the Hutu tribe raped and slaughtered their Tutsi neighbors, with whom they had previously peacefully coexisted; they were manipulated by their own government into committing the acts and desperate to be on "the right side" of history.)

In any event, these emissaries of the ayatollah believed that Satti's association with "imperialists" and her role in the introduction of family planning to the people merited her death. And with their pronouncement, she began to mentally prepare herself. Then, fate intervened. A cleric, who had been jailed during the Pahlavi regime, provided eyewitness testimony to the good works of Satti and her students in the prison of Qasr-e-Qujar, where he had been held. He also informed the men that Satti had been personally responsible for saving some women from being burned by a street mob. Because a trusted cleric knew of some of the positive developments brought about by Satti and the school, her death sentence was reversed and she was free to leave. It had been an extraordinarily close call.

Leaving Iran—For Good

Although the ayatollah had cleared Satti to go back to her school, she knew that she could not. It was only a matter of time, she believed, before her safety would be threatened again. After obtaining an exit visa, she left the country. It was March 1979. She has not been back since.

There is a belief in some religious traditions that we choose our parents. And if that is the case, then Satti chose well. It was her father, a forward-thinking man, who taught her that one always has to accept adversity and move forward. And in this most difficult of circumstances, she did.

After temporary stops in London (where she worked for the International Planned Parenthood Federation for several months) and Illinois (where Mitra was living), Satti made her way back to California, where she had come originally all those years ago. After taking the licensing exam, she became an investigator with Children's Services in Los Angeles County. I was curious to know how she felt about taking this job, after the groundbreaking work she had done in Iran. Her response was not what I expected: "It was very hard to acclimate because I had the idea that the United States was educated and they know better than to abuse babies, and has knowledge that they should not abuse. I could understand abuse in Iran with all the social problems. [But] these feelings [i.e., sexual abuse of children] were not revealed or it was pushed under the rug . . . in our classes [at the University of Southern California]." She remained in the job for twelve years and retired in 1992.

"And what happened to social work in Iran?" I asked. She responded, "They still have *madadkars* in Iran," but the Tehran School of Social Work no longer exists. When the revolution came, they closed the institutions of higher learning. When the University of Tehran reopened, some years after the revolution, a decision was made to provide social work education, housing it in the university's social science department: "The name *madadkar* is now very popular. I get a lot of papers from former students saying that social workers are [still] working with [the] poor." It is an astonishing legacy, when one considers that this woman, the profession's prime mover in Iran, had been gone from Iran for more than a quarter century.

Conclusion

Satti is now in her mideighties, but she looks younger and is quite fit. Her home is within blocks of the University of California, Los Angeles, campus and its extensive library, and she takes full advantage of their excellent courses in culture, philosophy, and other aspects of medieval, Renaissance, and Middle Eastern studies. She showed me her notebooks from these classes, filled with lecture material. It is obvious that she loves the opportunity to continue to learn. And she is fortunate that she lives in close proximity to other Iranian expatriates, to whom she can speak in her native language. In fact, when we went to an Iranian restaurant that she particularly likes for lunch, she ordered for me in Farsi. And—for the record—the food was delicious!

When I first read Satti's autobiography, it did not dawn on me that I would ever meet her. I am so glad I did. The book ends with Satti embittered by the destruction of a life's work. But she has every reason to be proud. Iran is a far better place for her having lived there, particularly for poor women and their families. And her beloved parents, so influential in her life, would undoubtedly be proud of a daughter who not only achieved great things but also moved forward with grace and purpose in the face of adversity and sorrow.

Reference

Farman Farmaian, S. (with Munker, D.). (1992). *Daughter of Persia: A woman's journey from her father's harem through the Islamic revolution.* New York: Crown.

About the Authors

Tigest K. Abye is program head for the Ethiopian Women Lawyers Association, Addis Ababa, Ethiopia. In 2006, she participated in the Second International Policy Conference on the African Child, whose principal purpose was to contribute to the ongoing international effort to effect attitudinal and policy change relating to physical, psychological, and sexual violence against girls. This conference resulted in the initiation of a pan-African movement opposed to all forms of violence against girls in Africa.

Mahasweta M. Banerjee, Ph.D., is associate professor at the School of Social Welfare, University of Kansas, Lawrence. She teaches quantitative and qualitative research at the BSW, MSW, and Ph.D. levels. Her research interests include economic empowerment of low-income people through microenterprise development and critiques of theories of justice such as those of John Rawls, Amartya Sen, and Martha Nussbaum. Recently, in the study "Capacity Building among Economically Disadvantaged People of West Bengal, India," sponsored by the U.S. Fulbright Commission, she tested the capabilities approach developed by Sen and Nussbaum.

Alice K. Butterfield, Ph.D., is professor at the Jane Addams College of Social Work, University of Illinois at Chicago. She is coauthor of *The Dynamics of Family Policy* (Lyceum Books). Her international research includes the emergence of the nonprofit sector and child welfare organizations in Romania, as well as participatory community development in Ethiopia. Since 2001, she has been involved in a university-to-university partnership to establish MSW and Ph.D. programs at the School of Social Work at Addis Ababa University in Ethiopia. She is coeditor of *University-Community Partnerships: Colleges and Universities* *in Civic Engagement* (2005) and *Interdisciplinary Community Development: International Perspectives* (2007). Butterfield is a leader of the Association for Community Organization and Social Administration and a member of the Council on Social Work Education's Commission on Global Social Work Education. In 2007, she received the Distinguished Alumni Award from Washington University in St. Louis.

Kathryn Collins, MSW, Ph.D., is an associate professor at the University of Maryland School of Social Work. The focus of her academic career is on social justice, disparities in access to trauma-based mental health services, and developing trauma-focused social work interventions for vulnerable and oppressed populations such as children, women, and families surviving poverty and chronic violence in the inner city. Collins's commitment to the field is long standing, with more than thirteen years of community-based clinical social work practice with children and families. She has numerous publications and has been the principal investigator or co–principal investigator on state and nationally funded research. Currently, she is co–principal investigator of the Substance Abuse and Mental Health Services Administration–funded Family Informed Trauma Treatment Center of the National Child Traumatic Stress Network. She has earned an extramural research award in the National Institutes of Health, National Center for Minority Health, and Health Disparities Loan Repayment Program for her research focusing on children from minority communities and their exposure to community violence. Collins is a former cochair of the Council on Social Work Educations' Council on the Role and Status of Women in Social Work Education. Further, she brings her research scholarship, practice, and life experience to the classroom, where she has received several teaching awards, including the 2008 Student Government Association Exemplary Faculty Member of the Year Award at the University of Maryland School of Social Work.

Jami Curley is an assistant professor at the School of Social Work at Saint Louis University in St. Louis. She holds a Ph.D. and MSW in social work from Washington University in St. Louis and a BA in sociology and psychology and business administration from Eureka College in Illinois. Her research focuses on the social and economic development of low-income families, including the impact of asset ownership on family, children, and individuals both in the United States and abroad.

Dorie J. Gilbert, Ph.D., is associate professor of social work and a faculty affiliate of the Center for African and African American Studies at the University of Texas, Austin. In addition, she is a visiting research scholar at the University of California at San Francisco, Center for AIDS

Prevention Studies. Gilbert's scholarly work focuses on the mental health, behavioral, and social consequences of structurally imposed stigma on vulnerable populations, with an emphasis on HIV/AIDS prevention for African American women. As a research associate with the Institute for the Advanced Study of Black Family Life in Oakland, California, Gilbert is certified in the African-Centered Behavior Change Model, a culturally congruent model based on the principle of reinstilling traditional African and African American cultural values into women to enhance health promotion behavior. As such, Gilbert's work is uniquely centered on advocating for prevention programs that emphasize African-centered philosophies of health promotion and disease prevention. Her research interests also extend to HIV prevention work in Ghana, West Africa.

Marceline Lazzari, Ph.D., has served in a variety of administrative positions in social work education and has taught and conducted research on issues related to field education, diversity, and leadership. She works from a feminist perspective that promotes inclusiveness, collaboration, shared responsibility, and shared leadership. Lazzari currently serves as the chair of the Council on Social Work Education's Commission for Diversity and Social and Economic Justice and served previously as the cochair of the Council on the Role and Status of Women in Social Work Education. She is professor and founding director of the social work program at the University of Washington, Tacoma.

Alice A. Lieberman is Chancellor's Club Teaching Professor of Social Welfare at the University of Kansas. She is the author and editor of numerous books, including *The Social WorkOut Book* (Pine Forge Press, 1998); *Social Work Practice with a Difference: Stories, Essays, Cases, and Commentaries* (coedited with Cheryl Lester, McGraw-Hill Higher Education, 2004); and the Social Work in a New Century series (Routledge/ Taylor and Francis IIe, forthcoming). She has also been co–principal investigator on several federal initiatives funded by the Administration for Children and Families.

Patricia O'Brien, Ph.D., is associate professor of social work, Jane Addams College of Social Work at the University of Illinois at Chicago. For almost twenty years, she has been studying the issues of women's reentry from prison to the community. She is the author of *Making It in the Free World: Women's Transition from Prison* and many articles investigating the nexus of interpersonal and social conditions that influence women's choices and access to resources. In addition to her scholarship and research, she teaches practice and theory graduate courses, serves on the board of directors of Chicago Legal Advocacy for

Incarcerated Mothers, is cochair of the Council on Social Work Education's Council on the Role and Status of Women in Social Work Education, and is a consultant with the National Institute of Corrections.

Deborah L. Padgett, MSW, Ph.D., is associate professor and chair of the Department of Social Work at the University of Wisconsin, Milwaukee. She teaches courses in macro practice, group work, and ethics, and her research interests are in administration and leadership.

Irene Queiro-Tajalli received her BSW in Argentina, her MSW in Iran, and her Ph.D. in social work from the University of Illinois at Urbana-Champaign. She is the executive director of undergraduate education and interim executive director of labor studies at the Indiana University School of Social Work. She has extensive experience working with clients from diverse backgrounds, including Latinos, Native Americans, and Iranians. Her volunteer positions have been at the local, state, and national levels. Queiro-Tajalli served for two terms as commissioner for the Commission on Accreditation and several terms as commissioner for the International Commission, Council on Social Work Education. Currently, she serves as the chair of the Latino Social Worker/Human Services Providers Network of Indiana. She is the president of the DANESH Institute, as well as a certified site visitor for the Commission on Accreditation, and a member of the Committee on Racial and Ethnic Diversity, National Association of Social Work's Indiana Chapter. Her current public presentations and writings focus on community organizing, social movements in Argentina, aging, online teaching, educational assessment, and Latino women.

Uma A. Segal, Ph.D., is professor and director of the baccalaureate program in the School of Social Work at the University of Missouri, St. Louis. She holds a research fellow position in its Center for International Studies and is a clinical social worker, licensed in the states of Missouri and Texas. Her areas of research interest and publication are immigrant and refugee concerns, Asian American acculturation, and cross-national issues in family violence. In 2004, Segal was appointed editor of the *Journal of Immigrant and Refugee Studies* and has moved toward making it a premier journal on international and interdisciplinary studies in migration. Segal's teaching now focuses primarily on organizational functioning and human behavior. In 2007, she joined the Universidade do Minho, Gestão do Economia, Braga, Portugal, as an adjunct professor and the Universidade Fernando Pessoa, Center for Minority Studies, Porto, Portugal, as an external collaborator. She has been an invited guest speaker on child maltreatment at Oxford University and at several universities in Japan and India.

Margaret Sherrard Sherraden, Ph.D., is professor, School of Social Work, University of Missouri in St. Louis, and research professor, Center for Social Development, Brown School of Social Work, Washington University. Her research, publishing, and teaching focus on access and equity in domestic and international social policies. Her research studies include rural health policy in Mexico, birth outcomes among Mexican immigrants, microenterprise in low-income U.S. families, matched savings accounts for low-income adults and children, and international volunteering and service. She is lead author, with Cynthia K. Sanders and Michael Sherraden, of *Kitchen Capitalism: Microenterprise in Low-Income Households* (SUNY Press, 2004), and lead author, with Amanda Moore McBride and Sondra Beverly, of the forthcoming book *Striving to Save in Low-Income Households.*

Susan S. Tebb is a professor in the School of Social Work at Saint Louis University. She received her Ph.D. in social work from the University of Kansas and her MSW from Wayne State University in Detroit. She received a BA in psychology from Ottawa University in Kansas. Tebb has centered her research interests on family caregiving. She has written a few books and more than forty articles or book chapters in this area. She has been a social worker for more than forty years, working with many diverse family configurations in adoption, medical social work, court mediation, and caregiving situations.

Julia M. Watkins is the executive director of the Council on Social Work Education. Previously, she served from 1993 to 2003 as president of the American University in Bulgaria. Watkins received an MSW and a Ph.D. in educational psychology from the University of Utah. She previously was a professor of social work, dean of the College of Social and Behavioral Sciences, and interim vice president for academic affairs at the University of Maine. She has been a fellow of the American Council on Education and is a member of the Phi Kappa Phi Honor Society. Watkins has a record of scholarship and university service and has served on the boards of many nonprofit organizations. She was president of the Association of American International Colleges and Universities from 1998 to 2000 and president of the Alliance of Universities for Democracy from 2000 to 2002. She was elected a lifetime honorary member of the Board of the New Symphony Orchestra, Sofia. She is an expert in higher education and quality assurance in higher administration.

Hilary N. Weaver, DSW (Lakota), is a professor in the School of Social Work, University at Buffalo (State University of New York). Her teaching, research, and service focus on cultural issues in the helping process with a particular focus on indigenous populations. She currently serves as president of the American Indian Alaska Native Social Work Educators Association and president of the Board of Directors of Native American Community Services of Erie and Niagara Counties. Weaver has presented her work regionally, nationally, and internationally, including at the Permanent Forum on Indigenous Issues at the United Nations in 2005, 2006, 2007, and 2008. She has numerous publications, including the recent text *Explorations in Cultural Competence: Journeys to the Four Directions* (2005). Weaver has received funding from the National Cancer Institute to develop and test a culturally grounded wellness curriculum for urban Native American youths, the Healthy Living in Two Worlds program.

Index